T0360914

OPEN DOORS

The **Nordic Institute of Asian Studies** (NIAS) is funded by the governments of Denmark, Finland, Iceland, Norway and Sweden via the Nordic Council of Ministers, and works to encourage and support Asian studies in the Nordic countries. In so doing, NIAS has been publishing books on Asia for the last three decades, with more than one hundred titles produced in the last decade, many of them in cooperation with Curzon Press.

Open Doors

Vilhelm Meyer and the Establishment of General Electric in China

by
Christopher Bo Bramsen

Routledge
Taylor & Francis Group

LONDON AND NEW YORK

Nordic Institute of Asian Studies

First published in 2001
by Routledge
2 Park Square, Milton Park,
Abingdon, Oxon, OX14 4RN

Routledge is an imprint of the Taylor & Francis Group

Transferred to Digital Printing 2006

Typesetting in ITC New Baskerville by NIAS Publishing

British Library Cataloguing in Publication Data
Bramsen, Christopher Bo
Open Doors : Vilhelm Meyer and the establishment of General
Electric in China
1.Meyer, Vilhelm 2.General Electric Company - History
3.Danes - China - Shanghai 4.Shanghai (China) - Social life and
customs - 20th century 5.China - Economic conditions -
20th century
I.Title
951'.04'092

ISBN 0-7007-1404-9

Publisher's Note
The publisher has gone to great lengths to ensure the quality
of this reprint but points out that some imperfections in
the original may be apparent

Contents

Figures

Preface

Vilhelm Meyer was my mother's father. He died several years before I was born. Naturally I had heard tales about his exciting life in China. But it was Sven Riskær, the managing director of the Danish Industrialization Fund for Developing Countries (IFU), who really opened my eyes to Vilhelm Meyer's impact on the extensive industrial development that had taken place in China during the early part of the century.

In 1990 Riskær told me that he had recently been to China visiting Danish development projects. Here he had come across a publication celebrating the twenty-fifth anniversary of the firm Andersen, Meyer & Company, Ltd (A. M. & Co.) of Shanghai, published in 1931. The president of the company had been the Danish Vilhelm Meyer. Riskær had been impressed by Meyer's contribution to China's industrial development during the first third of the 20th century. In comparison with the vast and numerous projects undertaken by A. M. & Co. over the years – building power plants, factories, railroads and bridges and creating outlets for a large import of machinery, motors, trains and trucks from the United States and Europe – the projects in China carried out by present-day Danish development organizations such as Danida and IFU paled into insignificance. Riskær's observations made me want to know more about Vilhelm Meyer's life and work in China.

Vilhelm and his wife Kirsten Meyer left behind very little in writing about life in China. Their third daughter Anette Ricard has given a vivid description of the girls' happy childhood in China in the book Mist on the Window Panes (1959). And their fourth daughter, my mother, Marie-Louise Bramsen, has described it in a chapter in a book on Danish homes in the 1920s and 1930s (1977). Besides these publications and the anniversary book mentioned above, I had no knowledge of any other source material.

At this point I was made aware of letters and photographs by a young Danish girl, Gerda Nielsen, who had been employed by the Meyer family in Shanghai from 1920 to 1923 and who during her entire stay had diligently written letters home to her mother in Denmark. These letters were now in the historical archives of the city of Faaborg. They contained a great deal of detailed information about the daily life of the Meyer family and the Danish community in Shanghai.

Using these sources as my starting point, I proceeded to piece together all the fragments I was now in possession of so as to form a whole. New clues turned up. On visits to America and China in 1991–92, I followed various new leads, such as information about changes in A. M. & Co.'s corporate structure, which had taken place over the years. I was unable, however, to locate the company books anywhere. Gradually all the different elements merged into a coherent picture of the life of Vilhelm and Kirsten Meyer and the role played by Andersen, Meyer & Co. in the industrial development of China.

This book is the result. It is not a thesis about the economic impact of A. M. & Co. on China's modernisation in the first part of the twentieth century, with lots of footnotes and references. The approach has been more holistic. Vilhelm and Kirsten Meyer are the main characters of the book, but their lives are seen against the backdrop of the economic and political developments taking place in China during the early decades of the twentieth century. The book also describes the development of Andersen, Meyer & Co. Furthermore, it shows the evolution of Danish–Chinese relations as we follow the Danish community in Shanghai, which with a population of 400 was the largest Danish community in the Far East. In addition we trace the development of Sino–American commercial relations, which began in earnest at the beginning of the twentieth century.

This book was first published in Danish in 1993. The following year I took up the post as the first Danish Consul-General in Shanghai at the re-opened Royal Danish Consulate General. After a year in Shanghai I was transferred to Beijing.

On 1 September 1995, while presenting my credentials as Danish ambassador to China to President Jiang Zemin in Beijing, I was quite surprised when the president told me that he was aware of my family roots in Shanghai and that he remembered my grandfather's company 'Shen Chang Yang Hang'.

While living in Shanghai and Beijing I have gathered more information about the Meyer family and Andersen, Meyer & Co. In Beijing I met Professor Lin Hua, who agreed to translate the book from Danish into Chinese. The Chinese version of the book was published in Beijing in 1996 and again in 1998. It is with great pleasure that I am now able to present the book about Vilhelm Meyer in English. The translation, made by an old American friend in Denmark, Joan Høberg-Petersen, follows the original Danish version, but there are many additions. Furthermore, the present edition has more illustrations than the original Danish version.

The title of the book, *Open Doors*, refers to the fact that Vilhelm Meyer was a firm believer in the American policy of keeping China open to all foreign countries on an equal and competitive basis, instead of carving China up into special exclusive zones of interest for a limited number of countries. The title also refers to the Meyer family's house in Shanghai which was always open to a wide range of different people – Scandinavian, English, American and Chinese friends alike.

Vilhelm Meyer was born in 1878. This was the year when the American inventor Thomas A. Edison was working on his incandescent lamp and when he founded his Edison Electric Light Company to support his lighting research. The founding of this company marked the beginning of a corporate lineage, which a few years later led to the creation of the General Electric Company, G. E. In 1906 Vilhelm Meyer became the agent for G. E. in China, thereby contributing to bringing electricity and all the new innovations in electrical appliances into China. This book thus also gives an account of how G. E. came to China, thereby recounting the early corporate history of the General Electric Company in China.

Vilhelm Meyer died in 1935 in Shanghai and A. M. & Co. was taken over by its main business partner in the United States, the General Electric Company. This book is a tribute to the role of the Danish, American and Chinese inventors, engineers and business people who took an active part in the industrial development process in China during the first half of the 20th century.

Beijing, May 2000
Christopher Bo Bramsen

Figure 1: On 1 September 1995, the author of this book, Christopher Bo Bramsen, presented his credentials, signed by Her Majesty Queen Margrethe II of Denmark, to the President of the Peoples' Republic of China Jiang Zemin, thereby becoming Denmark's ambassador to China.

Acknowledgements

While working on this book I received excellent assistance and advice from many sides. Various people have been helpful in terms of both source material and illustrations. At the risk of forgetting one or two, I would like to thank the following for their invaluable assistance: Preben Ahlefeldt-Laurvig, Thea Ahlefeldt-Laurvig, Wava Armfeldt, Rose-Marie Barton, Henrik Bjørk, Christen and

Aase Black, Bo Bramsen, Bolette Bramsen, Kjeld Erik Brødsgaard, Thomas Duer, Er Dongqian, Mei-Mei Ellerman, Else von Essen, Tobias Faber, William and Alice Friis-Møller, Inger Gericke, Dan Gregersen, Guo Yongle, Flemming Hasle, William Heering, Mette Holm, Joan Hornby, Kim and Birgitte Hueg, Niels Høyer, Jing Ying, Tess Johnston, Mads Kirkebæk, Kirsten Krarup, Tage Kaarsted, Knud and Ruby Langaa-Jensen, Ole Lange, Tyge Lehmann, Li Ning, Lin Hua, Lisa Lee Liu, Lars Lunn, Henning Malmgren, M.G.I. Melchior, Klaus Carsten Pedersen, Bo Rasmussen, Carl Ricard, Lennart Ricard, Sven Riskær, Wilhelm von Rosen, Ulla Skipper, Bent Suenson, Ib Topholm, Monika Thowsen, Elsebeth Troels-Smith, David Wang, Betty Wei, Frank P. Wardlaw, Charlotte Wilhelmsen, Zhang Longhai, Zu Lirong and Clemens Stubbe Østergaard.

A special thanks to Højesteretssagfører C.L. Davids Legat for Slægt og Venner which made it possible to carry out certain source studies in the United States. Thanks also to Thomas B. Thriges Fond for supporting the translation of the book into English.

I am also indebted to Barbara Vibæk of Gads Publishing House, who originally gave me invaluable advice on how to put it all together. I would also like to thank Joan Høberg-Petersen for doing such a splendid job of translating the book from Danish into English, and Liz Bramsen and Leena Höskuldsson of the Nordic Institute of Asian Studies and Sandra Jones for their professional editing of the book. Finally, I wish to extend particular thanks to my wife, Gudrun, and our little son Vilhelm. Their support, patience and inspiration during the writing of this book have been invaluable.

Transcription of Chinese Characters

When Europeans and Americans began trading with China, they soon felt the need to transcribe Chinese characters into Roman letters. In some cases Europeanized names were used, such as Canton and Amoy. A comprehensive system of transcription called the Wade–Giles system was developed in the nineteenth century by Sir Thomas Wade and H.A. Giles. This is the system used in such personal names as Chiang Kai-shek, Mao Tse-tung and Chou En-lai and in the names of cities such as Peking, Tientsin and Nanking.

After the People's Republic of China was founded, a new system called pinyin was developed in the mid-1950s, the purpose of which was to make phonetic transcription more accurate in relation to the spoken Chinese language. In pinyin the three personal names mentioned above are written as Jiang Jieshi, Mao Zedong and Zhou Enlai while the spellings Beijing, Tianjin, Nanjing and Guangzhou are used for the names of the cities of Peking, Tientsin, Nanking and Canton.

In this book, as a rule, the pinyin system is used in connection with place names so as to enable the reader to recognize the areas in modern China. However, some of the old spellings, such as Peking and Canton, are so well established that they are not transcribed into pinyin.

ONE

A Wedding in Shanghai, 1909

A Voyage to China

13 June 1909.

So much has happened since the last time I wrote! I shall now pack this book away with all the other things to be sent to Shanghai tomorrow – where I shall live with Vilhelm. This is the last time I write as Kirsten Bramsen. Next time I shall be Vilhelm's wife. I depart on the 19th or 20th of September arriving on the 24th of October. Papa accompanies me.

Kirsten closed her diary and put it in the large trunk. It was a beautiful, leather-bound volume given to her by her Norwegian grandmama in July 1901. This was the last entry she was to make. A new chapter in her life was opening before her and she would have no more time for or interest in a diary.

In September Kirsten embarked on the long voyage from Copenhagen to Shanghai accompanied by her father, Aage Bramsen. Kirsten's mother, Ottilie, did not wish to go along. It was too far away, and was Kirsten really sure she wanted to marry and live so far away from Denmark? No announcement had been made in Copenhagen of either the engagement or the wedding. Aage Bramsen, the director of an insurance company, had informed his business associates that he was accompanying his eldest daughter on a journey to China for health reasons. Father and daughter had agreed that if Kirsten were to regret her decision to marry Vilhelm Meyer, the young Danish entrepreneur, when she got to Shanghai she could simply return to Denmark with her father.

Aage and Kirsten travelled by train from Copenhagen to Genoa in Italy where they boarded the *Prinzess Alice*, a German passenger steamer. The voyage from Genoa to Shanghai lasted over four weeks, but it was a wonderful experience for both of them, sailing through the Suez Canal and on to Aden, Ceylon, Penang, Singapore and Hong Kong.

Shanghai

The 25-year-old young woman standing on the deck with her father was agog with excitement. They were approaching the mouth of the great Chinese river, the Yangtze. The sea was no longer blue, but a muddy yellow. The flat coast emerging on the horizon and the innumerable Chinese junks and foreign merchant ships signalled that this was the main artery leading into the heart of the vast Chinese empire.

The ship sailed into the estuary and up the Whangpoo River towards Shanghai. Kirsten Bramsen had left Denmark and Europe behind and had finally arrived in China to marry her great love, 31-year-old Vilhelm Meyer. Kirsten's father had respected his eldest daughter's decision that Vilhelm was to be the man in her life. Vilhelm had gone out to China in 1902 when Kirsten was 17 years old. The two young people had written to each other frequently in the intervening years.

In the summer of 1906 Vilhelm had returned to Copenhagen in order to finance the establishment of his new firm in Shanghai, Andersen, Meyer & Co. The two young people met several times during his stay and agreed to marry once Vilhelm was well established in Shanghai. Vilhelm's affairs went well and when he visited Denmark in 1908 they agreed that the time had come. The wedding was to take place in Shanghai in October 1909.

And here were Kirsten and her father standing on the deck with all the other passengers watching Shanghai appear further up the river. How fascinating to watch all the ships and the European-looking buildings facing the river! Neither father nor daughter had ever been to China before. But Aage Bramsen was aware that it was on this famous stretch of waterfront, The Bund, which they were now approaching, that his brother William Bramsen, who was five years his senior, had helped land the Great Northern Telegraph Company's cable on the coast of China under cover of darkness before the final concession rights had been officially granted. He remembered, too, that it was here in Shanghai that another elder brother, Ludvig Bramsen, while travelling around the world in 1904, had received the distinct impression that young Vilhelm Meyer was something of an adventurer. And now he himself had come out to China to marry his daughter off to that very young man!

As the ship steamed up the Whangpoo River, the otherwise so determined Kirsten felt a moment of anxiety. This was a vast and foreign land with its exotic, pulsating port, a place where she did not know a single soul. Was Shanghai really going to be her future home? Then she caught sight of Vilhelm down on the wharf among the milling throng of Chinese, Europeans, Americans and Japanese. There he was, waving, his straw hat in one hand and a large bouquet of flowers in the other. Kirsten, overwhelmed by a mixture of panic and excitement, went down to her cabin. Vilhelm was one of the first on board and they fell into each other's arms. All Kirsten's doubts vanished completely as Vilhelm accompanied her and her father down the gangway.

The wedding was to take place three days later. Vilhelm spent the intervening time showing his bride-to-be around Shanghai. In the French section they shopped for hats at a French modiste, who had just arrived from Paris with the latest models. Vilhelm presented Kirsten with the most magnificent wedding bonnet he could find. Large and white with white plumes, it was the last word in elegance for a fashionable wedding. Aage Bramsen, however, was shocked by the young people's extravagance. Why did they buy such an expensive hat when they were in much greater need of furniture for their future home? Kirsten smiled at her father 'You can always buy furniture, but you don't find a hat like this every day!' Besides, Kirsten loved to get presents and Vilhelm loved to give her presents! So why spoil the young couple's fun?

A Wedding at the Consulate General

The wedding took place on 27 October 1909 in brilliant sunshine. The wedding ceremony was performed at the Royal Danish Consulate General on Whangpoo Road right by the river. Theodor Raaschou, the Consul-General, was on leave in Denmark at the time so his Norwegian counterpart, Thorvald Hansen, officiated at the ceremony as acting Danish Consul-General. Vilhelm had been appointed Danish vice-consul in Shanghai a few years earlier and he felt completely at home at the Consulate General. And since Kirsten was half Norwegian, getting married in such a Danish–Norwegian setting didn't strike her as particularly exotic, even though she was a long way from her family and friends in Copenhagen. Thorvald Hansen reverently read aloud the words of the marriage ceremony in which the young couple pledge each other eternal love and support. He then asked each of them, in the name of the Danish State, if they would take each other as their lawfully-wedded spouse. Having received their affirmative replies, he then declared Mr Vilhelm Octavius Meyer and Miss Kirsten Bramsen henceforth 'united in holy matrimony in accordance with the laws of the State of Denmark'. The newly weds beamed and the protocols were signed. Among the witnesses were two of Vilhelm's friends from Shanghai, Michel Speelman, a Dutch banker, and Captain J.J. Bahnson of the Great Northern Telegraph Company.

The reception that followed took place at Michel Speelman's house. Here Vilhelm and Kirsten received a great number of the city's foreign inhabitants as well as Vilhelm's Chinese business associates. They were a lovely bridal couple – the tall groom, already a prominent, popular Danish businessman in Shanghai, with his open smile and his powerful, personal charisma and the lovely bride graciously enchanting all the guests with her mild, clear blue gaze. As the long line of guests filed by, she looked kindly and directly into the eyes of each one. In the local newspaper, *The North China Herald News*, the wedding was announced as follows:

Marriage

MEYER–BRAMSEN on October 27, at Shanghai,
before Th. Hansen, Esq., Consul-General for Norway,
Acting Consul-General for Denmark, Vilhelm Meyer,
Danish Vice-Consul, son of Louis Meyer, Esq., of Copenhagen,
to Kirsten, daughter of Aage Bramsen, Esq., of Copenhagen.

The newly-weds moved into a house on Avenue Road in the International Settlement not far from The Bund. This was to be their permanent residence for the rest of their lives. They were to experience Shanghai in the years when the city was the Western world's main gateway to China. They would also live through the vast political upheavals that were to take place in China and they would see the city become the centre of a massive commercial effort as roads, bridges, railways, telegraph lines, power plants and factories were built, giving a great impetus to China's industrial development.

Figure 2: After a long engagement, Vilhelm Meyer and Kirsten Bramsen were married in Shanghai on 27 October 1909. The bride's father, Aage Bramsen, an insurance company director, was also present.

TWO

The Early Years, 1878–1902

The Meyer Family

Vilhelm was born on 14 June 1878 in Copenhagen. He was the eighth child of Louis and Thea Meyer, commemorated by the middle name Octavius. He had five elder brothers, Albert, Viggo, Ernst, Holger and Otto and two elder sisters, Anna (who was Ernst's twin sister) and Emma. After Vilhelm there was another brother, Emil, who died at the age of 2. Then came the twins, Jutta and Olga, and finally the youngest member of the family, Emilie, who would henceforth always be called Mille. Thus Vilhelm grew up among five brothers and five sisters.

He was descended from a family of Jewish merchants (see Appendix). How-ever, his parents, Louis and Thea Meyer, did not attach great importance to their Jewish origins and several of their eleven children, including Vilhelm, mar-ried non-Jews. Vilhelm was a lively, happy boy, full of self-confidence and charm, growing up in the 1880s along the canals of the old part of Copenhagen. His father, Louis Meyer, was head of the trading firm Beckett & Meyer.

It was common for large, wealthy Copenhagen families to spend the summer months in the country, typically from May to September. The Meyer family was no exception. In 1881 Louis Meyer bought a house at the seaside resort of Skodsborg, 15 miles north of Copenhagen, which was to be the family summer residence for the next 25 years. The house had originally been the dining hall of Skodsborg Castle, once in the possession of King Frederik VII, and came with extensive grounds and gardens. Alterations were made when the Meyer family moved in. A tower was added and the date 1881 A.D. written on the wall in large letters, still recalls how the house was remodelled in order to make it into a suitable summer residence for Louis and Thea Meyer and their 11 child-ren. Louis left the dining room untouched: Frederik VII's monogram above the windows and the numerous coats-of-arms on the walls remained intact.

The Meyer family was one of the first families to move so far away from the city in the summer. For 16 years Louis and those of his children who attended school in Copenhagen went by horse and carriage to the closest railway station located at Klampenborg, a few miles away, and from there into town. It was not until 1897 that the family could take the train all the way. There is a descrip-tion of the family carriage journeys from Skodsborg to Klampenborg in a book on Louis Meyer, written by Sievert Gunst in 1943. Louis is seated in the carriage together with the smaller children while his older sons follow on tall bicycles with large front wheels and small rear wheels:

Figure 3: Louis Meyer, a Copenhagen wholesaler, was married to Thea Friedlænder in 1867. The couple had a total of 12 children. This picture of Louis and Thea was taken in 1888.

All along the way down Strandvejen Louis Meyer picked up friends and acquaintances also on their way to catch the early train. Everything took place with such precision that it was said that the Strandvej families set their clocks by the passing of the Meyer cavalcade. At a few minutes to eight they all rolled up in front of old Klampenborg station, which is still there, close to the woods, and only then could the train leave. This was the rule which, as everyone knows, is proved by the exception. Once and only once was the Meyer family delayed. The station-master, Lieutenant Lissner, friend to all the summer families, could not bring him-self to send off the train without Louis Meyer and his entourage. Finally he had to give the departure signal but at that very minute the cavalcade appeared where the road turns down towards the station. He resolutely stopped the train and everyone got on. But, alas, another passenger was displeased with such favouri-tism and lodged a complaint, with the result that the stationmaster was officially reprimanded.

Emilie, the youngest member of the family, later described the family's summer residence in the following manner:

> Skodsborg, ah, how lovely it was! Big – lots of rooms. The everyday dining room table was also a billiard table, there was a screwing mechanism and the top could be removed. It could seat 16. And then there was the large dining room with high windows under Frederik VII's monogram, and on the wall the coats-of-arms from all different countries. There was the dumbwaiter to the kitchen and the speaking tube. What a treat for us children. Candles in all the bedrooms – there were eight of them – the water was pumped up by Morten, our gardener, in a large tank down in the kitchen. And then it was brought upstairs to all the rooms in large pitchers. Hot water? No, we didn't have any of that. The cellars, oh, let me tell you about them, there was a dark cellar, 'the shoe cleaning cellar', where Jørgen cleaned and repaired all our shoes. Then came the laundry cellar, a huge one with a big mangle, an enormous kitchen with a wood-burning stove and the pantry, where mother prepared sandwiches every morning, or rather the kitchen maid buttered the bread for the entire staff and mother put the cold cuts on it. Then came the china cellar. Cupboards all the way to the ceiling filled with glasses, china and cups. Then the cold cellar with the icebox, where Kristine always made mayonnaise on Sundays – one drop of oil after another. That took three hours every time – and after that a large jam cellar. Then there was the wine cellar with a heavy, locked door and finally the vegetable cellar.
>
> The staff of servants consisted of a kitchen maid, house maid, chambermaid (Kristine), servant, coachman – in addition there was a permanent gardener, who lived in a house in the garden with his wife and children, and three others to care for the garden (who didn't live with us); of these, Hanne helped with the washing up. It must have been huge, but we children never felt it. We were brought up in a spartan fashion, which was well done. Carriages, dogs, tennis court, beach, well, it was all there, of course.
>
> When the kitchen maid had been there for 22 years she married Jørgen, who had been there for 19. Sine became a pensioner after 28 years and Kristine died in service after 42 years with us. By then she was a member of the family.

Thea Meyer was in charge of the daily management of the large establish-ment. There were dinner parties, too, and pleasant evenings spent in playing cards, first hombre and in later years the new card game, bridge. The family often went to the theatre – Louis and Thea would sit in the front row and the older boys would sit up in the balcony. Thea was mild and kind and became quite plump over the years. She loved to write verse and could whip up a rhyme at the drop of a hat. At family parties, in Skodsborg or in Copenhagen, members of the family would often write songs for the occasion.

The New House by the Harbour

In the 1880s the firm of Beckett & Meyer bought a warehouse at the Copenhagen Harbour, in Kvæsthusgade, at the far end of the Nyhavn section. The firm had grown so large by 1891 that a new location had to be found. Louis Meyer had the warehouse in Nyhavn torn down and built a new building on the site. The new house was arranged with offices on the second floor and an apartment on the third and fourth floors for the big family of 11 children, aged 9 to 23, most of whom still lived at home. It had been difficult for Louis to get permission to build so close to the waterfront but he had finally succeeded. The house was a stately one with the most modern facilities and the best view in town of the harbour, the Royal Dockyards and Christianshavn on the other side.

Figure 4: At an early age Vilhelm made it clear that people would have to give way to him! One day when he was 3 years old he sat down on the same chair as his mother. 'Me bother you?' asked the little boy. When Thea nodded, Vilhelm replied with a disarming smile, 'Then you move you!' He is shown here in 1880.

Vilhelm was 13 and his sister Emilie 9 years old when they moved to Kvæsthusgade. In Emilie Heering's subsequent reminiscences she describes the family home by the waterfront:

> The house in Kvæsthusgade was very large. It was built so that the kitchen and the office stairs were located in the front entrance gateway and the main entrance was at the back across the courtyard. The sitting rooms and Mother and Father's bedroom faced Kvæsthus Bridge, Havnegade and Christianshavn. It was beautiful. Here, too, Father was ahead of his time. Electricity and central heating were almost unheard of then. The WC had not been invented yet.
>
> On the second floor were the study, two sitting rooms, a large, dark dining room facing the courtyard, the butler's pantry, a kitchen, three maid's rooms and privy, pantries and the wine room. There was a staircase between the main entrance hall and the fourth floor: Mother and father's bedroom, an extra study, six bedrooms and our sitting room, wardrobe room and bathroom and two almost-

Figure 5: The family's four residences over the years can be seen on this card printed for Louis Meyer's 80th birthday. On the top left is Læderstræde no. 11 and on the top right Kvæst-husgade no. 6, Copenhagen. At the bottom left is the Skodsborg summer residence which had once belonged to King Frederik VII – at that time it had been known as 'Villa Rex'. The family's Vedbæk summer residence from 1906 to 1929, 'Villa Padre', is shown at bottom right.

WCs. Quite splendid and new. You could turn on an electric light on the main stairs at the back and turn it off in the entrance hall. You could turn on the electric light on the kitchen stairs on every floor but you had to turn it off before continuing. We often used the kitchen stairs when we came home from a ball so as to avoid having to cross the courtyard.

At home Vilhelm, as the youngest son, had a special place in his mother's heart. His sense of fun could always make her laugh and he could twist her around his little finger with his boyish charm. In the Meyer family, great importance was attached to coming to meals on time. A rebuke awaited late-comers and the unfortunate late arrival had to offer appropriate apologies. Vilhelm was the only one able to get around it. He would dash into the dining room, look around in great surprise and exclaim, 'What! Started without me, have you?' Or he would present a completely incredible excuse, making the whole family laugh. His elder brothers would occasionally be annoyed at the way their youngest brother managed to avoid getting into trouble, but they forgave him as from time to time he would also rally to his brothers' defence.

Figure 6: Louis and Thea Meyer had their large family photographed in August 1892 for their silver wedding anniversary. Here are the 11 children with their husbands and wives and the Meyer grandchildren, with 14-year-old Vilhelm standing at the centre of the picture.

Vilhelm's Commercial Apprenticeship

Vilhelm went to preparatory school and continued his education at the Commercial College, founded in 1888 on the initiative of C.F. Tietgen, the great Danish financial and industrial magnate. The building was known as the 'school palace' and it was the most up-to-date school building in town with central heating and electricity. Vilhelm took his preliminary examination in 1893 and after a year at another business college in the same building received his diploma in 1894.

Trade and commerce soon became key words in Vilhelm's daily life. Outside his window in Nyhavn he could see the large merchant vessels which plied the seven seas sailing in and out of Copenhagen harbour. Right across the harbour, at Christianshavn, docked the ships belonging to his grandfather's family firm, Moses & Son, G. Melchior. And just below his windows there was the constant, great bustle of goods being carted in and out.

The merchants and other businessmen of the capital met every day at the Copenhagen Stock Exchange where they exchanged information and cut deals. Everyone knew Louis Meyer with his long whiskers and big cigar. Vilhelm listened eagerly to his father's tales of life on the Exchange and was very interested in becoming a businessman himself. In accordance with the Meyer merchant family tradition, Vilhelm embarked on his practical career at an early age. At the age of 16, upon completion of his diploma, he was apprenticed to the iron merchant, Albert Berendsen, head of Sophus Berendsen Ltd, in Amaliegade. The owner's father, Sophus Berendsen, had founded the company. Interviewing Vilhelm for the job, Albert Berendsen tested young Meyer's mathematical skills by asking him to multiply 17 by 19. When Vilhelm took out paper and pencil to perform the operation Berendsen asked him if that was really necessary as he himself could do it in his head at the age of 10. 'I could, too, when I was 10', replied Vilhelm – and was hired on the spot!

He advanced rapidly from apprentice to Albert Berendsen's private secretary. The business was then experiencing a burst of growth, importing rolled iron girders and sectional iron primarily from Belgium. With iron warehouses located around Copenhagen the firm played an important role in the construction boom taking place at the time. Vilhelm learned a great deal about practical trading and extensive contracting. Young Meyer's daily rounds in the Copenhagen of the 1890s were confined within a very limited area – home, school and work all lay within a few hundred yards of each other. It was now time to go abroad as part of his education not only to learn foreign languages and commercial skills, but also to try to make his own way in the world. So it was that in 1898 he went to Antwerp in Belgium, where he worked first in a coal company and then in a shipping firm.

In addition to his interest in business, Vilhelm had developed a magnificent singing voice. While in Belgium he took a trip to Paris where he took singing lessons from Jean de Rezké, the well-known French opera singer, who told him that with the proper instruction his baritone would become superb in time. He had the stature of an opera singer, too. As we shall see, Vilhelm became an excellent singer, but he never had any wish to make a career of it.

Vilhelm returned to Copenhagen in early 1899 where he was hired as bookkeeper and correspondence clerk to his mother's brother, Moses Melchior, now the senior partner in the old family firm, Moses & Son, G. Melchior. One day when old Uncle Moses, the director, was looking for some papers, he found a collection of small eggcups in Vilhelm's writing desk. This called for an explanation and Vilhelm reluctantly admitted that in the china shop downstairs there was a highly attractive young lady whom he enjoyed chatting up during the lunch break. To prevent her from getting into trouble, he bought a little eggcup at every visit simply because it was the cheapest article in the store.

In the summer of 1900 Vilhelm became the firm's travelling representative in Denmark. He was now 22 years old. In an interview in 1931 Vilhelm recalled how at that time he travelled around the country with one case of tea and one case of rum and how important it was to have a grasp of his work down to the smallest detail:

> The whole secret of running a large business is to build it up from the bottom, paying the greatest attention to every detail. I have never forgotten my two cases, which were easy to take in with a glance, and even though our affairs in China have gradually become quite wide-ranging, I nevertheless maintain that I have a thorough grasp of them.

Kirsten Bramsen

Kirsten Bramsen was born on 31 May 1884. Her parents, Aage and Norwegian-born Ottilie Bramsen, lived outside Copenhagen in Frederiksberg. Three more children were born in the following years, Luis, Agga and Aagot.

Vilhelm met Kirsten upon his return from Belgium. She was at school at the time. She was 15 and he was 21. Vilhelm thought so well of her that he asked his 17-year-old sister Emilie to cultivate her acquaintance. Emilie and her slightly older twin sisters, Olga and Jutta, had previously helped their brother, who was something of a ladies' man, to initiate contacts with girls with whom they did not really have anything in common. But in this case the contact not only resulted in a happy marriage for Vilhelm and Kirsten, but also a lifelong friendship between Emilie and Kirsten.

The two girls' fathers, Louis Meyer and Aage Bramsen, knew each other from the Copenhagen business world where commerce and insurance went hand in hand and where everyone met regularly on the Stock Exchange. The two girls began to spend a great deal of time together. Vilhelm did not always know when Kirsten was visiting Emilie in Kvæsthusgade. But he could recognize her blue coat in the entrance hall. Mrs. Meyer thought that such clothes were a bit extravagant. In the large Meyer family there was no room for such excesses. Emilie, however, could see nothing wrong with beautiful Kirsten being well dressed. Many years later, Emilie said that Kirsten was so beautiful that even a sheet would look like a ball-gown on her, whereas on the Meyer sisters a sheet would just go on being a sheet!

At Christmas 1901 the romance between Vilhelm and Kirsten began in earnest. He was 23 and she was 17. On Boxing Day Kirsten went into town with her cousin Rigmor. Here they met Vilhelm who accompanied the two young ladies. As always Vilhelm was fascinated by Kirsten's grace and smile and Kirsten fell for Vilhelm's charm and wit. As they walked along, chatting, they realized they were going to the same ball on 5 January. In her new diary Kirsten wrote: 'Oh, I really like him and I think he likes me, too. We've promised to think of each other on New Year's Eve at midnight. Let's see who remembers, he or I. Probably both of us.'

Kirsten spent New Year's Eve at home with her family. Among the guests were her uncle, Alfred Bramsen, his wife, Vilhelmine, and their two children, Henry and Karen.

Figure 7: In 1883 Aage Bramsen married Ottilie Grip in Bergen, Norway. The couple settled in Frederiksberg, an area of Copenhagen.

Henry is an odd character. He's not at all such a rowdy the way everyone says. I wish people would mind their own business. We had great fun the whole time. Karen played three small pieces for us, among other things. She plays very beautifully … When the clock struck 12 we all stood up and touched glasses and wished each other 'Happy New Year' – and I kept my promise to a certain person, too.

Figure 8: Aage and Ottilie Bramsen had a total of four children. Six-year-old Kirsten is shown here with her siblings, Ib, Agga and Aagot, photographed in 1890. The eldest of the four, pretty Kirsten, developed into a responsible girl who kept both feet firmly on the ground.

Both Kirsten and Vilhelm were full of expectation when they arrived at the ball on 5 January 1902. Vilhelm and Emilie sat at the same table as Kirsten. After dinner there was dancing. As they were waltzing together, Vilhelm told Kirsten that he was a bit angry at the host for not letting him be seated beside her at dinner. Kirsten wrote in her diary that she would have liked to ask the host, too, but had been afraid of his teasing her if she did. And she couldn't admit this to Vilhelm.

As they danced Vilhelm told her that over the past few months he had become more and more interested in going out to China. He didn't really know how or when he would be able to leave, but he was sure that there were ample opportunities in the vast Chinese empire for young foreign businessmen. He confided in her that he would try to get a job at the Danish East Asiatic Company's new office in Shanghai. Kirsten could well understand that Vilhelm wanted to travel and see the world, but she was sad, too. Smiling down at her, he told her that everybody would surely forget him when he was gone. 'But I won't!' wrote Kirsten in her diary.

THREE

The Call of Shanghai, 1899–1902

The View of Copenhagen Harbour

As a salesman for the firm of Moses & Son, G. Melchior, Vilhelm had travelled regularly in Denmark. His anchor point, however, was the house in Nyhavn from which he could watch Danish ships loaded with Danish goods set sail for foreign ports. Later they would return to Copenhagen harbour, bearing fascinating cargoes from exotic lands.

Vilhelm's interest in foreign trade and particularly in the opportunities that were opening up in China were aroused in earnest at this time. Three Danish companies occupied his thoughts in this connection. In the eighteenth century, commercial relations between Denmark and China had been primarily influenced by the Asiatic Company. In the nineteenth century the Great Northern Telegraph Company, founded on the initiative of financier C.F. Tietgen, had established extensive Sino–Danish cooperation in the area of telegraphic communications. And now at the dawn of the twentieth century, H.N. Andersen's East Asiatic Company marked a new epoch in Denmark's trading and shipping relations with the Far East.

The Danish Asiatic Company

Vilhelm had read about the Royal Chartered Danish Asiatic Company, which had replaced the East India Company founded in the seventeenth century. In 1730 the Asiatic Company had sent its first Danish Chinaman, the *Cron Printz Christian*, to Canton.

Canton was the only city in China open to foreign trade at the beginning of the eighteenth century. European ships were permitted to cast anchor at Whampoa Island in the Pearl River, at the entrance to the city. Danish ships moored near a small island, which in time came to be known as Danes Island. European trading companies were also allowed to build so-called 'factories', i.e. trading houses located on the piece of land on the river adjacent to the city walls of Canton, allotted by the Chinese for that purpose. The transportation of goods between the factories and Whampoa Island took place on small river sampans. The Asiatic Company's head office in Denmark was situated at Asiatisk Plads on the islet of Christianshavn in Copenhagen.

The captains of the large merchant ships were responsible for navigation, while the so-called 'supercargoes' were in charge of purchasing goods in the Far East. In the early years the supercargoes sailed out to China and back again. However, it was considerably easier to let the buyers remain there. From 1742

Figure 9: European traders were early granted access to the Chinese port of Canton. However, they were not allowed to enter the country and each nation had to set up a 'factory' at a specified location in the Canton harbour. The factories of the foreign countries can be seen in this painting from 1790. The Danish factory and flag is on the far left.

to 1791 the Danish supercargoes stayed in Canton where they bought the goods to be sent home on the next ship to Copenhagen. As can be seen in many old paintings of Canton, the Danish flag waved for many years outside the Danish factory, situated at the far left of the 13 factories in Canton.

Vilhelm was fascinated by the old 'Chinamen', the magnificent, large trading ships that went to the Far East, and by the Danish traders and seamen returning home with profitable bargains. Danes had made their mark in the field of trade and shipping and Vilhelm wanted to follow this tradition.

Kirsten's father used to tell how his great-grandfather Peder Lassen (his mother's father's father) had served in the Asiatic Company. From 1779 to his death in 1806 he had made a total of nine voyages to India and the Far East. Each voyage normally took 16–18 months. Peder Lassen had been made supercargo prior to his departure for Canton in 1794 on board the *Dannemark*. As was common practice at the time, this position gave him the right to ship a considerable amount of goods home with him at his own expense. Here was an excellent opportunity for a fine profit. The *Dannemark* was in Canton for two months in the autumn of 1794 and was back in Copenhagen in the summer of 1795.

The next voyage began in the autumn of 1795 on board the *Princess Charlotta Amalia*. Twice the ship lost all its masts in heavy storms and the difficult voyage was not completed until 1797, but the value of the cargo brought back from China left nothing to be desired – 915,000 rigsdaler. Then in 1801–02 Lassen was off to China again, this time on board one of the most renowned ships in the company's fleet, the Christianshavn. Finally, on his last voyage in 1805–06 on board the *Prinsesse Louise Augusta*, the ship brought home 717,000 pounds of tea and 20,000 pieces of Nanking porcelain.

But Aage Bramsen also pointed out that even though Peder Lassen survived his nine voyages to India and China for the Asiatic Company, he never got to

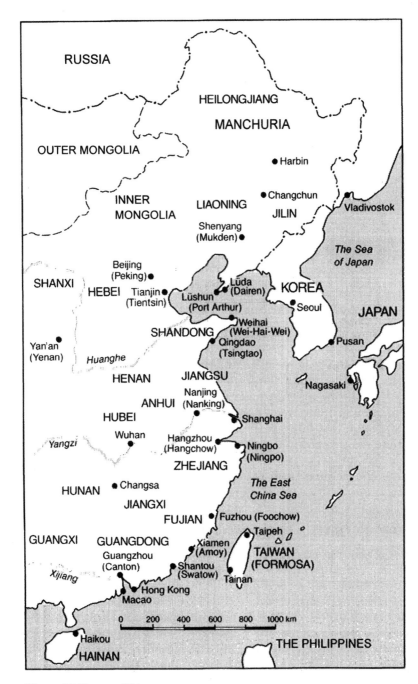

Figure 10: Eastern China

Figure 11: At the end of the eighteenth and the early part of the nineteenth centuries, Copenhagen residents could examine shipments of tea, silk and porcelain brought back from China displayed in the large store room in Eigtved's Warehouse, built in 1748.

enjoy his retirement at home in Denmark, which he had so much been looking forward to. His wife, Mette Christine, a shipmaster's daughter, died in Copenhagen in 1805 during his last voyage and he himself died shortly after his return to Copenhagen in 1806. He was only 53 years old at the time.

Peder Lassen lived through the flourishing period of trade at the beginning of the nineteenth century when Danish trade with China was particularly profitable. In the following years the Asiatic Company lost ground, keenly feeling the competition from British merchant ships in particular. After 1814 only a few Danish ships were sent to the Far East and they all operated at a loss.

The Great Northern Telegraph Company

Vilhelm was also intrigued by the Great Northern Telegraph Company founded in Denmark in 1869 and now the largest Danish firm in China. In the company's anniversary publication of 1894 he could read how in the course of a very short time Great Northern had established an extensive telegraphic network in Europe. The company had also laid down a telegraph line running from Europe to the Pacific Ocean parallel to the Trans-Siberian Railway, which was under construction. Great Northern's submarine cables secured the continued link from the Russian port of Vladivostok to Nagasaki in Japan and Shanghai and Hong Kong in China.

First Lieutenant Edouard Suenson had been sent to China in 1870 at the age of 27 to make preparations for laying out Great Northern's submarine cables

Figure 12: Peder Lassen (1753–1806), Kirsten Bramsen's great-great-grandfather, was a supercargo employed by the Asiatic Company. He sailed to the Far East a total of nine times.

between Russia, Japan and China. The young naval officer had served in the French navy in the Far East and had an excellent knowledge of conditions in China and Japan.

At the time of Suenson's departure, Great Northern was about to send cable ships to China. The Danish navy placed the frigate *Tordenskjold* at the disposal of the project. Waldemar Raasløff was responsible for this somewhat unusual arrangement. Having negotiated the Danish–Chinese commercial treaty in Tianjin in 1863, he was now Minister of War and prepared to support Tietgen's and Great Northern's plans for China. The *Tordenskjold*'s mission was to transport a small portion of the necessary cables to the Far East and perform deep-sea soundings in the waters where the cables were to be laid down. The bulk of the cable rolls, all of which were produced in England, were to be transported to China on the British cable ships, the Great Northern and the Cella.

They were adventurous young men, the Danes who presented themselves to Tietgen in 1870, eager to take part in the construction of the Great Northern cable lines to the Far East. In this connection Aage Bramsen could tell Vilhelm about yet another of the family's early Chinamen. Aage's older brother, William, had been one of the Danes sent to China by Tietgen in 1870. One day 19-year-old William Bramsen had suddenly announced to his astonished friends at the Students' Union in Copenhagen that he was going to China on the *Tordenskjold*. Coached by William on the best way to approach the great Tietgen, several of his friends also joined Great Northern. The group of young men, known as 'the Chinese', had been trained as telegraph operators prior to their departure from London in the summer of 1870.

European ships had always had to sail around Africa on their way to India and the Far East. However, the Suez Canal had opened in 1869. The *Tordenskjold* was the first Danish ship to sail through the canal. In September 1870 the Danish frigate arrived in Hong Kong followed by the two British cable ships. Lieu-

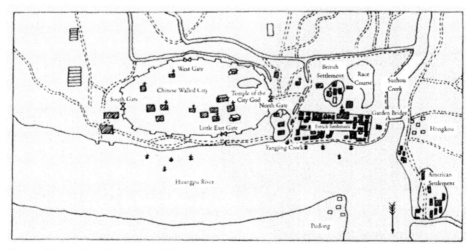

Figure 13: In this 1853 map of Shanghai the old section of Nantao is seen behind the city walls. The French Concession is to the north (on the right). Then comes the British area and on the northern side of the bridge is the American enclave. These two areas were merged in 1863 to form the International Settlement, which continued to exist until 1943.

tenant Suenson, who had arrived earlier, had negotiated the unresolved problems of concession with the Hong Kong authorities and in October the first cables could be pulled ashore at the beach at Deep Water Bay.

In November the *Great Northern* left Hong Kong for Shanghai. The ship sailed up the Yangtze and cast anchor outside Wusong, where Suenson, who again had arrived before the others, picked up the young Danes in a large sailboat. The company's new house on The Bund in Shanghai was now put to use. There were rooms for the staff as well as offices for the company's future activities. On the ground floor there was a common dining and sitting room. The young Danes relaxed in the evening particularly by playing or listening to music. William Bramsen played the cello and several of the others were excellent pianists. Thus did the Great Northern Danish community establish itself. For many years it would leave its mark on the commercial life of Shanghai.

The cable ship laid down a cable from Wusong to the island of Gutzlaff, 40 miles off the coast. The rocky little island, named after a German missionary with only a lighthouse and a small dwelling, was to become the central junction of Great Northern's cable lines along the coast of China. The link with Hong Kong was thereby established.

However, Suenson had not straightened out all the formalities involved in laying out the cable from Gutzlaff to Wusong and up the Whangpoo River to Shanghai. The original plan had been to land the cable on the land allotted to the English commercial house of Jardine, Matheson & Co. in Wusong. The Peking authorities had already refused British negotiators permission to bring the cables ashore as they were strongly opposed to allowing such foreign devilry into China. The provincial authorities also felt their independence threatened by the idea

Figure 14: William Bramsen (1850–81), Kirsten's father's brother, helped to lay the Great Northern telegraph cable in China in 1870. Afterwards he was employed as secretary to the management of Mitsubishi in Tokyo. The Japanese firm sent him to London to study law, but in 1881 he died there of pneumonia at the age of only 30.

of the new, rapid means of communication gaining a footing on land. Francis Bulkeley Johnson, partner in Jardine, Matheson & Co. in Shanghai as well as the acting Danish consul, got cold feet at this point and begged out of the Danish project. Suenson then entered upon a secret agreement with the French authorities to land the cable at the French naval station at Wusong.

A great deal was at stake – in the race between the European telegraph companies it was imperative to get in first. Young Suenson therefore decided to go through with laying out the final cable section to Shanghai without the go-ahead from Peking. His young telegraph operators, including William Bramsen, were ready to assist in the dangerous operation.

On the moonlit night of 8 December 1870, the end of the cable was brought ashore at Wusong. Here two small tugboats silently assisted in laying out the cable in the water along the bank of the Whangpoo and on into Shanghai. The end of the cable was then buried in the riverbank on the piece of Bund land acquired by Great Northern. All traces of the Danish landing were removed and for several months only the handful of participants who had taken part in the nightly expedition were aware that the first telegraph cable had been laid in the Heavenly Kingdom. Suenson sent a message by courier to the Russian border town of Kiachta and from there by telegraph across Siberia, informing the head office in Copenhagen that the operation had been successful. Tietgen was delighted at the news.

Suenson succeeded in getting the necessary Chinese formalities settled in April 1871. It was now up to the Danes to show the Chinese that it was actually possible to communicate with Hong Kong. In Denmark, Professor Hans Schjellerup, at the request of a Chinese delegation visiting Denmark in 1869, had drafted a proposal for a Chinese telegraph dictionary. In combination with a survey done by the Shanghai harbourmaster, Frenchman M.S.A. Viguier, Great Northern could now use Schjellerup's principles to draw up a telegraph dictionary consisting of 5,454 Chinese characters arranged according to the traditional 214 radicals. Each character was assigned a number. Chinese merchants in the two key ports could communicate with each other by sending a series of consecutive numbers, which were then translated back into characters at the other end. Doubt and suspicion rapidly gave way to admiration and enthusiasm when it turned out that the connection actually worked! In May several Chinese merchants in Shanghai wired orders to their agents in Hong Kong. A week later the Chinese merchants visited Great Northern's office, jubilantly announcing that they had cut some excellent deals.

Figure 15: The frigate *Tordenskjold* was the first Danish steamer to navigate the Suez Canal in 1879. A number of young Danes, including Kirsten's father's brother, William Bramsen, were aboard on their way to China to work as telegraph operators for Great Northern Telegraph Company. The *Tordenskjold* is shown here off the coast of China. Today this painting by Vilhelm Arnesen hangs in the Great Northern headquarters in Copenhagen.

In the following months submarine cables were laid out from Shanghai to Nagasaki and on to the Russian port of Vladivostok. Cables were being laid out along the coast of China at the same time that Great Northern's men were completing the final stages of the overland telegraph line from Europe to Vladivostok. How proud the Danish firm was on 1 January 1872, when it was able to open its doors for commercial telegraphic dispatches between Europe and the Far East! Messages from Copenhagen to Shanghai, which had formerly taken several months by sea, could now be transmitted by relay stations across Siberia in a few hours. First Lieutenant Georg Dreyer assumed the position of Great

Northern's Shanghai manager. His wife came out to join him in August 1872 and the Danish community in Shanghai was hereby established in earnest.

For Great Northern the following years in China were marked by a continual build-up of the overland telegraphic network. The company arranged the training of Chinese telegraph operators, using Danish instructors. In time several Danish employees joined the Chinese telegraph service. The Danish system of converting the Chinese characters into Morse telegraph codes soon came into general use in China (and became topical again more than 100 years later when the Chinese characters had to be converted into computer language for purposes of electronic data processing).

Figure 16: The European and American businessmen who settled in Shanghai from the middle of the nineteenth century built large, beautiful houses on the towpath along the Whangpoo River. The path had formerly been used by Chinese coolies pulling the heavily laden grain junks up the river. The British called the muddy towpath The Bund, a word they had brought with them from India. Before long the fashionable houses on The Bund had become Shanghai's major business district. This picture taken in 1869 shows what The Bund looked like when Great Northern established its Shanghai cable office there.

The East Asiatic Company

Whenever Vilhelm passed Great Northern's head office at Kongens Nytorv in Copenhagen, he cast a respectful glance at the green, bronze statue of Electra, bearer of a ball of light, standing on the top of the building. He was well aware that Great Northern was still the largest Danish company in China and that employment in such a firm might very well help him realize his dream of going to Shanghai. However, he wanted to go as a businessman and consequently felt that the newly founded East Asiatic Company was probably his best bet.

He embarked on a study of E.A.C.'s history. H.N. Andersen, the company's director, had founded the firm of Andersen & Co. in 1884 with headquarters

in Bangkok, the capital of Siam. After a few years the brothers Frederik and
Emanuel Kinch were made partners in the firm. H.N. Andersen moved back to
Copenhagen in 1896, where he founded the East Asiatic Company the following
year. The new firm was still based on activities in Siam, but was also taking steps
to expand its sphere of activities since in the future the company would also be
staking a great deal on international shipping. As implied in the company name,
not only Siam, but all of East Asia was to be the primary target of its expansion.

When H.N. Andersen founded E.A.C. in 1897, he was well aware that if Denmark were to stake a claim in the Far East, this would involve more than posting
a few agents in the most important seaports. If Denmark were to have an impact,
she would have to show her colours more noticeably. Henrik Cavling, journalist
for the newspaper *Politiken* and a good friend of Andersen's, agreed. On the front
page of *Politiken* in November 1897 he published an article under the headline
'The Danish Flag on the Seven Seas', in which he wrote:

> The personal competence of citizens of small nations is often increased by ex-
> posure to the greater world. It is astonishing how many Danes have acquired
> outstanding positions in foreign parts from whence they bring back new im-
> pulses to the mother country. But the mother country does little or nothing to
> encourage and support such fellow countrymen even though their feelings for
> home have grown more intense as the distance increases.

Cavling emphasized the importance of sending one of the navy's ships to promote Danish trade and enterprise abroad:

> Not a single Danish man-of-war has passed through Singapore since 1870 when
> the *Tordenskjold* was in China. There is currently within the Danish business com-
> munity an awakening interest in the cities along the coasts of India and China.
> The East Asiatic Company will further increase this interest. In Siam, where Danish
> influence is particularly noticeable, they have never seen a Danish warship and
> in Shanghai, where the Great Northern Telegraph Company occupies a position
> of great prominence, they have not received an official visit from the home
> country in the past 27 years.

In the article Cavling also comments on the unfortunate consular conditions
then prevailing: 'Danish consuls out there are usually men of foreign nationality. Most of them have the impression that Denmark is on the moon. It would
do no harm if we shot them up a bit at regular intervals.' Cavling concludes
with the following earnest call to action: 'May these lines call forth a comment
on the conditions touched upon here and the expediency of sending a man-of-
war to Far Eastern waters.' The article was read in Copenhagen and the request
was acted upon. The Danish Chamber of Commerce in particular hurried up
the proceedings. In the spring of 1899 Hørring's Conservative government
petitioned the Danish Parliament for funds for the cruiser corvette, the
Valkyrien, with Prince Valdemar in command. The Liberal Party in Parliament
felt that the business community ought to cover some of the costs and that the
portion of the expenses defrayed by the state should be covered by the Ministry of the Interior, which at the time protected the interests of the business
community, rather than the Ministry of the Navy. The Liberals then gave their

Figure 17: Prince Valdemar (1858–1939) was commander of the *Valkyrien* on the Far Eastern voyage of 1899–1900.

support to the plan to send the corvette on a promotional campaign to the Far East. The newly appointed Minister of the Interior, Ludvig Bramsen, brother of Aage and William (see Genealogical Table, Appendix) was thus formally responsible for the expenses defrayed by the Danish government in connection with the *Valkyrien* voyage departing in October 1899.

The *Valkyrien* in Shanghai

Vilhelm had watched the *Valkyrien* and E.A.C.'s big, new steamship the Annam leave Copenhagen for the Far East. Henrik Cavling of *Politiken* was among H.N. Andersen's guests on board the Annam. After a stopover of a few weeks in Bangkok, most of the participants returned home while H.N. Andersen and Prince Valdemar continued on to Saigon, Hong Kong, Canton, Fuzhou and Shanghai. Cavling also covered this stage of the voyage to the Orient. He committed his impressions to paper in the book *Østen* [The Orient] published in 1901. Vilhelm read it with interest, receiving a full and topical impression of conditions in China. During the *Valkyrien*'s stay in Shanghai several banquets and other functions were arranged. Jacob Henningsen, Great Northern's local manager, who had gone out to China with William Bramsen on the *Tordenskjold* in 1870, gave the first party. Jacob Henningsen and H.N. Andersen had known each other as boys in Nakskov where Jacob, who was from one of the city's wealthier families, had been a loyal friend to Hans Niels, whose family was not well off. This prompted H.N. Andersen, who had not proposed a single toast throughout the entire journey, to propose a toast at the Henningsen dinner, which, according to Cavling, 'bore the stamp of his strong feelings for home'.

Figure 18: The *Valkyrien* sailed to the Far East in 1899–1900 to show the Danish flag. The cruise was initiated by Danish entrepreneurs and business people, who – under the leadership of H.N. Andersen, the president of E.A.C. – were eager to invest in new export markets in the Far East. The Danish warship shown here was drawn by Princess Marie, who also first launched the ship. She was married to Prince Valdemar, the ship's commander on the voyage.

The Danish community in Shanghai (there were about 100 Danes living there at the time) gave a magnificent banquet for the crew of the *Valkyrien* as well as visitors from Denmark. A total of 200 guests sat down to dinner surrounded by Danish flags and escutcheons, with royal monograms on the walls. At the far end of the hall were draped large national flags of Denmark, Norway, Sweden and France. The French flag was in special deference to the godmother of the *Valkyrien*, the Princess Marie, born in France and married to Prince Valdemar. The next day a detailed description of the festivities appeared in the *The North China Herald News*, in which it was mentioned that during the dinner there had been many speeches and toasts 'as is the Danish custom'.

Figure 19: From 1869 until the Communists took power in 1949, the Great Northern Telegraph Company was the largest Danish firm in China. This picture, taken at the turn of the century, shows the Great Northern telegraph station in Shanghai. Jacob Henningsen, its renowned manager, stands at the centre of the photo.

The Shanghai Municipal Council then gave a full dress ball at the town hall. Cavling noted that none of the European and American participants seemed to be over 50: 'The purpose of staying in China is to acquire the largest possible fortune in the shortest possible time and when that goal is achieved, the older people go back to Europe with a light heart, making room for new youth.' The Danish reporter also noticed that all the guests belonged to pretty much the same social group:

> There is no elegant class here to claim homage and attention and disturb the natural flow of things. Here anyone can drain the cup of pleasure unaffected by any other humours than his own. Of course, among the ladies there is the eternal rivalry for the prize of elegance and beauty. The rivalry is increased by the fact that the ladies are not only fighting for their own social position of power, but for their nationality.

The highest Chinese authority in Shanghai, the Taotai, also hosted an elegant banquet, and finally the officers of the *Valkyrien* were themselves the hosts at a dinner at the British Country Club attended by all the foreign dignitaries in town. But apart from the waiters in their blue jackets, no Chinese were present – Chinese guests were not admitted to the club.

Great Northern's station in Shanghai was now the company's biggest office in China. The staff at the turn of the century consisted of approx. 200 people, including around 30 Danes. The remaining 70 or so Danes in Shanghai were

Figure 20: Jacob Henningsen (1849–1913), who was among the first telegraph-operators to go to China, travelled there in 1870 aboard the frigate *Tordenskjold*. He became manager of the Shanghai station in 1883 and was the author of several books on life in China during the final years of the empire.

not employed by Danish firms, but in positions as master mariners, pilots, insurance agents, or were employed as officials in the Chinese customs and telegraph services. Several of them were married to Chinese women.

One of the Danes living in Shanghai was old Captain Petersen-Høj. He had helped lay out the first cables in China and was now a senior captain in the large shipping company, China Merchant Steam Navigation Company. Old-Petersen, as he was called, had been made a mandarin. This was also true of Knud von Lindholm, one of the many Danes working in the Chinese customs service; he lived in China from 1888 to 1925. The title of 'mandarin', which was subdivided into nine different classes, was granted to civil servants as well as military officers.

'Send Danish Youth Abroad!'

On his return to Copenhagen from his voyage to the Far East, H.N. Andersen submitted in April 1900 a written report on business conditions in all of Eastern Asia to the Danish Chamber of Commerce. The main message was clear: there was a large market in the Far East just waiting for Danish enterprise. In the foreword to the report he urged the members of the Danish Chamber of Commerce to rise to the occasion:

> With the *Valkyrien* we have begun to look afar and it is to be hoped that we will continue to keep our eye on the goal so that the links forged on this occasion will not once again be broken. The Danish people are not only a farming nation, but also a commercial and seagoing one. Let us make use of our favourable position

Figure 21: Henrik Cavling (1858–1933) was employed by the Danish newspaper *Politiken* in 1885. He went on many trips abroad, including a voyage to the Far East in 1900–01 with H.N. Andersen, the president of E.A.C. He shared H.N. Andersen's dream of sending young Danish merchants to China to promote Danish exports.

and avail ourselves of the opportunities arising therefrom to turn the areas mentioned in my report to our country's greatest possible advantage.

In his report H.N. Andersen emphasized the vital importance of having people in the field if a firm wished to be competitive with the firms of other European nations. Only by 'creating a home on the spot' was it possible to gain the necessary insight into the goods traditionally used by the natives and the goods they might find use for in the future. Cavling touched on the same idea in his travel book *The Orient.* Writing about the Danes in Shanghai, he said that many of them worked for Great Northern, and were to be highly commended for their hard work and accuracy. But Cavling also found that the young Danish telegraph operators were somewhat cowed by the endless monotony of their jobs and were marked by a mechanical sense of duty, which was slowly destroying their spirit of enterprise. Very few of them had a sense of adventure or the courage to try anything new.

He further lamented the fact that there were no young Danish merchants going to China on their own so as to get their share of the promising new markets. And it was no use pleading that Denmark was a small country. It was precisely the smaller countries that could turn the mutual rivalry of the larger countries to their own advantage, as Edouard Suenson's great feat in the field of telegraph communications had shown, for example. Perhaps education was partly responsible, wrote Cavling:

> Nothing arouses the boys' interest in foreign climes. What do our educators tell us about the greatest empire in the world? Nothing, for they know nothing. Add to this the complete indifference on the part of ministers and leading politicians

to the aspect of education that broadens the child's horizons. We don't have many citizens of the world in Denmark. One need only recall the comic furor of opposition at the thought of dispatching the *Valkyrien*! In the end a subscription had to be circulated and when the man-of-war left Denmark it was by subscription! A subscription ship sailing to the Orient bearing the Danish flag!

Cavling thought that the most gifted boys should be sent to England to learn English instead of drilling Latin and Greek verbs. 'Send Danish youth abroad! Will they forget the fatherland? Never! Nowhere in the world does youth learn a deeper love of country than when it is able to do credit to the fatherland.' This call to send the young abroad was characteristic of the pragmatic imperialism that marked the thinking of many well-established Europeans. In fact, the Western world was even supposed to be responsible for initiating the development of poor countries overseas. Kipling's poem 'The White Man's Burden' from 1899 concisely expounds this philosophy:

> Take up the White Man's Burden.
> Send forth the best ye breed.
> Go bind your sons to exile,
> To serve your captives' need;
> To wait in heavy harness,
> On fluttered folk and wild.
> Your new-caught sullen peoples,
> Half devil and half child.

H.N. Andersen's visions as presented to the Chamber of Commerce and Cavling's call to young Danish merchants to travel to the Far East were the subject of lively debate on the Copenhagen Stock Exchange. In their home in Nyhavn, Louis Meyer, the merchant, and his enterprising, youngest son also discussed the new opportunities opening up in China.

E.A.C. Opens Offices in China

In view of the growing Russian interest in Manchuria, H.N. Andersen felt that E.A.C. might profit from the commercial opportunities now opening up. Work on the Trans-Siberian railway from Moscow to the Pacific had been started in 1891. The final section to Vladisvostok, running through Manchuria, which belonged to China, was not yet completed. Allowing the Russian railway to pass through Manchuria would shorten it by 400 miles. An agreement to that effect was signed by the Russians and the Chinese in 1886 and the railway was scheduled for completion in 1903. The necessary capital had been raised in 1895 through the establishment of the Russo–Chinese Bank, which, thanks to contributions from a number of French banks, was able to put up 6 million gold roubles in initial capital. Both the bank and the railroad company, Chinese Eastern Railways, were French enterprises on paper. In reality, however, they were controlled by the Russian government in St Petersburg. In return for Chinese concessions to Russia in Manchuria, the Sino–Russian pact contained a defence alliance against Japan, their new common rival in the Far East.

In 1897 Russia had forced China to make the two ports of Port Arthur (Lüshun) and Dairen (Dalian) in Manchuria available for the next 25 years. From the naval base at Port Arthur, which is ice-free all year round as opposed to Vladivostok, a rail link could be established through Mukden (Shenyang) and Harbin to link up with the railway line from Moscow to Vladivostok.

Given the new railway network stretching across Siberia, the Great Northern telegraph lines reaching to the Far East and China's huge market potential, H.N. Andersen was convinced of the desirability of E.A.C. establishing branches in China. The British were well-ensconced in Southern and Central China, Canton and Hong Kong being the most important ports. E.A.C. ought therefore to turn its attention primarily towards Shanghai, China's most important commercial centre, and to the other ports along the coast to the north, including the Manchurian ports. Because of his close cooperation with Russia, it was natural for H.N. Andersen to follow in the wake of the Russian expansion into Northern China. He had excellent connections in St Petersburg, including the Russian imperial family. Tsar Nicolas II was the son of Dagmar, daughter of King Christian IX and thus the nephew of Prince Valdemar and Princess Marie, with whom H.N. Andersen was on excellent terms. He succeeded in negotiating contracts for the transportation of Russian railroad materiel on E.A.C. vessels from Russian ports in the Baltic to Port Arthur and Vladivostok.

In connection with the Boxer Rebellion in China in the summer of 1900, E.A.C. entered a contract to transport 12,000 Russian soldiers and military supplies from the Russian Baltic ports to Port Arthur, Dalian and Vladivostok. The company earned a substantial profit in this period.

In August 1900 Frederik Kinch, director of E.A.C., left for Shanghai, in order officially to open the company's main branch in the Far East there in November. The new office was housed in the business street along the river, at The Bund no. 4. Frederik Kinch's first job was to make sure that the ships that had transported Russian troops and matériel to the Far East could get freight to take back to Europe.

There was also other profitable business to be done. Early in 1901 Kinch, acting on orders from the E.A.C. head office in Copenhagen, bought a piece of land at the harbour in Shanghai, where he had warehouses and a small shipyard built. Chinese Eastern Railways, the Russian railway company in Manchuria, had set up a shipping department interested in buying these new facilities. The sale, which took place in November 1901, was particularly profitable for E.A.C. and the balance sheet of 1901 boded well for the newly opened branch. In the course of the first year after establishing its Shanghai branch, E.A.C. opened new sub-branches in Hankou up the Yangtze River and in Port Arthur, Dalian, and Niuzhuang (Yingkou) in Manchuria. Denmark had thus acquired another important firm in the Far East in addition to Great Northern Telegraph Company. The two Danish companies had both chosen Shanghai as their headquarters in China.

To Vilhelm the message was quite clear. There seemed to be great opportunities in China for a young Dane trained in business. He felt drawn to Shanghai, attracted by the idea of making an impact in China.

FOUR

Setting a Course for Shanghai, 1902

Vilhelm Applies for a Position at E.A.C.

Vilhelm had confided to Kirsten on 5 January that he wanted to leave the old family business Moses & Son, G. Melchior to go to China. A few days later he set about putting his plan into action. He presented himself to the head office of East Asiatic Company for more information about the possibility of working at the company's newly established branch in Shanghai. He was 23 years old, had already had several years of practical experience in various firms both in Denmark and abroad and was in possession of excellent references. At E.A.C. Vilhelm was told that there were no openings at present.

Figure 22: From 1899 to1908 the E.A.C. headquarters were located in the Copenhagen Free Port. It was here that Vilhelm was hired by E.A.C. in 1902 and later – in 1906 – entered into an agreement with H.N. Andersen for a loan to A. M. & Co.

But then in February Vilhelm was called in for an interview by H.N. Andersen, the president of E.A.C., who wanted to speak to the young China enthusiast. This meeting, which took place in the president's office in the E.A.C. building, was very formal, however. Vilhelm was not asked to sit down, but had to remain respectfully standing throughout the entire interview. Seated behind his large desk, Mr Andersen informed Vilhelm that there was a position for him at the Shanghai office. He stated clearly what he expected of young Meyer. To begin with, Meyer was to be fully conscious of the responsibility that such an opportunity implied. Second, it must be clearly understood that although the work did allow for a certain amount of independent action, he must at all times obey orders from Copenhagen, attach great importance to the minutest of details and exercise the greatest economy in his daily work.

H.N. Andersen further impressed upon him that although, as the youngest representative of the firm in China, Meyer as an individual was of little or no importance, nevertheless his behaviour as a Dane and an employee of E.A.C. was very important indeed. Loyalty and obedience to the firm's ideas and policies must always come first. There would be a great deal to do in Shanghai and if Meyer entertained any romantic notions about the Far East as a place where a white man could spend his life in self-indulgence and luxury, he either had to forget them fast or else remain at home in Denmark. Meyer would certainly have more to do than he had ever had before. And as for luxury in China, he would receive a salary he could live on, but which would allow for no extravagances. The salary would be determined by the managing director, Frederik Kinch, upon arrival in Shanghai.

Figure 23: As a young sailor in the early 1870s, H.N. Andersen (1852–1937) arrived in Hong Kong, where he became fascinated by the rapid pace of developments in the Far East. In 1884 he established the firm of Andersen & Co. in Siam, present-day Thailand. In 1897 he took steps to establish the East Asiatic Company, which in time would become one of the largest Danish firms.

In conclusion H.N. Andersen referred to his old motto, 'The will to succeed'. 'If at E.A.C. we are satisfied with your abilities and your will to succeed in the course of the next couple of years, then it is highly likely that we will employ you permanently. I wish you good luck.' He then indicated by a brief nod that the interview was at an end. But Vilhelm did not immediately withdraw. The president of the East Asiatic Company had just informed him what lay ahead, but he had been somewhat taken aback at the tone of the monologue. He had come to the interview with great expectations regarding the splendid opportunities in China. And although he didn't expect the company president to share his enthusiasm, he had nevertheless counted on a certain friendliness. In the firms where he had worked in recent years the everyday tone between employer and employee had been naturally kindly and encouraging. Vilhelm was also a bit put off by the warning note he had felt underlying H.N. Andersen's remarks. It almost seemed as if he had been addressing a refractory schoolboy.

Figure 24: Eager to go to Shanghai, Vilhelm applied for a position with E.A.C. early in 1902. On 15 March 1902, the day he left Copenhagen, Vilhelm gave his closest friends a photograph of himself so they would not forget him. He did not return to Denmark again until a visit in the summer of 1906.

Vilhelm hesitated a moment before leaving H.N. Andersen's office. Then he summoned up his courage and made his own statement. He would of course do his utmost in Shanghai to protect the company's interests and he was truly grateful for the great opportunity he was being given. But he assumed that since East Asiatic Company was at liberty when it came to giving him permanent employment, this freedom would also apply to himself when he addressed the question at a later date.

The president glanced at Vilhelm with his steely grey eyes and then at the papers on his desk. 'Your assumption is correct, young man, but not very sensible', he said brusquely. No more was said. The interview was over. Although the meeting had not seemed particularly harmonious, H.N. Andersen nevertheless wrote to Frederik Kinch that he had employed Vilhelm Meyer to work in the Shanghai office and that the young man had given the impression of being unusually pleasant and bright.

In theory this was a normal three-year contract in accordance with the terms usually stipulated in E.A.C. employment contracts. Employees wishing to leave the job prematurely had to pay for their home voyage themselves. But in

Vilhelm's case both he and E.A.C. wanted as free an agreement as possible and there was thus no written contract of employment.

After a few days' work at the E.A.C. office in the free port area, Vilhelm took his leave of his family and friends in Copenhagen in March 1902. He told Kirsten that he would not be back for at least three years. But they had photos of each other and they would both write. Kirsten was miserable. She was young and in love and also extremely anxious about Vilhelm's entire project. On the other hand she realized how important it was for Vilhelm to go abroad and try his luck in the world. Vilhelm's friends had given him a silver cigarette case as a farewell gift. On the inside of the lid was inscribed:

> To Vilhelm Meyer
> 14 March 1902
> from your Danish friends

Vilhelm went by train from Copenhagen to Genoa, Italy, from where he had booked passage on the German ship, the *Prinzess Irene.* The passenger ship sailed through the Suez Canal to the Far East with the classical stopovers in Shanghai, Indochina and Hong Kong. E.A.C. covered the price of a second-class ticket to Shanghai, but Vilhelm wanted to travel in style and therefore bought a first-class ticket, footing the difference himself.

Among the books Vilhelm had with him on his long voyage were the new book *The Orient* by the journalist, Henrik Cavling, and two books on everyday life in China written by Jacob Henningsen, Great Northern's Shanghai manager for many years. Sitting on deck he lost himself in tales of the great ancient empire towards which he was heading, following in the footsteps of other Danes who had been there before him.

Canton, Shanghai and Peking

Apart from the foreign factories in Canton, China had for many years maintained its ban on trade with European nations. In 1839 the Chinese government had put a stop to the import of opium into Canton. The British merchants had no wish to discontinue this lucrative trade and the tense relations between England and China resulted in the so-called First Opium War in which the British Navy was victorious. The Chinese were forced to sign a peace treaty in 1842, which, among other things, gave England control of a small rocky island at the mouth of the Canton River. This became the British Crown Colony of Hong Kong. The treaty also allowed the British to use the ports of five Chinese coastal cities, Canton, Xiamen (Amoy), Fuzhou, Ningbo and Shanghai as bases for British trade with China. According to the treaty, British subjects had the right to take up residence in the five cities with a view to engaging in trade without Chinese interference or limitations.

In Shanghai the British were allotted an area of about 50 acres by the river. By the end of 1843, 25 British businessmen had already settled in the area, built 11 houses and been visited by 40 foreign commercial vessels. The following year the United States and France signed similar treaties with the Chinese government and the two countries were also allotted areas in the other open Treaty Ports.

In 1844 Shanghai consisted of a Chinese section surrounded by the old city wall built in 1553, a French area north-west of the city wall, a British area and an American area in the Hongkou district on the northern bank of the Suzhou River. (See Fig. 13) Leading European businessmen had built spacious commercial houses on The Bund, the waterfront street along the river, and in the following years Shanghai developed into a large and dynamic commercial centre.

By 1843 the British trading company, East India Company, had gained control of the China trade – the same year that the Danish Asiatic Company had found it necessary finally to discontinue operations. Danish merchants had not given up, however. They had continued trading with the Far East, shipping their goods on foreign vessels.

Figure 25: Admiral Steen Andersen Bille (1797–1883) commanded the corvette *Galathea* on a voyage around the world in 1845–47. He carried out a number of diplomatic, consular, commercial and scientific tasks. In Shanghai in 1846 he installed Nicolas Duus as the first Danish consul in Shanghai. Bille returned to Shanghai in 1864 in order to formalize the Danish–Chinese treaty that had been negotiated the previous year.

In the 1840s it was vital for Danish merchants to have consular agents appointed to protect Danish interests in China. Denmark had appointed three consuls on the coast of China, in Hong Kong, Canton and Shanghai. Partners in the large British commercial firm of Jardine, Matheson & Co. often served as the Danish consul, as Donald Matheson did in Canton, for instance. In Shanghai, however, the first Danish consul was the Danish merchant Nicolai Duus of the firm Duus, Pawle & Co., appointed in 1845.

The Danish naval officer, Commander Steen Andersen Bille, was in charge of a scientific expedition that circumnavigated the globe in 1845–47 on board the Danish corvette *Galathea*. In August 1846 the ship docked in Shanghai. It was the largest ship ever to have sailed all the way up to the city and the *Galathea* was greatly admired by foreigners and Chinese alike.

During his stay in Shanghai Bille introduced Nicolai Duus, the newly appointed Danish consul, to the local Chinese governor and for the first time the Danish flag was hoisted in Shanghai. Bille considered Shanghai a most charming and pleasant city, finding the Chinese population there much friendlier than in Canton. He noted in an account of his journey that while the modern European section was airy and elegant and the houses there beautiful, the Chinese section behind the city wall was very crowded and nasty.

In 1856 there were again complications between China and the Western commercial nations. This led to new hostilities – the Second Opium War – and the subsequent defeat of the Chinese forces. According to the new treaties of 1858 between China and England, France, Russia and the United States respectively, these countries were granted the exclusive right to establish legations in Peking, the capital of China. The principle of exterritoriality was recognized for citizens of these countries, which meant that they were under the jurisdiction of the courts and legal systems of their home countries and not subject to the Chinese legal system. In addition a number of new Chinese treaty ports were opened to the four nations.

The *Taiping* Rebellion

The imperial Chinese government not only had to deal with foreigners wishing to take part in China's development by force. Many people within the vast empire's own borders, who wished to have an impact on developments, rebelled against the Peking government. In 1851 a rebellion broke out in Guangxi province, which took 14 years of fierce fighting to put down. The rebel Chinese rallied around the 'Heavenly Kingdom', opposing the Manchu Qing dynasty in Peking, which had ruled China since 1644 and whom they considered foreign rulers. In 1853 the *Taiping* rebels took the old Ming capital, the fortified city of Nanjing. After a veritable blood-bath, in which all the Manchus and their supporters were killed, the Yangtze River ran red with blood.

In Shanghai it was imperative for the handful of foreign settlers to keep out of the civil war. After the fall of Nanjing they decided to set up a corps of volunteers, the Shanghai Volunteer Corps. In the course of the following years, the volunteer marksmen protected Shanghai's international district, first from the imperial forces of the north and later from the *Taiping* rebels of the south.

In 1863 it was decided that the British and American sections should be merged into one International Settlement. The French Concession had the status of a colony and France had therefore no wish to allow the French section to be incorporated into the new Anglo-American district.

The *Taiping* rebels were not put down by the imperial forces until 1864. In this period the foreign Shanghailanders were given a foretaste of the precarious situation they were often to find themselves in during the subsequent military confrontations between Chinese warlords, nationalists, communists and Japanese forces.

The Danish–Chinese Treaty

After the major Western powers had gained a number of new business concessions in 1858, Copenhagen, too, wished to improve Denmark's chances of engaging in trade with China. The Danish chargé d'affaires in Washington, Lieutenant-Colonel Waldemar R. Raasløff, was sent to China in 1863 on a special mission to negotiate a Danish–Chinese Agreement on Friendship, Trade and Shipping. The Danish diplomat stayed at Astor Hotel in Tianjin where he succeeded in negotiating a treaty, which on the whole corresponded to the Great Powers' treaties of 1858. Article 1 reads as follows:

> There shall be, as there has always been, peace and friendship between His Majesty the King of Denmark and His Majesty the Emperor of China; and their respective subjects shall equally enjoy, in the dominions of the High Contracting parties, full and entire protection for their persons and property.

The treaty ensured that all formalities enabling Danish commercial firms to enter a number of Chinese ports were now in order. This applied to the traditional ports up along the coast and along the Yangtze River. In addition, ports on the islands of Taiwan and Hainan were now also opened to Danish ships. As was the case for similar treaties between China and other Western nations, Denmark had insisted on a clause to the effect that the Chinese would not use the Chinese character for 'barbarian' to refer to Danish subjects in any official document!

In July 1864 Steen Bille, now vice-admiral, had again gone to Shanghai, this time to exchange ratification instruments for the treaty concluded with the Chinese government. Bille was impressed by the way the foreign businessmen in Shanghai had developed the city since the last time he had visited the city, 18 years before. The Bund was now characterized by opulent Western buildings, such as the new club building, the Shanghai Club. This was not only the Shanghailanders' most exclusive club, but also the favourite hotel and boarding house for newly arrived Europeans and Americans.

Bille also noticed something else, which was to become more and more pronounced in Shanghai over the years: new arrivals from abroad were completely preoccupied with their economic ventures:

> With the exception of missionaries and the military, they only come out here to make money. They pursue their goal from morning to night, which makes them highly inaccessible both physically and mentally. During the daytime you can't get near them because they're constantly working and in the evening they're so tired that they have no mind for any conversation of general interest.

In his book *The Orient*, Cavling noted how the foreigners in Shanghai had developed their own independent city council, the Shanghai Municipal Council, in the International Settlement:

> In terms of municipal affairs, the English and American Settlement is a European city. It is run by a Municipal Council consisting of nine members, including not only representatives of the nationalities mentioned, but at one point there was even a Danish Shanghailander, too. In the different sections of the city the streets have American, English and French names respectively and as you walk through the streets it is easy to tell the different nationalities by type and dress.

Figure 26: Waldemar Raasløff (1815–83) was Denmark's envoy to Washington in 1859–66. From there he went to China in 1863 to negotiate an agreement that would give Danish citizens in China the same rights that Britain and France had gained. In 1866 he was made Danish minister of war. In this capacity he backed sending the frigate *Tordenskjold* to China in 1870 to assist the Great Northern Telegraph Company.

In their daily dealings Europeans feel as though they belong to the same city. Around 6,000 Europeans live in Shanghai's foreign colony. But they enjoy a higher social position than if they were 6,000 ordinary European citizens. The European community in the Far East is not weakened by a proletariat. Europeans are clerical workers, merchants, shipowners and bankers. This is a civilian population, which in its commercial and social development remains unaffected by the authoritarian spirit of Western society.

It is of special interest to note how these 6,000 civilians, left to their own devices, have formed and developed a modern society. The Europeans who came out here brought with them an image of Europe. But no matter how deeply this image may have been imprinted on their minds, they transformed it according to their needs. The result is a miniature Europe with no established church, military or public authorities. There were things from the old society that the Europeans had no use for here – the rattling of swords, titles, orders and official high rank. The citizens of this city have as little use for governors and retired colonels as for knights and court tailors and court shoemakers. They have created a simple, social organism, which they manage like a bank.

Cavling then develops the comparison with a bank, explaining how every year the Europeans elect a board of directors to manage the city's finances.

The city is completely autonomous even though it is situated in a foreign state. Being elected to the Municipal Council is, of course, the highest honour that can befall a mortal in Shanghai. The council levies taxes, imposes duties, and is in charge of public works. The city has its own police force consisting of around 50 Europeans and six times as many Chinese and Indians, the so-called Sikhs, who resemble walking bamboo sticks with a motley turban on the top end. It also has its own prison, its volunteer fire brigade with five fire engines and a fire station, its own highway authority in charge of maintaining the electric street lights, its own health police, market halls, public slaughter-houses and its own small volunteer army consisting of 300 infantry, artillery and cavalry. The city has its own gasworks, waterworks, hospitals and a theatre seating 800 and finally a ceremonial hall at the town hall, which more than any of the city's other monumental adornments reminds the traveller of Europe. Ladies and gentlemen gather there for magnificent balls renowned throughout the entire Orient.

There are surely very few places in the world where so many new social events take place and where rumours are spread and discussed so eagerly as in Shanghai. The relations between men and women are different than in the West. The tone is free and unceremonious, whether the ladies and gentlemen meet on the tennis court, on a hunting expedition up the river, on a summer excursion to Japan or at the races in Hong Kong. This is the main reason for the social explosions, which often ruffle the smooth surface of life in the Paris of East Asia.

The social dynamite is all the more dangerous as the city is primarily inhabited by young people.

Far from Copenhagen

In his book *Djung Rhua Dji* Jacob Henningsen, the manager of Great Northern for many years, writes that although strictly speaking the Chinese did not have the right to live in Shanghai's international districts, they nevertheless moved there by the thousands. The greater degree of political freedom and the economic security that the Chinese could enjoy in the foreign sections was the primary attraction for the many new Chinese arrivals.

> Inasmuch as the Chinese are hardworking, thrifty and law-abiding citizens and as they appreciate in full measure the advantages they enjoy under European protection, they are an uncommonly important and welcome factor in the well-being of Shanghai. Some of them are in service or have business relations with the Europeans, but the great majority are small tradesmen or artisans, whose houses and neighbourhoods make up more than three-quarters of the settlement area.

Henningsen, who had lived in China from 1870 to 1900, was very fond of China, but also emphasized the fact that most foreigners throughout their entire stay in Shanghai dreamed of spending their final years in the country of their birth.

> Life in Shanghai is indeed very pleasant materially speaking, but this is the only compensation for spending the best years of one's life in surroundings that are not truly congenial, in a kind of voluntary exile, never giving up hope of 'going home' after the job is done, perhaps not before many long years have passed, and where it is the custom at least once a week to drink a glass in silence for 'absent friends', 'sweethearts and wives' and 'the old folks back home'.

Henningsen also describes the social life of Shanghai:

> There is a great deal of entertaining and the British, who make up the great majority of resident Europeans, set the tone, of course. The winter seasons are full of dinner parties, balls, concerts and theatre performances, while riding to

hounds, cricket, football and other outdoor activities delight the young. Twice a year, in the spring and autumn, there are horse races in which the small Mongolian horses must bear the brunt, and in the summer an international regatta. The river is alive with yachts and houseboats, on which the sportsmen of Shanghai go for long hunting trips up country by means of the ubiquitous canals leading to inexhaustible hunting grounds, accessible to anyone, and so rich in game – deer, pheasant, partridge, wild boar, snipe, ducks and geese – that it is not unusual for a hunting party of three or four to return after a few weeks' hunting with a thousand pieces of game.

And then there was the European Park down by the river, a most popular meeting-place. On the surface, life in Shanghai was idyllic, but Henningsen had to admit that as a Dane he sometimes felt far away from home. For an employee of Great Northern, the head office in Copenhagen seemed especially far away.

In the summer even though the thermometer reads 30 to 35 degrees ladies and gentlemen meet for the eternally young lawn tennis, tea, ice punch and flirtation, and then, after a cold shower and a good dinner, stroll down to the public garden, where, sprawled in our long, comfortable cane chairs, we continue the last two diversions of the afternoon while listening to the waltzes of the municipal band – and wishing we were 10,000 miles away.

For when it comes right down to it, Shanghai is too far away from Copenhagen.

The Boxer Rebellion

At the turn of the century rebellion was smoldering beneath the surface of the vast Chinese empire. There was discontent on several levels. The southern Chinese were hostile to the northern Chinese Manchurian regime in Peking. The rural population was hostile to the wealthy Chinese mandarins and merchants in the cities. And the commercial foreign interests in China, which increasingly had come to characterize the nineteenth century, had led to a growing xenophobia among the Chinese.

China had lost the Sino–Japanese war of 1894–95. Korea was then given its independence, but as part of the Japanese sphere of influence. The Manchurian government in Peking had had to relinquish Taiwan to the Japanese victors and to open a number of commercial ports to the Japanese. In order to pay war indemnities to Japan, China had to borrow money from the Europeans, who in return had been given further territorial concessions in China. Japan had made sure that according to the terms of the peace treaty, the Chinese treaty ports would not only allow trade, but also industrial development, i.e. the construction of factories. This was to have an especially great impact on Shanghai, where the large cotton mills manned by cheap Chinese labour and fuelled by cheap coal imports from Japan had already meant a heavy industrialization of the growing port.

In 1897 Germany had used the murder of two German missionaries as a pretext for occupying the port of Qingdao and extorting a 99-year lease for the entire Shandong province. As mentioned above, Russia had obtained a 25-year lease that same year for the naval base at Port Arthur and the commercial port of Dalian, with permission to build the railway through Manchuria from Vladivostok to Port Arthur. All of Manchuria was thus in the Russian sphere of influence.

The British for their part had quickly focused on the area surrounding the vast Yangtze River. In 1898 the British lease of Hong Kong was extended by 99 years until 1997. The British had also taken over the Chinese naval base in the Shandong province, Wei-Hai-Wei, which became the main British naval base in the Far East. According to the treaty with China, the British were to maintain control of the base for as long as Russia was in possession of the naval base at Port Arthur. Thus from both sides British and Russian naval forces were in control of the entrance to Peking's vital port, Tianjin.

France, which had already taken over Indochina, had acquired Yunnan province in the southern part of China as its sphere of interest. Fujian province had similarly fallen into the Japanese sphere of influence.

At the end of the 19th century the secret organization 'Yihctuan', which means the fist of justice, and is therefore known to foreigners as the Boxer Movement, gained widespread support in China. In addition to growing numbers of traders, the number of missionaries had also greatly increased. Early in the year 1900 there were more than 3,000 Christian missionaries in China. In German-dominated Shandong province alone more than 1,000 churches had been built. It was in this province that the Yihetuan rebels struck in the spring of 1900. Churches were torched and many foreign missionaries were killed along with their Chinese co-believers. The Boxers also vanquished the imperial soldiers sent to the province to put down the rebellion.

As the *Valkyrien* was on its way home to Denmark in the spring of the year 1900 after a successful visit to a peaceful China, the Boxer Rebellion spread. In June a Boxer force of many thousands of Chinese attacked the foreign population of Peking. Houses and churches were burnt down and many foreign missionaries and Christian Chinese were killed. The old empress dowager Cixi joined the Boxer Rebellion, issuing orders to the provincial governors to kill all foreigners. In Peking roughly 900 foreigners, half of whom were in the military, and 3,000 Chinese Christians took refuge in the foreign missions in the Legation Quarter.

The foreign governments formed an alliance consisting of England, Germany, France, Italy, Austria, Russia, Japan and the United States. They sent a relieving force of 2,000 to Peking. But for 55 days the legations were besieged by Boxers as well as by regular Chinese units. The foreigners were totally cut off from the rest of the world.

A large number of foreign forces convened in the port of Tianjin and in the middle of August an international force of approx. 20,000 men launched an attack on Peking. The foreign soldiers liberated the besieged foreigners. But they also availed themselves of the opportunity to loot Chinese palaces and temples, plundering art treasures, which were then shipped back to Europe in great numbers.

The Boxer Rebellion spread to other parts of China including Shanghai, where the atmosphere in the international sections was tense. One of Great Northern's Danish telegraph operators, Einar V. Jessen, wrote in his memoirs:

> Then came the difficult year 1900 with the Boxer Rebellion aimed at all whites. We had an awful lot of work and at the same time the summer of 1900 was the hottest yet in the brief history of Shanghai. Most foreigners let themselves be

recruited by the international or rather British voluntary military corps. I joined the French voluntary corps, which was later reinforced by Anamitic soldiers from Saigon and was then called 'Infanterie de la Marine Anamite'. I was given a fine uniform and a rifle of the good, old sort. We did guard duty, night drills and shooting practice.

The night-time guard duty was often quite tense. The worst guard duty I remember was standing a whole night by the French cathedral. A Dutchman was with me. We were surrounded by a swarm of almost naked, sweating coolies armed with bamboo sticks. They came very close to us, spat on us and yelled insults at us. But if we moved so much as an arm or a leg the whole crowd jumped back a few steps. We were hit on the head by stones quite a lot, but fortunately we were wearing white tropical helmets which took the worst blows. We were pretty worn out after a night like that. There was just time for a bath at home and then back to the telegraph station.

Jessen further wrote that the Shanghai consuls advised that all women and children should be evacuated. All ships to Japan were packed with 'refugees'.

After the foreign troops had taken Peking and liberated everyone besieged in the Legation Quarter, the Chinese government had to accept a humiliating peace treaty signed in September 1901.

Russia used the Boxer Rebellion as a pretext to capture Mukden (Shenyang) and Harbin with a view to taking over the three northern provinces, which put together constitute Manchuria. Russian expansion to the east, the primary aim of which was to ensure Russian access to Vladivostok, was now a vital element in the foreign policy of Tsarist Russia.

Arriving at Shanghai

It was clear to the 23-year-old Vilhelm that he was heading for something of a powder-keg. China was the most populous country in the world. It was a country in which ancient imperial and feudal traditions were in conflict with the desire for industrial development – a land where civil war and rebellion were smouldering just below the surface and where several foreign governments were doing all they could to influence political and economic developments. He could not understand the imperialistic conduct of Europe and Japan in China. He was better able to identify with the American attitude, which opposed the division of China and the special rights that the Japanese and the Europeans had gained for themselves. The Americans were worried that this development would continue to the detriment of U.S. exports to China and influence in the Far East. They supported free world trade. In 1899 and 1900, Secretary of State John Hay – through diplomatic notes to the European coun-tries and Japan – had explained in detail the American Open Door Policy, which contained two main tenets: the integrity of China and the equal treatment of all foreigners in China. Instinctively Vilhelm believed in the concept of Open Doors.

After several weeks at sea the *Prinzess Irene* approached Shanghai. Vilhelm was prepared for what awaited him on the last stretch from Wusong to Shanghai's famous waterfront, The Bund, described so vividly by Cavling on his trip to the Orient two years before:

Figure 27: The steamers that took passengers from Europe or the United States to the Far East in the early part of this century were large. In the spring of 1902 Vilhelm travelled to Shanghai on board the German vessel *Prinzess Irene*.

As you sail in from the sea what meets the eye on the right-hand side of the river are a number of factories and a long row of palatial merchants' residences. Between the merchants' homes and the river stretches the spacious, airy street The Bund, which is justly the favourite place of pilgrimage and pride of all Shanghai. The Bund, which terminates in a beautiful park, is just as busy as any main European thoroughfare. In the park the slanted eyes of Chinese amahs watch over the pale progeny of the Europeans. The sidewalks are alive with ladies and gentlemen dressed in white, their light-coloured hats emerging from among the red parasols. Again European speech is heard and ladies in provocative costumes bring San Francisco to mind. The European impression is further enhanced by the sight of the glittering horses and carriages and the cabs as light as a feather hurrying in all directions along the asphalt. Yes, truly there is something here, which in passing recalls Paris.

As the steamer slowly glides up the river it is easy to tell the American Settlement from the British – then you pass the French Concession. The first two nations do not own their land. They have leased it, paying the Chinese an annual rate. The French, on the other hand, were given a piece of land in 1853 because they had helped the Chinese government put down the *Taiping* rebels. The French Concession is thus subject to the authority of the French government. Legally speaking, all Europeans are under ex-territorial law, that is, the consuls are the highest legal authorities and execute the laws of their own countries.

Vilhelm stood on deck, gazing at Shanghai. The autonomy granted to British traders in 1843 and later extended to new arrivals from a number of other nations, including Denmark, had lasted for almost 60 years. How much longer could this unique arrangement continue? He wondered what the future held in store for him in this big and exotic city.

FIVE

Young Man in China, 1902–1904

East Asiatic Company in Shanghai

Vilhelm arrived in Shanghai on 18 April 1902. Ivan Andersen, the E.A.C. book-keeper, was waiting on the wharf to welcome him. Andersen was somewhat old-er than Vilhelm and had already been in Shanghai for a year. The two young men were to work at the same office and although quite different in appear-ance, Andersen being plump and Meyer tall, the two got along well. Directly after his arrival, Vilhelm reported to the E.A.C. office to start his new job with Frederik Kinch, the managing director. The ship had been delayed for several days and Kinch blamed Vilhelm for the delay. Vilhelm was taken aback and annoyed as he had had no means of getting there any faster.

In addition to Kinch and Andersen, E.A.C.'s small Shanghai staff consisted of Adolf Petersen, in charge of imports, Adolf Aistrup, in charge of the cotton section, and E.S. Petersen and R. Berner. In addition, the Shanghai branch employed a Chinese middleman ('comprador'), Ho Soy Dong, and his staff as well as some Chinese clerks.

There were many pitfalls for young Europeans in Shanghai at the turn of the century. Einar V. Jessen, the Danish telegraph operator mentioned earlier, gives the following description in his memoirs of his youthful years in Shanghai:

> Shanghai was a very difficult city for weak souls. Spirits, wine and beer were im-ported tax free. You never paid for anything in cash, you just signed a chit. This was the case in all shops – the jeweller's, the tobacconist's, the tailor's, the shoe-maker's, restaurants, etc. The comprador of the foreign firms was the firm's pay-master and the go-between to the Chinese business world. He would cover the chits, both large and small, and on payday would present the debtor with the lot. And then you had to be in the comprador's good graces in order to get him to extend your credit to the first of the following month. Young people stationed in Shanghai could get into serious trouble and risk being sent home if they could not pay their debts. Certain deviations were tolerated during a young man's first year in a British firm, for example. Starting up a lasting relationship with a Chi-nese woman, however, meant instant dismissal. There was an unwritten law in the international business world that alcohol was only drunk in the evenings and you were sober when you turned up for work the next morning.

Vilhelm was prepared to live sensibly without too many excesses. But he quick-ly realized that the conditions of payment would present difficulties. Kinch re-fused to pay him for the time he had spent travelling from Denmark and Vil-helm soon became aware that in Shanghai the monthly salary of US$ 150 that he was to receive would not be enough to make ends meet if he were to live reasonably comfortably. He felt badly treated by his new boss from the start. In the small Danish community in Shanghai it was a common subject of conversation that Frederik Kinch was a difficult man to work for. E.M. Melbye, a Dane in Shanghai employed by a British firm, wrote in 1902 to a friend in Denmark that in his opinion Kinch might be an able businessman, but he was not a good employer and the atmosphere at the E.A.C. office was reprehensible. In his letter the same Melbye referred to the newly arrived E.A.C. employee, Vilhelm Meyer, as exactly the kind of young man Shanghai needed, but who was made to work for the lowest salary offered by any of the European firms in town – a salary on which it was impossible to live without getting into debt. Vilhelm was given a slight raise just at the time the letter was sent. Kinch agreed to give Vilhelm half-pay for the time he had been en route from Denmark. In addition, Vilhelm's monthly salary was increased by $15, and an additional $30 a month was paid out as an advance on commissions and bonus.

Figure 28: Frederik Kinch (1863–1926) became H.N. Andersen's partner in Siam in 1884 and was one of the founders of E.A.C in 1897. In 1900 he became head of the E.A.C. Shanghai office, where Vilhelm was employed from April to September 1902.

Melbye's letter was brought to the attention of H.N. Andersen at the head office in Copenhagen and events began to snowball. Without mentioning Melbye by name, H.N. Andersen wrote to Kinch in 1902, including extracts of some of Melbye's critical remarks. He then asked Kinch to consider raising the salaries of the office staff. H.N. Andersen also wrote to Vilhelm Meyer, whose name had been explicitly mentioned in Melbye's letter, again without naming his informant. He wrote that as the president of E.A.C., he had to take precautions against the spreading of defamatory rumours and assertions about the company. He would, however, await Vilhelm Meyer's own explanation of the case.

H.N. Andersen's letters to Kinch and Meyer arrived at the Shanghai office on 8 September 1902. Vilhelm immediately hurried to his employer's office to assure him that he had made no defamatory statements about either Kinch or E.A.C. It was true that he had probably told friends privately that he could not live on $150 a month, but in the meantime the problem had been solved. Meyer was happy working for Kinch and believed that Kinch's kind treatment of him after the salary question had been resolved meant that Kinch was satisfied with his work at the office.

He put this in writing in a letter to Kinch with a copy to H.N. Andersen in Copenhagen. But Kinch grew impatient. Three days later he insisted that Vilhelm supply him with the name of the Dane in Shanghai who had started the allegations. If Kinch was not in possession of the name within the next two days, Meyer would be suspended from his job. Vilhelm found this an impossible task. There were over 100 Danes in Shanghai, so how was he to know who had written the notorious letter? He therefore stuck to his original written statement and informed Kinch that he was unfortunately unable to provide the desired information.

This response was deemed unsatisfactory. On 12 September Kinch assembled the Danish staff at the E.A.C. office and informed them of what had happened. Before the entire staff, Kinch let the newest staff member in the office know that he was on suspension, effective immediately. Vilhelm was outraged at this treatment and informed Kinch later that day that he considered the suspension to be a definitive dismissal. He also declared that later, when the truth – that he had not originated the accusations – became known, he would not seek re-employment in the company.

Melbye, who heard about the whole affair the same day, immediately went to Kinch to inform him that he was the one who had written the letter. He pointed out that not once had Vilhelm Meyer uttered a defamatory word about E.A.C. or about Kinch. The letter to Copenhagen was based on impressions he had received through his long acquaintance with the entire Danish staff of E.A.C. It was impossible for Kinch himself to be ignorant of their dissatisfaction. Melbye told Kinch that he considered him to be a competent man, but that as an employer he did not treat his employees properly.

Both Kinch and Vilhelm wrote to H.N. Andersen giving their versions of the course of events. Vilhelm felt injured since his only point of criticism had been the conditions of payment, which certainly did not live up to the promise of 'a salary you can live on'. Furthermore H.N. Andersen had asked for Vilhelm's own explanation of the matter before making any decisions as to the possible consequences of Melbye's letter. Vilhelm felt that he had a right to have H.N. Andersen's 'justification' in the case. He also realized, however, that if he were to succeed in Shanghai, he would have to change course at once and find employment elsewhere. He therefore approached the Russo–Chinese Bank. Kinch was loyal in this connection, replying to a query from the bank that young Meyer was an excellent and trustworthy employee. A few days later Vilhelm was hired by the bank. The correspondence with Denmark took several weeks and it wasn't until November that a reply arrived from H.N. Andersen, who could not understand Meyer's wish for 'justification'. He no longer considered it a problem as he had been informed that Meyer had obtained new employment in Shanghai. However, he was willing to discuss the entire matter at some later date when Meyer was in Copenhagen.

H.N. Andersen informed Kinch that he could not completely ignore Meyer's explanation that he had not made any defamatory statements about Kinch or about the East Asiatic Company. He also informed him that the merchants Louis Meyer and Moses Melchior, who had both been informed of the case, considered it both humiliating and unfair to suspend young Meyer in the presence of the entire staff for an offence he insisted he had not committed.

Kirsten in Copenhagen

In Denmark Kirsten thought anxiously of her Vilhelm far away in China. The situation was not entirely promising. In particular, Ottilie Bramsen, Kirsten's mother, was not enthusiastic at the idea of having young Meyer as a son-in-law. Vilhelm, who seemed to be something of an adventurer in her eyes, had not yet given proof of being able to provide for her daughter. But Vilhelm and Kirsten corresponded. The etiquette of the period did not permit a young lady to receive letters from a young gentleman without the letters previously being read by her parents. The young people therefore agreed to get around primarily Ottilie's curiosity by having their letters pass through the hands of a few close friends and relatives. The most frequent messengers were Vilhelm's cousin Christian Hvidt and Kirsten's cousin William Heering. At Christmas 1902 Kirsten was feeling low. She wrote in her diary:

> There is not a single person I can really talk to, so it is often quite trying. Oh, how I miss Vilhelm! I could talk to him about anything and he could help me and explain so many things to me that I have to bear alone now.

But corresponding with Vilhelm was a great comfort.

> It is a great relief to me to write to my best friend. Oh, it makes me so happy to think I have him. I don't need anything else. Even though he is so far away he is nevertheless always much closer to me than all the others here. I'm always thinking of him, dear, dear friend. If only I would get a letter from him again soon, then I always liven up and am so happy. No one can understand why but I have my reasons. It will probably be here soon.

Her musings on New Year's Eve 1902 read thus:

> Well, well, I wonder what the New Year will bring? It is almost a year now since Vilhelm left. It has passed so quickly and yet so slowly. Imagine three years – it's a long time. How much may have changed by then?

In January 1903 Kirsten wrote:

> Sitting here with Vilhelm's picture right in front of me. Oh, how I long to talk to him, just to have him near me. Oh so terribly far, far away, he is my own best friend. If I had only had some writing paper I would have written to him now for

Figure 29: In 1902 Aage and Ottilie Bramsen moved into a villa at Evaldsgade no. 5 where they lived until Aage's death in 1921. The house, facing Peblinge Lake in Copenhagen, is used today by DR, Denmark's Radio.

> I only write when I feel like it. It's not something you can do on command – at least not to Vilhelm. How I long for his letters!

And on January 23 she wrote:

> Again it's been a long time since I've written here, but when I write to Vilhelm I don't write here. Oh how happy I am! I received his letters on the 20th at the Melchiors. Christian Hvidt brought them. Two of them at the same time. Christian is really so sweet. I am so glad that there is one person who really knows about us. I can always go to him. If anything goes wrong I am sure he will help me. Oh, how happy I was to get those letters! Truly there's no need to say more!

The Russo–Chinese Bank

When Vilhelm had to seek new employment in September 1902, a mere six months after arriving in China, it was no whim that made him turn to the world of banking. He had noticed that many of the Western businessmen in Shanghai did not understand the vital banking aspects of international trade with China.

It was Michel Speelman, Vilhelm's Dutch friend, who persuaded him to apply for a position with the Russo–Chinese Bank. Speelman had come to Shanghai from Amsterdam as a 20-year-old and had now been at the bank for five years. The two young Europeans, who became life-long friends, were well versed in the most important aspects of trade and finance in China at this time. The previous year the Bank had erected a large, opulent building at The Bund no. 15 and this was where Vilhelm began his new job as 'confidential telegraph and exchange assistant'.

Figure 30: This is what Shanghai's Chinese streets looked like when Vilhelm arrived in China in 1902. The telegraph poles are a testimony to Great Northern's activities in the area, but there are no cars or trams as yet.

The financial conditions in China were not easy to fathom. The copper coin, the so-called tjen, also called 'cash' by Europeans, had a square hole in the middle. It had been in use for several centuries and served as a medium of exchange for daily necessities. A string could be drawn through the copper coins, which could then be joined together in rolls of 100 coins. But the value of the coin was so small that an enormous number of coins were necessary for large payments.

This is when silver was used. When it weighed one Chinese *liang* it was called a tael, and a lump of silver, in the form of a shoe weighing between 10 and 50 taels, was used as a medium of exchange. The individual merchants and banks hallmarked the small bars themselves. The silver originated primarily in Mexico. In the late nineteenth century the Chinese began to produce coins from the silver, which they called 'Mexican dollars' valued at a little under one tael.

All Chinese banks issued their own bank notes and foreign banks followed suit, starting with the Hong Kong and Shanghai Banking Corporation. A great deal of China's trade with foreign merchants was settled in Mexican dollars, whereas the tael was used as an accounting unit within China. In addition, American dollars and the British pound sterling were also in circulation in China.

Jacob Henningsen, Great Northern's Shanghai manager, offers a critical description of the Chinese currency system at the time, which he felt was sorely in need of reform:

> Fortunately it would appear that in the not too distant future the odious practice will be remedied. The tendency towards centralization which has taken root

in China in recent decades, and which has already brought forth the telegraph out of the earth while the railways are beginning to follow in its wake, will gradually revolutionize local conditions. The first consequence will be that China will be forced to adapt a monetary system. How, for instance can one run a railway when it takes half an hour at a time to count the payment in 'tjen' and a coolie to carry the sum or else you have to bring your own scales or silver scissors in your pocket in order to cut off the amount while you dispute the weight with the ticket agent? The time is not too remote when the government in Peking, as it slowly proceeds on its irreversible march towards progress, will be forced to coin its gold and silver bars in legal tender, and call in the millions of false and counterfeit 'tjen' now in circulation. It will have to establish guaranteed government banks authorized to issue bank notes, and regulate the overwhelming number of financial transactions among the numerous and enterprising members of the business community.

Sanitation in Shanghai at the turn of the century was unspeakable. Like many others, Vilhelm did not escape a bout of typhoid fever. He fell ill in the spring of 1903. For a long time he was so lethargic and groggy that he was incapable of doing anything at all. Writing home was impossible. In Copenhagen Kirsten and young Christian Hvidt grew very anxious:

> Christian could not understand either what has come over Vilhelm – it's been such a long time since we both heard from him. Oh, what would we do without Christian? But a letter *must* arrive soon, otherwise I don't know what I'll do.

Kirsten heaved a sigh of relief when Vilhelm finally gave a sign of life. In May 1903 she wrote: 'Vilhelm has been so terribly ill, the poor dear. Thank God that's over now, I hope. Letter from him arrived on April 29 describing his illness. I hope he's completely recovered by now.' Once he was on his feet again Vilhelm travelled to the Vladivostok branch of the Russo–Chinese Bank on the Pacific coast of Russia. During his four-month stay he visited the island of Sakhalin and the section of Siberia north of the Amur River. In Denmark Kirsten took drawing and German lessons. In September 1903 her parents gave her permission to go to Dresden, where she continued her drawing instruction. It was a dream come true and Kirsten enjoyed being able to pursue her artistic interests. She stayed at a boarding house with other girls her age and in the evenings they eagerly joined in the theatrical and musical life of the city. She continued to correspond with Vilhelm, openly now, and the bond between the two – so far from each other in Vladivostok and Dresden – grew closer and closer. In October 1903 Kirsten received a long awaited letter from Vladivostok:

> But here's the best part. I received a long letter from Vilhelm. It certainly took forever to get here! He's well. That is fortunate, I am so happy, so happy. It's been such a long time since I heard from him. – Went down to the drawing room this evening. Happy! Absolutely overjoyed. It *has* been trying, waiting so long.

However, Kirsten returned from Dresden in 1904 earlier than planned. In a letter to her parents she happened to mention that in one of the classes they were sketching nude models. This was intolerable, particularly for the somewhat Victorian Ottilie. Kirsten was ordered to return to Copenhagen immediately!

E.A.C. Changes Course

In April 1902 when Vilhelm began work at E.A.C. in Shanghai, Frederik Kinch's instructions from home had been 'full-steam ahead and expand'. The company had embarked on a coast and river trade with a total of four steamships, including two of the company's own new ships, the *Bintang* and the *Anamba*, which arrived in September 1902 from Europe. One of the Shanghai branch's main activities was to transport coal to Port Arthur for use on the Russian railways in Manchuria. E.A.C. had also succeeded in getting itself appointed as the Shanghai, Hankou and Niuzhuang agents of the Russian Chinese Eastern Railways steamship department. Now, however, the Russians wanted to take over the agencies themselves.

In June 1902 the first signs of a change in policy arrived from the head office in Copenhagen. H.N. Andersen no longer wished to invest large amounts of fixed capital in China. He wanted to slow down. Kinch's problem, however, was that he had already entered into a number of agreements in accordance with the original instructions. 1903 was no easier. The amount of freight transported to and from Europe on E.A.C.'s own ships was significantly reduced owing to heavy competition from other shipping firms. In the spring of 1903 Frederik Kinch was called home to a meeting at the head office. It was resolved at a meeting of the board of directors in April that investments in China should be reduced. However, it was also resolved that the fixed investments in Port Arthur should be increased.

In November 1903 things finally came to a head between H.N. Andersen and Frederik Kinch. H.N. Andersen also had a falling-out with Emmanuel Kinch in Bangkok at this time. This was the beginning of a dispute between H.N. Andersen in Copenhagen and the two Kinch brothers as to who was responsible for the disappointing results in China and Siam. In December 1903, Frederik Kinch was telegraphically instructed by Isak Glückstadt, chairman of the board of E.A.C., to close down the branches in Niuzhuang (Yingkou) and Dalian. Furthermore, economic commitments in Port Arthur and Shanghai were to be reduced.

The Russo–Japanese War

After his stay in Russia, Vilhelm returned to Shanghai around New Year 1904. Here he worked as secretary to the Russian bank director in charge of the bank's cable and exchange office. His work in the bank was now marked by the war between Japan and Russia, which had been looming on the horizon for a long time. Both countries wanted to exploit China's weakness and gain control of Manchuria and the rivalry between the two now flared into the open in an area belonging to neither of them.

The Japanese made the first move in the confrontation. In February 1904 the Japanese submarine fleet attacked the Russian warships in Port Arthur. Although the surprise attack resulted in Japanese casualties, too, the Japanese succeeded in hemming in the Russian fleet and could now land their troops and initiate a siege of Port Arthur.

Figure 31: Kirsten's father's elder brother, Ludvig Bramsen, minister of the interior 1899–1901, embarked in 1904 as a widower on a voyage around the world, arriving in Shanghai in March. Fifty-six-year-old Bramsen had promised his brother Aage to meet young Vilhelm Meyer, but the meeting was not a success. Ludvig viewed Vilhelm as a somewhat rash adventurer and Vilhelm found Kirsten's uncle rather stiff and old-fashioned. They had no way of knowing that two of their children would later marry each other – for Ludvig's youngest son, Bo Bramsen, married Vilhelm's youngest daughter, Marie-Louise, in 1941. (See genealogical table in the Appendix.)

When the ice broke up in the port of Vladivostok, the Japanese naval superiority was so great that the Russian ships could not leave that port either. It was consequently decided in St Petersburg to send the Baltic fleet to their aid. A Russian naval force, consisting of 35 ships, did not leave until October 1904 and had to take the long route, passing south of Africa, since sailing through the Suez Canal was considered too risky. Although Japanese soldiers succeeded in taking Port Arthur on 2 January 1905, followed by Mukden (Shenyang), the Baltic fleet was nevertheless ordered to continue to Vladivostok.

It was not until late May 1905 that the Russian warships finally arrived in the Tsushima Strait between Korea and Japan, where the Japanese navy was lying in wait. It was an unequal battle between the outdated Russian vessels, badly damaged after the long sea voyage, and the modern Japanese ships, which had introduced radio communications while the Russians were still using optical signals. It was a clear victory to Japan. Only three Russian ships out of the large Russian fleet reached Vladivostok. The rest were either sunk or captured by the Japanese.

During the war Vilhelm Meyer worked for the Russo–Chinese Bank. On several occasions he had to travel from Shanghai to Port Arthur, transporting large amounts of cash to the Russian port. He was also appointed to the position of private secretary to Mr Davydoff, the general manager of the bank in Shanghai

The White Man's Burden

In his poem 'The White Man's Burden' mentioned earlier, Kipling gives voice to what the European and American spirit of the times felt to be the white man's duty to the overseas nations. The train of thought was that the white man was duty-bound to take it upon himself to ensure that other peoples were also given the opportunity to enjoy the spiritual and material advantages of Western civilization. Vilhelm, however, was aware of the two-edged sword built into any attempt at helping other countries. Any effort could be interpreted as interference and any profit made by foreign firms could be seen as imperialism and economic exploitation.

Although China had a much older culture than Europe and the United States, it had not experienced the period of rapid industrialization seen in the West. To Western eyes, China thus seemed an underdeveloped country with a small ruling elite and large masses of poor peasants, workers and coolies.

Vilhelm had quickly realized that for the man who acted competently and responsibly, there were excellent opportunities to make money. There were, of course, both foreign and Chinese businessmen only interested in grabbing as much for themselves as they could. But there were also businessmen who realized that the Chinese economy could only be developed by the responsible introduction of Western capital and industrial know-how and by assuring the country's workers decent wages and working conditions. So long as 'the white man' refused to recognize the necessity of such a balance, he would be contributing to the collapse of the Western commercial foundation in China. The

Figure 32: All throughout his life Vilhelm was fond of music. He had a beautiful baritone voice and also enjoyed playing the piano. He is shown here in his house in Shanghai in 1905.

special status that foreigners had obtained in China, particularly in Shanghai's International Settlement, was at the root of the revolt against all foreigners, which seemed inevitable if no allowance were made for the rights and needs of the ordinary Chinese.

The so-called unequal treaties, which China entered into with several Western nations in the second half of the nineteenth century, are on display today at the Museum of the Chinese Revolution in Peking. These treaties gave the Western nations a number of advantages with nothing in return for the Chinese. The Sino–American Treaty of 1858 and the Danish–Chinese Treaty of 1863 are among the documents on exhibit.

Holger Rosenberg, the Danish travel book author and the first European to travel by land from Burma to Shanghai at the beginning of the twentieth century, discussed the question of historical inequality with Chung Li, a young Chinese revolutionary, in Shanghai. In his book on China, Rosenberg has young Chung Li recount the dilemma facing the Chinese as on one hand they feel contempt for the white man's material attitude to life, yet on the other admire his power and singleness of purpose:

> You Europeans are hard and cruel and yet I admire you. I envy you nothing. I don't care much for the God you worship, not because his teachings are wrong, perhaps, but because his teachings do not make better human beings. I want nothing to do with all your technology and mechanics. They may make life more pleasant, but not one single person is happier because of them. I am not acquainted with your social system. It may be better than ours, but its representatives that are sent to China give no indication that it is motivated by higher ideals. You have hurt and insulted us, trampled on every Chinese person's con-

cept of law and justice, enriched your own nations at our cost and treated China as an oppressed country and the Chinese as a nation of slaves. And yet I admire you. I admire your power, your energy, your singleness of purpose. I might come to see things differently if I visited Europe, which I hope to do.

Alas, revolutionary Chung Li never got to see Europe. He was killed by government soldiers shortly before the revolutionary forces succeeded in overthrowing the old empire.

Working in the bank and on his long journeys in China, Vilhelm acquired a first-hand knowledge of the vast Chinese empire. He met Chinese people from many different walks of life, both those in power and those who owned nothing. He was aware of the enormous social conflicts and understood the necessity of involving the Chinese in the process of development in which so many foreign business people were eager to participate. Vilhelm felt that the time was now ripe for him to realize what had been his true goal in China from the beginning – he would establish his own firm.

SIX

Andersen, Meyer & Company, 1905–1906

The East Asiatic Company Winds up its Affairs

The Russians lost the war with the Japanese, and the board of directors of the E.A.C. in Copenhagen were forced to realize that they had backed the wrong horse. In July 1904, when there was no longer any doubt as to the outcome of the war, the board sent a telegram to Frederik Kinch, ordering him to shut down all branches in China, including the Shanghai branch, by the end of the year. In Shanghai this meant that all stock had to be sold off so as to enable the new local agent, the Netherlands Trading Company, to take over the remaining assets.

Frederik Kinch was recalled at the beginning of 1905. He brought with him the branch's account books and upon arriving in Copenhagen in April had an unpleasant confrontation with the board when he was assigned responsibility for the recent losses in China. The board of directors of E.A.C. had an internal report drawn up in May. According to the report, the heavy losses incurred by the China branches were primarily due to poor management and inadequate execution of the head office's orders. The losses were later assessed at approx. DK 2.7 million. Kinch felt badly treated by E.A.C. and resigned at the end of May with immediate effect. Kinch then wrote his own report, which he presented to the board in August. He pointed out the contradictions inherent in the policy that H.N. Andersen and the board wished to pursue in China. He emphasized that the reason for his investing so heavily, albeit unsuccessfully, in Port Arthur had been that the head office in Copenhagen had instructed him to do so. The Russo–Japanese War was partly to blame, too, and Kinch therefore maintained that they could not simply place the entire responsibility on his shoulders.

This counter-attack made a certain impression on the E.A.C. directors. In September 1905, shortly after the formal conclusion of the Russo–Japanese War in Portsmouth, Maine, in the United States, a truce was also declared in Copenhagen between H.N. Andersen and Frederik Kinch.

A New Danish Trading Firm

In Shanghai, by the time Frederik Kinch was recalled to Copenhagen, Vilhelm had acquired such an excellent knowledge of the trading and financial aspects of commercial life in China that he decided to leave the Russo–Chinese Bank and start out on his own. He resigned from his post as of 1 March 1905. He was just 26 years old.

Figure 33: On his return from Denmark in 1906, Vilhelm had borrowed enough capital to start up the firm of Andersen, Meyer & Co. In this picture he is seen in the centre flanked by Andersen and Petersen and their European and Chinese staff.

The E.A.C. head office in Copenhagen had adhered to their plan of closing down the Shanghai branch; consequently several of Vilhelm's former Shanghai colleagues at E.A.C. found themselves out of work. It must be admitted that they were hardly the company's most impeccable employees. Adolf Aistrup had embezzled US$ 20,000 from the Shanghai branch. The police had been notified of the fraud and he had then disappeared. Several of the others owed the office quite a lot of money. This was true of Ivan Andersen, the bookkeeper, who had run up a debt of DK 3,500 and Adolf Petersen, who owed the office DK 6,100, which he had withdrawn without the permission of the general manager Kinch.

However, Vilhelm wanted to work with Danes in Shanghai and proposed to Ivan Andersen and Adolf Petersen that the three should go into business together. The two E.A.C. men thought it an excellent idea and a document was drawn up on 10 March 1905, in which the three agreed to start a new firm in Shanghai under the name Andersen, Meyer & Co. The firm's initial capital was to consist of 30,000 taels, which was to come from Andersen (20,000 taels) and Meyer (10,000 taels.) They also agreed that prior to the official opening, Andersen, Meyer and Petersen 'were to carry out the necessary preliminaries in the interests of the firm and if possible conduct the business of an agency to the extent that this can be done without running any form of financial risk'.

They borrowed 1,000 taels from the Chinese money-lender, Wong Shun Tsze, to cover start-up expenses, including 250 taels for each of the three gentlemen. 'Settling of accounts for incurred expenses and profits shall be given over to the new firm and liabilities assumed by the said firm.' On the basis of this modest initial capital, the three young Danes moved into an office consisting of a single room at Siking Road 2 near The Bund early in the summer of 1905.

The Russo–Japanese War had not yet ended, enabling Vilhelm to get a contract to buy war equipment for his former employer, the Russo–Chinese Bank. This was to be the only time Vilhelm ever traded in military goods, and he didn't like it. In all the following years spent in Shanghai, dealing with huge industrial plants and products, he totally refrained from dealing in weapons and other military equipment. In addition to the name Andersen, Meyer & Co., the newly established firm also had to have a Chinese name. It was not the custom in China, as it is in the West, for the firm to be named after its owners. Firms were instead given a designation, a so-called hong name, describing the principles and ideals of the firm. Names such as 'High Integrity', 'Honesty and Prosperity' and 'Mutual Benefit' were not uncommon. Great Northern Telegraph Company was called Da Bei, 'Great North', while E.A.C. had chosen the name Bao Long meaning 'Magnificent Treasure'. Two Danes, Jacob Jebsen and Heinrich Jessen, had given their firm, Jebsen & Co., the Chinese name of Jie Cheng, 'Rewarding Success'. The old British trading company, Jardine, Matheson & Co. called itself E Wo, 'Happy Harmony', and its competitor, Butterfield & Swire, had chosen the hong name Tai Koo (Da Gu) which meant 'Great and Ancient'. Foreign companies often added 'Yang Hang' to their hong name, meaning 'foreign trading company'. To this very day E.A.C. is known in China as Bao Long Yang Hang and Jebsen & Co. as Jie Cheng Yang Hang. After consultation with Chinese friends, Andersen, Meyer and Petersen chose a hong name that on one hand respected the inherited Chinese belief in the established order, but on the other hand contained a progressive element, pointing toward the future. The firm thus came to be named Sun Chong (originally written Sun Cheong, in pinyin Shen Chang), based on the Chinese characters for caution and prosperity respectively. The four Chinese characters 'Sun Chong Yang Hang' were henceforth to be found on all the firm's writing paper as well as anywhere else where the name of the firm figured in Chinese.

Several important European and American firms that were already established in Shanghai were sceptical about the small, newly-founded Danish firm. The three owners, however, were optimistic. It was not entirely out of the question that the new firm would be able to take over part of E.A.C.'s business as it intended to close down all branches in China. The fact that E.A.C. nevertheless chose to remain in Shanghai did not hurt Andersen, Meyer & Co.

Vilhelm had also made contact with Jacob Henningsen, the former director of Great Northern, who had now started his own trading company in Denmark, the Asian Trading Company. It was agreed that Andersen, Meyer & Co. should be the agents of Henningsen's new company. Former Shanghai employees of Great Northern and E.A.C. had thus joined together with the purpose of expanding trade between Europe and China.

In August Andersen and Petersen left for Denmark while Vilhelm remained in Shanghai, where on August 26 the new firm was established. During their stay in Copenhagen, Andersen and Petersen contacted the business editor of the newspaper *Nationaltidende*, to inform him of their new enterprise on the day of its foundation. This resulted in favourable coverage the next day with the headline 'New Danish Firm Opens in the Far East':

> Yesterday on 26 August a new, Danish firm was started up in Shanghai of which it is surely safe to expect a great deal although the owners are wisely starting on a modest scale.
>
> The owners are three young men who, after a solid mercantile education, went to China four or five years ago, where they worked primarily in the service of the East Asiatic Company. They are now setting out on their own. The excellent foundation upon which they base their enterprise, consisting of an exact knowledge of the special conditions in China, guarantees that they will surely create a trading company that will not only do them credit but earn them a substantial profit as well.
>
> The business will be partly an import–export business. European and American goods will be imported into China; feathers, skins, silks, etc. exported to Europe. In addition, the newly-founded firm will be the general agent of the newly established Asiatic Trading Company for the whole of China.
>
> The new trading company can take pride in a number of important connections both at home and in London. The best banks in Copenhagen and London as well as several highly respected trading companies have opened their doors to them and inasmuch as they belong to a neutral and politically disinterested state, they can count on a certain amount of goodwill in advance.
>
> The firm consists of Mr Ivan Andersen, Mr Vilhelm Meyer and Mr A. Petersen. The first-mentioned is a son of Consul Andersen of Lemvig, the second of the merchant Meyer (Beckett & Meyer) of Copenhagen. All three have the kind of belief in their enterprise that works miracles and all are prepared for any eventuality.
>
> Only one of the founders is presently in Shanghai, namely V. Meyer, who has been getting things ready over there for the foundation of the new firm, which took place yesterday. As for the other partners, A. Petersen will return to China in a week, Andersen somewhat later, whereupon Vilhelm Meyer will return home in November for a brief visit.
>
> As has repeatedly been stressed in these pages, eastern Asia is *the* place for able Scandinavians to pursue excellent business opportunities.
>
> For our part in Denmark, we shall follow with great interest the progress of their firm in that distant land with best wishes for a favourable outcome.

Vilhelm did not manage to return to Denmark in the autumn of 1905, however.

The Danish Vice-Consul in Shanghai

Denmark was allowed to have consuls in the treaty ports. Nicolai Duus, the first consul in Shanghai, was a Dane, but in several cases British businessmen had been appointed honorary Danish consuls. After visiting China, Admiral Bille had pointed out already in 1864 that in time the Foreign Service ought to station a Danish Consul-General in China and that the consular posts in the other open cities should be filled by local Danish businessmen. The Consul-General ought to be the one to negotiate with the Chinese authorities, while the other consular agents, who were to be accountable to the Consul-General, could take care of consular business in the ports. In the description of his journey Bille writes:

> And it is my hope that at that time there will be many able Danish men, for they are the ones who should be given preference in selection. The way is clear, trade with China is open, there are fortunes to be made for hard-working men and the example is there before us. We have many highly esteemed countrymen out there who would do Denmark credit if selected for such positions.

Bille's thoughts were fairly straightforward and the Danish Ministry of Foreign Affairs in Copenhagen was no stranger to them. However, several years would pass before the system that Bille proposed was carried out.

Partners in the British firm Jardine, Matheson & Co. were often appointed to take care of Danish consular interests. This was the case, for example, in the 1860s–1880s in Shanghai when Jardine's impressive office building at The Bund no. 27 also served as the Danish Consulate.

The position of consul in Shanghai was of particular significance because consular officers, in accordance with the principle of ex-territoriality, also served as consular judges, i.e. the Danish judicial authority in cases involving Danish subjects in China. The Danish Ministry of Foreign Affairs in Copenhagen there-fore decided to send an envoy from the foreign service to Shanghai. Antonio Gustav Gottlieb Leigh-Smith arrived in Shanghai in 1896 as the first Danish civil servant stationed in China. He was to serve as Danish consul and consular judge.

In 1904 Consul Leigh-Smith was replaced by 42-year-old Peter Theodor Raas-chou, who was both a lawyer and an engineer and had run his own electrical manufacturing plant in London for ten years. Since 1902 he had served as Danish vice-consul in London. It was the general opinion in Copenhagen that with his solid legal and commercial background, Raaschou would be the right man for the job.

Theodor Raaschou and Vilhelm Meyer quickly hit it off. They were both committed to promoting commercial contacts between Denmark and China and both of them were also interested in music, Raaschou being a skilled violin-ist. The new consul approved of the young Danish businessman and felt that it would be a good idea if Vilhelm could contribute his services to the Danish Con-sulate as honorary vice-consul. Vilhelm agreed. Although the job was without pay, he was convinced that as vice-consul he could build up an extensive know-ledge of Danish-Chinese business dealings, which in the long run would be to his advantage. In his application Vilhelm gives the following reasons for his ap-pointment to a position that did not yet exist:

> I take the liberty of drawing your attention to the fact that I have an extensive acquaintance among the resident foreign merchants and in my daily dealings I have every opportunity to follow commercial developments on the China market. I believe that I would on occasion be of benefit to the Consulate by procuring information on commercial conditions, which might be of use to young Danes trying to find employment here.

Figure 34: From 1905 to 1909 Vilhelm was honorary vice-consul at the Danish Consulate in Shanghai. His main responsibility was to promote Danish exports and investments in China. The young Danish vice-consul is shown here in his uniform.

Raaschou sent young Meyer's application to the Foreign Ministry in Copenhagen in 1905. He stressed the vital importance of attaching an independent, young Danish businessman to the Consulate and gave the following justifications for expanding the staff, which had hitherto consisted solely of himself:

> All other consulates have at least one European assistant and it would be advisable for the Danish Consulate to be equally well equipped in that regard, since the smallness of staff is conducive to reducing the importance of the Consulate both in the eyes of the other consulates and, even more important, in the eyes of the Chinese authorities and merchants, accustomed to seeing high officials surrounded by large numbers of assistants of various ranks. Three Danish businesses have recently been started in Shanghai and various Danish interests are putting a great deal of effort into getting a share of the China trade. It would therefore be detrimental to their interests if such endeavours were not supported by an adequately equipped Consulate.
>
> If the Consulate's proposal to advance Danish interests by appointing young Danish business people is to be carried into effect, it is also vital to have a vice-consul who not only has daily dealings with the Shanghai business community, but who can also temporarily take charge of the Consulate if the consul is obliged to leave town.

In his letter, Raaschou also discussed the desirability of hiring Danish businessmen as honorary Danish consuls in other important Chinese trading centres. He himself could suggest some suitable candidates. At the end of his letter to the Foreign Ministry, Raaschou had the following to say about Vilhelm:

> Mr Meyer is the son of Mr Meyer the merchant, of the firm of Beckett & Meyer in Copenhagen. He is 27 years old and has recently started his own business. He speaks English, German and French fluently and has many excellent contacts among the merchants of various nationalities here in Shanghai.

In a letter dated 1 July 1905, signed by Rasmus Krag, permanent undersecretary of the Foreign Ministry, Raaschou was granted permission to hire Vilhelm Meyer. The Chinese Foreign Ministry in Peking also gave its permission for Vilhelm's appointment and in August, when the firm of Andersen, Meyer & Co. was founded, all the formalities were in order.

Vilhelm Meyer was now embarked on his career as Danish businessman and honorary Danish vice-consul in Shanghai, the biggest trading centre in China – a mere five years after H.N. Andersen of E.A.C. and Henrik Cavling of the newspaper *Politiken* had urged young Danish businessmen to go out to China, to go into business for themselves and assume the duties of Danish vice-consuls in the most important trading centres. On his daily rounds from his office on Siking Road along The Bund over Garden Bridge to Whangpoo Road no. 25, where the Royal Danish Consulate stood facing the river, Vilhelm was a happy and optimistic man.

Figure 35: Shanghai's well-known waterfront, The Bund, as it looked in 1906. The woodcut appears in A. M. & Co.'s *25th Anniversary Book*, published by the firm in 1931.

New Capital and New Contracts

Vilhelm loved being on his own in Shanghai, along with Andersen and Petersen. The entire Chinese market was open before them and goods from all over the world could be shipped to Shanghai. If new branches were going to be opened in China, the best place to start was the vital trading centre of Tianjin, near Peking. Vilhelm went to Tianjin in the autumn of 1905 to investigate the situation. Here he met 39-year-old Johan Wilhelm Munthe, an influential Norwegian officer from Bergen, who had been employed for several years by the Chinese Customs Service. During the Boxer Rebellion of 1900 he had volunteered for the Russian division and in August of that year had been among the first to climb the walls of Peking to liberate the legation quarter from the Boxers' siege. After the Boxer Rebellion he had been hired by the Peking general, Yuan Shikai, as aide-de-camp with the rank of colonel. The colourful Norwegian could tell Vilhelm many interesting facts about political and economic conditions in China.

But Vilhelm's plans to establish a branch in Tianjin were blocked by his somewhat delicate health. On 28 March 1906 he wrote to Colonel Munthe in Tianjin:

> I am sorry to have to write to say goodbye instead of returning to Tientsin this spring and starting up a new branch of our firm as planned, but, unfortunately, I have had the misfortune of having been stricken with appendicitis, which taken in connection with a case of enteritis has made it necessary for me to

Figure 36: Johan Wilhelm Normann Munthe was born in Bergen in 1862 and died in Peking in 1935. After initial training as a Norwegian army officer, he travelled to China in 1886 where he was employed by the Chinese Maritime Customs Service. In the war of 1894–95 against Japan, Munthe fought on the Chinese side as a volunteer. After the Revolution of 1911, Yuan Shikai made him his chief aide-de-camp in Peking, responsible for liaison between the Chinese government and the foreign legations.

return to Europe immediately – Carlsbad – to take a cure. I've been spending quite a lot of time in hospital or my own bed at home, but have fortunately had time to see to the business, which is making slow but sure progress. As soon as I'm back in the autumn, I hope to carry out our scheme to establish our firm in Tientsin and while I'm in Europe I will try to get commissions that would make us competitive with other firms.

Before his departure Vilhelm had the new company registered in Shanghai. This took place on 31 March 1906, henceforth considered the official date of the firm's foundation. As the founder of the firm of Andersen, Meyer & Co., Vilhelm was fully aware that the three Danes would require a more substantial sum than their initial few hundred dollars. He therefore intended to turn his stay in Denmark to good account by investigating possibilities of raising capital there.

Vilhelm arrived in Copenhagen in late April 1906. It came as quite a surprise when H.N. Andersen sent for him shortly after his arrival. Vilhelm recalled their previous, rather tense, conversation of four years earlier. In the interval he had been dismissed in Shanghai and had taken two other E.A.C. employees with him. On the other hand, he himself had asked H.N. Andersen for 'justification' after his dismissal, since he felt he had not been properly treated on that occasion.

Vilhelm went to the E.A.C. building in the free port area for his meeting with the head of E.A.C. Here in glowing terms he described his visions with

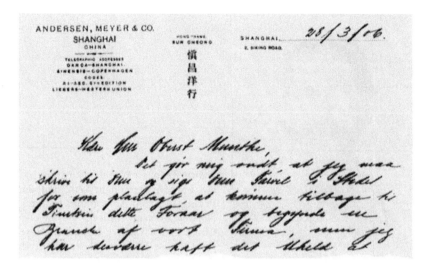

Figure 37: Vilhelm wished to establish A.M & Co. branches in other Chinese cities including Tianjin (Tientsin), which had always served as Peking's port. In March 1906 he wrote to Johan Munthe about the idea. Ten years were to pass, however, before A. M. & Co. opened its first branch office, in Tianjin in 1916.

regard to China's imminent industrial development and the opportunities open to a dynamic and goal-oriented Danish engineering and commission business in Shanghai. H.N. Andersen listened attentively. He then promised young Meyer to invest money in Andersen, Meyer & Co. In return, all the newly founded firm's supplies were to be transported on E.A.C. ships.

It may seem strange that H.N. Andersen was prepared to give Vilhelm a large loan to consolidate the new business since E.A.C. had already decided not to close down the Shanghai branch. This might have had to do with the fact that H.N. Andersen himself had had a dispute with Kinch in the interval and could see that Meyer had not been given a fair start in Shanghai. But there was probably another reason: if there was one thing H.N. Andersen esteemed above all else it was young businessmen with the will to succeed – men with drive, enterprise and commitment, or as he himself was subsequently to express it in his book *Tilbageblik* [Looking Back] of 1914:

> Young people with the will to succeed often do much better than others who may be more able, but who are lacking in willpower. Causes can apparently have relatively large effects: wanting to succeed in small things is good training for wanting to succeed in bigger things. The interplay or lack of interplay between will and ability, sense of duty or responsibility is vital for the education of young people and the development of their characters.

Getting Engaged in Copenhagen

After four years in the Far East it was wonderful to see family and friends again. The reunion between Vilhelm and Kirsten was tumultuous. They were both more mature now and felt they were made for each other. They discussed marriage, but Vilhelm was well aware that it was no use asking for Kirsten's hand in marriage before he had demonstrated his ability to support a family. As the owner of a newly established firm, however, Vilhelm seemed to be getting a grip on things and to be in a position where they could at least think of the possibility of marriage. It did not make matters easier that Kirsten would then have to move to Shanghai. A couple of years in the Far East might be all very well for a bachelor, but was this a life he could offer a wife and children? During his summer stay in Denmark, 28-year-old Vilhelm and 22-year-old Kirsten saw each other as often as they could. Vilhelm was a frequent visitor to the Bramsen family's summerhouse in Humlebæk.

Vilhelm left Copenhagen in October 1906. He had only been gone for a day when Kirsten received a huge bouquet of red roses and a telegram from Vilhelm from Hamburg. She wrote in her diary: 'It was awful having to lose him again – but this time he won't be gone for so long – and then it won't be such a long time before we can be together forever.'

Vilhelm and Kirsten had agreed to marry, but had not wished to make an official announcement of their engagement. Kirsten wrote the following about her parents' reaction:

> Strange that Mama and Papa are making such a fuss about it and are appalled that we won't announce the engagement. What business is it of anyone's, particularly since Vilhelm has gone? But people have to have something to talk about.

After Vilhelm's departure Kirsten became more closely attached to the Meyer family. She wrote in her diary on 30 October 1906 that she had been to a dinner at Emilie's where Mrs Meyer had given her a magnificent ostrich feather. 'It's terribly sweet of her. They are all so kind and nice to me. I hardly know how to repay them – by being good to Vilhelm, perhaps!' Kirsten had also noted the force of Vilhelm's will, as had H.N. Andersen. She wrote in her diary:

> He's strong – I am almost frightened to see how he gets his will across, but I don't mind. Ahh – I'll never forget what a lovely time we had last summer. He was often away, but then we were so much closer when we were together. I live and breathe for him.

Although several years were to pass before Kirsten and Vilhelm married, she was delighted that her cousin William Heering was going to marry Vilhelm's sister, Emilie. The ceremony took place the following spring at the Copenhagen town hall.

Figure 38: During Vilhelm's stay in Denmark in the summer of 1906, Louis and Thea Meyer gathered their 11 children in the summerhouse in Skodsborg. This was the first time since Vilhelm's departure in 1902 that the whole family had been together. But it was also to be the last; Thea Meyer died in January 1908. In the picture Louis Meyer is surrounded by his five daughters, Anna, Emma, Olga, Jutta and Emilie (Mille).

Figure 39: Thea Meyer with her six sons in Skodsborg in the summer of 1906. Ernst and Vilhelm (top), Albert and Viggo (middle) and Holger and Otto (bottom).

Contacts in the United States

Vilhelm returned to China via the United States. He was strongly attracted by the American Open Door policy towards China, as opposed to the European and Japanese partition of China into spheres of influence. Since he wanted to become better acquainted with American commercial life, he spent an entire month in New York, where he made arrangements to become the agent of several American firms capable of supplying technical equipment and complete plants to China. He had office facilities in Manhattan in the firm of Melchior, Armstrong & Dessau, 116 Broad Street, near Wall Street. This was a wholesale firm founded by three young businessmen, one of whom was David Dessau, a relative of Vilhelm's.

Figure 40: In 1904 Maurice A. Oudin became the first manager of the Foreign Department of the General Electric Company. In 1906 Vilhelm Meyer met with Oudin in New York and obtained his first contract with G.E. When the International General Electric Company was established in 1919, Oudin became vice-president of the company, with Gerard Swope as its first president. From 1923–29 Oudin was a member of the board of directors of Andersen, Meyer & Co.

One of the business sectors that fascinated Vilhelm was that of electrical power and electrical goods. He was impressed by recent American inventions and innovations in this field and by the way the discoveries of scientists like Thomas A. Edison and Elihu Thomson had been turned into business ventures. New ways of generating power and of transmitting and distributing electricity into people's homes were being used by companies to provide society with new products, such as lamps and electric motors. Vilhelm saw a huge market potential for such products in China's large population.

The General Electric Company (G.E.) had been established a mere 14 years before, in 1892, by merging the Edison General Electric Company with Thomson-Houston Electric Company. Charles A. Coffin was the first president of G.E. The company also had its own Foreign Department, with Maurice A. Oudin as manager since 1904.

During his stay in New York Vilhelm made contact with Mr Oudin. It turned out that G.E. could supply everything in electrical equipment and articles ranging from lamps to complete power plants. Vilhelm was made G.E.'s agent in China and over the years General Electric Company was to become the most important business partner of all his foreign suppliers.

When Vilhelm returned to Shanghai in the autumn of 1906, he was ready to take on the Chinese market in earnest. His health was restored, he had raised the necessary capital to consolidate the newly started firm, and he had managed to become the agent of General Electric and other American companies. Furthermore Kirsten had promised to join him in Shanghai as soon as he felt he could provide her with a secure and comfortable life. Now he had to show them back home – particularly the Bramsen family – that he was an able businessman capable of supporting a wife and family.

SEVEN

On His Own, 1907–1911

Vilhelm Becomes Sole Owner of A. M. & Co.

Back in Shanghai late in 1906, Vilhelm addressed himself to the problem of consolidating Andersen, Meyer & Co. There were now three addresses on the firm's writing paper:

> Shanghai: 2 Siking Road. Telegraph address: Danica
> New York: 116 Broad Street. Telegraph address: Desmayo
> Copenhagen: Kvæsthusgade 6. Telegraph address: Sinensis

It looked impressive. Andersen, Meyer and Petersen were pleased. Their small company was now represented on three continents!

Other Danish businessmen had established themselves in Shanghai at the beginning of the century too. The best-known of these was Laurits Andersen, who had gone to China as a 21-year-old machinist on board the *Cella*, the British cable ship transporting cables to China for Great Northern in 1870. As head of the large British American Tobacco Company, Andersen had become highly influential in the tobacco industry. At the turn of the century 'Elsinore', his huge house built like a castle with crenellated towers, was a favourite gathering place for the Danish Shanghailanders.

William Reedtz Funder was another Dane in Shanghai. He had established the auction firm of W. Funder & Company, which was to become one of Shanghai's leading auction houses. In addition there were businessmen such as Gordius Nielsen, Hillebrandt, and the former E.A.C. man, E.S. Petersen, each of whom had founded independent businesses. Vilhelm knew them all. The Danish community was a close-knit group.

In 1907 there were roughly 200 Danes in all of China, 130 of whom lived in Shanghai. Of the rest, 30 were missionaries, including 25 in Manchuria. Around 25 were employed in the Chinese Customs and the Chinese Telegraph Service in different locations in China. Finally there were around 15 entrepreneurs spread over a number of ports.

The total number of foreigners in Shanghai in 1907 was approx. 60,000. More than half were British. Only 1,500 met the requirements for election to the Shanghai Municipal Council. The British formed a large majority on the Council, always holding six or seven seats. The Americans usually had one seat. It was characteristic of the composition of the Municipal Council that its members were generally recruited from the large trading companies such as the British Jardine, Matheson & Co. and the American Russel & Co.

As vice-consul, Vilhelm was particularly interested in finding out what kind of articles Danish firms were importing to China. In response to a consular questionnaire that he put in circulation, his own firm replied that their main imports were butter, cigars, margarine, Tuborg beer, cherry brandy and, recently, vacuum cleaners from Titan A/S. Andersen, Meyer and Petersen, however, were not impressed by the Danish exporters' efforts on the Chinese market, which demanded a completely different kind of marketing and targeting than had hitherto been the case.

We should imagine that the best proposal for Danish trade lies in China's importation of machinery and small manufactured articles. In order to get into the Chinese market it is however necessary that the Danish merchants make big sacrifices, which they have so far been unwilling to do.

V. MEYER

Figure 41: Vilhelm had his name written in Chinese, composed phonetically of the three characters Ma Yi Er. Here are the three characters of Vilhelm's *ex libris*, the frontplate of Vilhelm's numerous books. He had brought several of the books with him from Denmark, including the collected works of the contemporary Norwegian author Henrik Ibsen.

Ivan Andersen, the former E.A.C. bookkeeper, was no longer happy in the trading business and therefore left the firm in 1907, obtaining employment in the Shanghai Horse Bazaar, an old, well-respected transport firm, involved since 1851 in the renting and selling of horses and carriages, but now on the brink of expanding the business to include automobiles. The position of secretary in a well-established firm suited him better than the far riskier job of director of the small, newly established Danish firm.

Several years later Ivan Andersen, who came from the small Danish town of Lemvig, changed his name to Iwan Dolgorouckoff, claiming that his mother descended from the Russian noble family of Dolgorucki. Although this statement was actually true, many of his Danish friends were highly sceptical and smiled at Andersen's pompous change of name. A number of years later, after the Russian revolution of 1917, when white Russians were pouring into Shanghai, Dolgorouckoff performed great humanitarian services for the numerous Russian refugees. He converted to Catholicism and was appointed papal chamberlain by the Vatican.

The two young Danes who had given their names to the firm of Andersen & Meyer in 1905 were thus only partners for a short time, but they both remained in Shanghai all their lives and continued to be friends.

Vilhelm now began to consider in earnest how he, as a businessman, could assist China in the country's industrial development, which seemed to be imminent. He particularly wanted to be involved in large engineering projects, but was not sure whether he was financially strong enough to venture into that market. His first step was to approach the highly regarded Shanghai firm, Mssrs Fearon, Daniel & Co., with whom he built up a joint engineering department. Through F.D. & Co.'s purchasing office in New York, Andersen, Meyer & Co. could now buy American machinery in complete units, to be sold in Shanghai. The following year Andersen, Meyer & Co. took over the piece-goods import from the well-established English firm in Shanghai, Sale & Co. Ltd, and started to import large quantities of primarily staple goods from Manchester, for which there was a good market in China.

Writing to Kirsten in Copenhagen, Vilhelm confessed that getting the new firm started was harder than he had imagined. No matter how much he wanted Kirsten to come to him in China, he felt he had not yet achieved the level of financial security necessary to start a family. Kirsten wrote in her diary in September 1907:

> Vilhelm may come home this winter, but it is very uncertain and business has not been good so there is no question of our getting married yet. He's slaving away and I was so sorry that he hasn't had better luck. He deserves it. Now that Andersen is gone we hope things will go better.

Vilhelm did not see his beloved Kirsten again until the summer of 1908 when he returned to Denmark. He felt by then that he had finally attained sufficient financial security to be able to provide for a wife and family.

He proposed to Kirsten, who accepted without hesitation, and they agreed that the wedding should take place the following year. Aage Bramsen understood that Vilhelm was the only man that his eldest daughter would ever marry. He did not oppose the match, although Ottilie thought the whole thing quite mad; there were so many sensible, potential young husbands in their Copenhagen circle. Why did Kirsten simply have to marry Vilhelm and settle so far away in China?

Vilhelm's visit to Denmark that summer was a short one. Reports from Shanghai that Adolf Petersen, the remaining partner, was mixing his own finances with those of the firm made Vilhelm hurry back to Shanghai. In Shanghai Vilhelm had it out with Petersen, who was forced to leave the firm, heavily indebted to Vilhelm. It also turned out that in 1905, when Petersen had entered the firm with Andersen and Meyer as the impersonal '& Co.', he had not informed E.A.C. of the fact and for a time had continued to draw his salary.

Although Vilhelm became the sole owner of the firm in the late summer of 1908, he did not change its name. For one thing the name had become a fixed element in the Shanghai business world. For another the name Andersen, as opposed to Meyer, indicated that it was a Danish firm. The name of Andersen, both H.N. Andersen and Hans Christian Andersen, was not unknown in the Orient. In Shanghai there were also Laurits Andersen, the tobacco manufacturer mentioned above, and his brother Captain Robert Andersen, who for many years was an employee of the Chinese Pilotage Service in Shanghai. The outcome was that the original name of Andersen, Meyer & Co. was maintained throughout the life of the firm.

Yuen Ming Yuen Road

In the course of a few years A. M. & Co. had become a well-established and fast-growing firm and Vilhelm felt that the time had come to find more suitable office space. In the autumn of 1908 the business moved to two new rooms in Yuen Ming Yuen Road no. 4. The following year it took over the adjacent building and two other buildings on the other side of the street. These four buildings, nos 4, 5, 6 and 8, became the firm's permanent headquarters. On the ground floor were the showrooms for the imported articles while the upper storeys served as offices. No. 4, the building in which Vilhelm's own office was located, was an impressive, dark red building with blue and white striped awnings over the windows.

Yuen Ming Yuen Road ran parallel to The Bund, not far from the British Consulate General. It was a good neighbourhood with a number of firms and banks. The street had been named after the imperial Summer Palace outside Peking, which had been destroyed by British and French soldiers during the final phase of the Second Opium War in 1860.

In the early years the firm had acted primarily as commission agent, involved in both the import and export trade. Now engineering contracts began to crop up and the General Electric Company in New York became A. M. & Co.'s main supplier. Electricity was a prerequisite for all the new electric household articles that were being manufactured. Vilhelm had made an agreement with G.E. that he would set up the first G.E. light plant in China. This major engineering project was carried out in 1908 by Andersen, Meyer & Co acting as an agent of the General Electric Company. The plant, built in Mukden (Shenyang), the capital of Liaoning province in Manchuria, was to be the first of a long line of power plants and factories built by the firm all over China.

Vilhelm had a firm grasp of the Chinese business system thanks to his early years in Shanghai. He knew that it was impossible to get on in China without a totally reliable middleman. As mentioned above, ever since the arrival of the first European traders in China, the system of compradors (Chinese merchants who could speak English) had prevailed. Vilhelm chose Mr Joh, a highly competent Chinese, as comprador for Andersen, Meyer & Co. Several years later in 1915, Vilhelm noted to his satisfaction that Joh was practically the only comprador who emerged unscathed from the difficult transition from empire to republic.

Vice-Consul Meyer's Report on Business Conditions

As Danish vice-consul in Shanghai, Vilhelm not only had a thorough understanding of the kinds of commodities that were of particular interest to Danish-Chinese trade, but was also well-informed about all other trade taking place in Shanghai. The Consulate had grown in prestige and importance. The Foreign Ministry acknowledged this in 1909 by upgrading the Shanghai Consulate, making it a Consulate General and by appointing Theodor Raaschou as Consul-General. There was no Danish legation in Peking as yet and it was thus the Danish Consulate General in Shanghai that reported to Copenhagen on political and economic developments in China.

In the summer of 1909 Raaschou asked Vilhelm to draw up a report on business conditions. Although this was normally the job of foreign service officers, Vilhelm, finding it an interesting task, assumed it willingly. In the report, covering the period from 1 July 1908 to 30 June 1909, Vilhelm paints a picture of Chinese market conditions as they appeared in 1909.

It is emphasized in the report that the stagnation characteristic of the imperial economy in 1907 had continued in the following years. European trading firms in China thus did not operate under optimal conditions. Falling exchange rates in relation to Western currencies made it difficult for Europeans and Americans importing goods and commodities to China. It is true that the fall of the exchange rate benefited exporters, but export was primarily the province of Chinese firms. The monetary system was chaotic and the situation had not been improved by the fact that Chinese banks had begun individually to issue bank notes without the reserves necessary to cover their obligations. Finally Vilhelm pointed out that China seemed to be increasingly interested in producing the sought-after consumer goods herself. What he proposed should be done was a reorientation of imports from manufactured goods to machinery and raw materials.

Vilhelm could not refrain from commenting on the moral code of some Chinese merchants:

> However, before China can succeed as a manufacturing country, Chinese moral concepts must undergo a significant process of education and they must stop the trickery which is always rampant whenever they export goods. There is scarcely a single article exported from here – both natural products as well as natural commodities – that has not been the object of manipulation of one sort or another and which therefore always demands the closest scrutiny before delivery or unloading.

He further pointed out the enormous developments taking place in the field of railway construction. Railways were being built all over China and the import of tracks, sleepers, railway bridges, locomotives and carriages was rising sharply. It was especially the United States, Great Britain and Belgium that had gained control of the market.

> There is no doubt that the coming years will see a large importation to China of all articles connected with railway construction and if Danish producers wish to have a share in the business, they must obtain good agents in China very soon and make it worth their while to prefer to sell their articles rather than their competitors'. This will undoubtedly cost money initially – for advertising, travel expenses, etc. – but market developments will without any doubt bring about a

pay-off on their investment, if their goods can compete with those of other countries in terms of quality and price.

Vilhelm also discussed the groups of commodities of special interest to Danish exporters. Both Australia and Siberia had become keen competitors in the field of butter exports. Australia, in particular, had gained an excellent initial position due to the large refrigerated holds on the new steamships.

Danish beer export to China was a mere 400–500 cases a month and there was the threat of competition, particularly from Germany and Japan. Other important Danish export goods were cigars, cherry brandy and cement. Vilhelm suggested that Danes should focus more on canned foods and the export of motors and machinery. Exporters should then establish sales depots in China so customers wouldn't have to wait three or four months for their commodities. China's export goods consisted primarily of such articles as tea, silk and tin as well as beans and bean cakes from Manchuria. As for the shipping industry, it was characterized by a surplus of tonnage and resulting low freight rates.

Vilhelm drew up the report in the course of September and October. He wanted it to be finished before his wedding, which it was. He handed in the report at the Consulate on 27 October 1909, his wedding day. The Danish Ministry of Foreign Affairs acknowledged the comprehensiveness of the report by asking Mr Raaschou, the Consul-General, to 'convey the thanks of the Ministry to Mr Meyer, vice-consul, for his report on business conditions, which has been read with the greatest interest'.

Vilhelm had now spent seven years in China. He had put a great deal of effort into learning the Chinese way of thinking, Chinese customs and the language. His openness, tolerance and sympathetic insight – qualities that were not typically associated with foreigners in Shanghai – stood him in good stead in his business and private contacts with the Chinese. This was not only true locally in Shanghai, but also in relation to the authorities in Peking.

He had made a serious study of China's trade, economy and monetary system and although in 1909 the state of the market was not entirely favourable in China, he nevertheless felt that he would be able to make Andersen, Meyer & Co. into a fine business. Of good heart, he looked forward to getting married and starting a family under distant skies.

The Meyer Family, 19 Avenue Road

Kirsten and Vilhelm were married on 27 October 1909 in Shanghai. Almost eight years had passed since Kirsten had first written about Vilhelm in her diary: 'Oh, I really like him and I think he likes me, too!'

Kirsten moved into Vilhelm's spacious house on Avenue Road in the International Settlement, a neighbourhood of large houses not far from the British Country Club. Vilhelm had lived there for a couple of years with two good friends. They had rented the building from a Chinese landlord. In light of the coming wedding they had drawn lots as to who should remain in possession. Vilhelm was the lucky winner and the newly-weds could now set up

Figure 42: Kirsten loved to paint and often made excursions outside Shanghai with her English friend, Mary MacLeod, looking for good, new subjects. The two are shown here painting one of Suzhou's characteristic bridges, surrounded by interested onlookers.

house there. It was a large mansion although not ostentatious by Shanghai standards, with a beautiful garden and a practical arrangement of the rooms. On the ground floor there were a large living room, a dining room, a library and a kitchen. A staircase ran from the hall to the first floor where there were bedrooms and bathrooms. On the top floor there were more rooms. Facing south towards the garden were covered verandas to provide welcome shade during the hot summer months.

There were annexes next to the house which were used by the family's Chinese servants. First of all there was 'Number One Boy', hired by Vilhelm in 1903 and who, in accordance with Shanghai tradition, was in charge of the rest of the household staff.

Kirsten quickly felt at home in her new surroundings and the active social life of the Shanghai foreign community. One of her best friends was Mary MacLeod, an Englishwoman married to Ronald Neill MacLeod, Vilhelm's lawyer in Shanghai. She was several years older than Kirsten, but they shared a common interest – they both loved to paint. Mary MacLeod was to be one of the fixed stars in Kirsten's life in Shanghai.

Vilhelm realized that his daily work in A. M. & Co. would take up all his time. He therefore wrote to Consul-General Raaschou, asking him to accept his resignation from the position of Danish vice-consul in Shanghai.

> It is with great regret that I make this request, but my private business takes up so much of my time that I feel I cannot assume any additional responsibilities.

Figure 43: The house on Avenue Road remained the Meyer family's point of anchor through-out their years in China. Here we can see the characteristic veranda arches on both floors.

Since my business may make it necessary for me to request official aid from the Consulate, I feel that my position as vice-consul would in many cases make this extremely delicate, both for you and for me.

Please be assured that I will always be delighted to assist the Consulate to the best of my ability and I urge you to avail yourself of my services whenever they may be of use to you.

Thanking you for the pleasant spirit of co-operation that has existed between us for the past five years and for the goodwill you have always shown me, I remain,

Your Obedient Servant

Vilhelm Meyer

Raaschou had to accept the fact that Vilhelm was no longer able to serve as his consular agent, but was grateful for the offer of assistance in individual cases. In his report to the Danish Ministry of Foreign Affairs regarding the young vice-consul's resignation, Raaschou wrote:

During the five years Mr Meyer has served as vice-consul, he has always demon-strated the greatest willingness to advance Danish interests, in particular by pro-moting the import of many Danish products, by helping Danes to find employ-ment and in his commercial reports.

Eric Scavenius, the Danish foreign minister, accepted the letter of resig-nation in a letter of 19 April 1910, asking Raaschou 'to convey to Mr Meyer the appreciation of the Ministry of Foreign Affairs for his excellent services during the time he held the position of vice-consul'.

Vilhelm and Kirsten's first child was born on 9 December 1910. It was a girl – the first of four daughters. The confinement took place at home, a few weeks prematurely. Mary MacLeod assisted at the birth and laid the frail little baby in a cardboard box lined with cotton wool where the newborn spent the first weeks of her life. She was christened Thea Ottilie Meyer after Thea Meyer, her paternal grandmother, who had died two years before, and Ottilie Bramsen, her maternal grandmother, who was alive and well in Copenhagen.

Vilhelm's affairs were going well and he and Kirsten had now set up house together and started the family they had both dreamt of and corresponded about for many years. In 1911 Kirsten made a trip to Denmark to show off her beloved daughter Thea to her family and friends.

Figure 44: Kirsten visited Copenhagen in 1911. Here are the three generations – Grandmama Ottilie Bramsen, little Thea and Kirsten.

EIGHT

From Empire to Republic, 1911–1914

The Final Chapter of the Empire

The imperial regime in Peking had for many years maintained control over the vast empire with an iron hand. Various rebellions had been suppressed, but the demand for political reforms had become more and more marked. A rising number of young Chinese had studied abroad, particularly in Japan, where recent developments had clearly demonstrated that it was possible to gain a knowledge of Western culture and democratic ideals without jeopardizing the country's own culture. Powerful revolutionary forces were lurking just under the surface all over the Chinese empire.

Figure 45: The Dowager Empress Cixi (1835–1908) ruled China with an iron hand from 1861 to 1908. Opposing the growing foreign influence in China, she supported the Boxer Rebellion in 1900. At her death the Dowager Empress handed over the power to the Manchu prince, Puyi, only 3 years old at the time. He remained on the throne until the Revolution of 1911. The life of Puyi was made into a motion picture in Bertolucci's *The Last Emperor.*

The Dowager Empress Cixi, who had ruled China ever since the death of the Emperor Xianfeng in 1861, knew that reform was necessary if the empire was to survive. In 1908 she had a provisional Constitution drawn up, which pro-

vided for elections to a National Assembly. The Assembly, however, was only intended to have an advisory function.

The dowager empress died shortly after the adoption of the Constitution.
She had chosen Puyi, the 3-year-old grandson of Emperor Xianfeng's brother,
as the successor to the throne to be the next Manchu emperor. His father, Prince
Jun, was to serve as regent for little Puyi. The reforms were to be carried out
the following year. However, it was soon clear that the newly elected parliamen-
tarians had gained no real influence on the policies of the Manchu government.

On 10 October 1911 revolution broke out in Wuchang, on the Yangtze River. This date, the tenth day of the tenth month, has gone down in history as
'Double 10' and is still celebrated in both China and Taiwan. It was a spon-
taneous revolution, spreading rapidly over the entire country. In the course of
two months 15 provinces declared themselves independent of the imperial
Manchu regime in Peking.

One of the young Chinese to oppose the empire at an early stage was Sun
Yat-sen. Born near Canton in 1866, he had studied in Hawaii and Hong Kong.
He founded a secret society in Canton in 1895, but was forced into exile after
several abortive attempts at rebellion. He had been one of the co-founders of
the Alliance Party, which was based on three principles: nationalism (directed
against foreign powers), democracy (directed against the Manchu regime)
and the common good (directed against the feudal economic system).

Sun Yat-sen, who was in the United States when the revolution broke out,
returned home immediately to lend his support. A republican convention was
held in Nanjing in December 1911, and on 1 January 1912, Sun Yat-sen was appointed president of the new republic. The Alliance Party was replaced by the
Nationalist Party, the Kuomintang, a name composed of the words *kuo* [coun-
try], *min* [people] and *tang* [party].

General Yuan Shikai, the Manchu regime's military leader in Peking, clearly
perceived the rise of the Kuomintang in the south as a threat. Taking a firm
hold on the child emperor's reins, he managed to persuade Prince Jun to have
his little son abdicate, thus allowing China to become a republic. Yuan Shikai
also negotiated secretly with the southern revolutionary leaders, gaining Sun
Yat-sen's acceptance of the idea that Yuan Shikai himself should take on the
office of president of the new republic. Sun Yat-sen went along with this arrangement to prevent the break-up of the vast empire.

In Peking Yuan Shikai promoted J.W.N. Munthe, his Norwegian military
aide-de-camp, to his general aide-de-camp and advisor in the Ministry of War
with the rank of lieutenant-general. Munthe was also made head of the crack
Chinese regiment that was to provide security for the Legation Quarter. He
was thus given the special role of liaison between the foreign diplomats in Peking and the new republican government.

At first there were few visible signs of the transition to the republic. The old
Manchu order that all Chinese had to wear a pigtail was revoked. But in many
places it took several years before the Chinese abandoned the practice. A new
five-coloured flag replaced the imperial dragon flag.

Figure 46: Yuan Shikai (1859–1916) was trained as an officer. At the outbreak of the Revolution of 1911 he was the man whom both Peking and the rebels could support. Yuan was proclaimed the new president of China in February 1912. Several years later he made a vain attempt to restore the imperial system with himself as emperor. He died of a kidney disorder in 1916.

By 1913 Yuan Shikai had already broken with Sun Yat-sen, openly opposing the principles represented in the Kuomintang. He staged a coup and dissolved Parliament. Once again there was a new despot in Peking.

The Triad Players

Shanghai had become the centre of China's revolutionary forces. The city's special international status made it a haven for anyone opposing the Chinese authorities. To the Europeans, however, the secret Chinese societies were a closed-off area, steeped in mystery. For more than two thousand years, as the oldest and largest empire in the world, China had experienced many imperial dynasties, which by conquest or coup had seized and maintained power over the vast empire. Naturally, any form of resistance from below had to be kept completely secret. A tradition thus arose at an early stage in the history of China for Chinese opposing the regime to join together in secret societies, the so-called 'triads'. To the Chinese the number three has always been particularly powerful, expressing the relationship between heaven, earth and man.

The revolutionary players, too, made use of the old triads as a base for their political aspirations. This interaction was vital, for the triads were able to provide the financial resources necessary to carry out the political goals. As we

Figure 47: The Soong family was the most influential family in the political life of China during the first half of the twentieth century. Charles Soong, his wife and their six children are shown here. The eldest daughter, Ailing, married the future minister of industry H.H. Kung. Soong Qing Ling married the Nationalist leader, Sun Yat-sen, and Soong Meiling married Chiang Kai-shek. The son, T.V. Soong, became Chiang Kai-shek's influential financial advisor and later minister of foreign affairs.

shall see, the triads were to play an important role in the political and economic development of China in the 1920s and 1930s. At the same time, however, a veritable gangster rule developed, particularly in Shanghai, which occasionally out-rivalled even the Chicago or New York of the time in terms of terror, violence and corruption.

In the Shanghai of the turn of the century there were a number of different triads functioning as brotherhoods, with secret initiation ceremonies and secret signals between members. Hong Pang, the Red Gang, which was the largest and most influential, was directed against the Manchu regime in Peking. The leader of the triad was Huang Jinrong, who, because of his pock-marked face, went by the name of 'Pock-marked Huang'. As the head of both the Chinese police and the French security police in the French Concession, Huang was the strongman of Shanghai at the dawn of the twentieth century.

The family that had the greatest impact on political developments in China was the legendary Soong family. Han Chao-shun was born in 1866 in Southern China. As a boy he went to Boston with his uncle, where a Methodist minister took charge of the young Chinese boy's education. He was baptized and took the name of Charles Soong. In 1886, when he was 20, he went to Shanghai as a missionary, where he married. In 1892 he founded a publishing house, Sino–American Press, which among other things published the Bible in Chinese. He taught Sunday school and helped found the YMCA in Shanghai.

In great secrecy Soong was initiated into the Red Gang as well as the triad San-ho Hui, the Three Harmonies. He now lived a double life. On the one hand he was a respectable Christian publisher, printer and Sunday school teacher. On the other he was a member of secret brotherhoods combated by the imperial police with any means in their power.

In 1894, 28-year-old Charles Soong met his contemporary, Sun Yat-sen, who was passing through Shanghai. The two young Chinese had a great deal in common. They were both born in Guangdong province in Southern China, spoke the same dialect, had been educated outside China and were members of the Three Harmonies. Sun Yat-sen told Charles Soong of his plans to overthrow the existing imperial regime and turn China into a republic and Soong was fascinated by Sun Yat-sen's stirring visions of the country's political future. Soong was becoming a wealthy man and the bonds linking Sun and Soong would later prove useful. In the following years when Sun Yat-sen was constantly on the run from the imperial police, he could count on financial support from his friend in Shanghai. Soong helped recruit Shanghai members to Sun's revolutionary movement and his printing house was secretly used to produce revolutionary campaign material.

Charles Soong had a total of six children – three girls and three boys. The girls, Ailing, Qing Ling and Meiling, went to an English girls' school in Shanghai and to college in Georgia in the United States while the eldest son Soong Tzuwen, who called himself T.V. Soong, studied at Harvard and Columbia. Most of the members of the Soong family played an important part in the political power struggle that was to characterize the following years.

When Sun Yat-sen returned to China in 1911 after the fall of the empire, Soong Ailing, his good friend's eldest daughter, became his secretary. She was especially useful to him in his English language correspondence and speeches.

Yuan Shikai in Peking considered the Nationalist leader Sun Yat-sen as his greatest rival. He wanted to destroy Sun's newly founded Nationalist Party, the Kuomintang, and in 1913 issued an order for his arrest. Sun Yat-sen went underground and travelled to Tokyo. Charles Soong decided to follow him there. Assisted by the Red Gang in Shanghai, Charles Soong and his entire family succeeded in leaving Shanghai on a boat to Japan, where they joined Sun Yat-sen.

During their stay in Japan, Charles Soong and Sun Yat-sen met H.H. Kung (Kong Xiangxi), a Chinese from a wealthy banking family who had been educated at Yale University in the United States. Kung was proud of his long pedigree – dating back 75 generations right to Kong Fu-tzu (Confucius). At the Soong family dinner table that evening there was an immediate rapport between the 33-year-old H.H. Kung and the 26-year-old Ailing, who both shared Sun Yat-sen's political visions. The two were married the following year, thus creating a further financial basis for Sun Yat-sen's Kuomintang.

Ailing's younger sister, the 21-year-old Qing Ling, took over the job of Sun Yat-sen's secretary. Sun was now 47 years old. Their bond was not only political; the two fell in love. When Charles Soong found out that his best friend wanted to marry his daughter, he vehemently opposed the match. Qing Ling left home, however, and married Sun Yat-sen.

Figure 48: Sun Yat-sen and Soong Quing Ling in Shanghai in 1922. The couple remained true to their revolutionary ideals all their lives. Their villa in the French Concession in Shanghai is a museum today.

Du Yuesheng was another young Chinese from Shanghai who was to play an important part in the political game marking the inter-war years in China. Du Yuesheng was born in 1888 in the Pudong district on the Eastern bank of the Whangpoo River. His father was a coolie and the family had grown up in the poorest slum district. His parents died while he was still a boy and his youth had been marked by violence and various gangster jobs such as opium dealer and hired killer. Before he was 15 he was a member of the Red Gang, where the sharp, cunning youth caught the eye of Pock-marked Huang, the boss.

Figure 49: Du Yuesheng (1888–1951) grew up in Shanghai where he made the Green Gang the most influential of all the Triads. He became the city's undisputed gangster boss by dealing in opium and prostitution. He was an invaluable support to Chiang Kai-shek, his contemporary and the friend of his youth.

Du proposed to Huang that Shanghai's biggest triads should merge – the Green Gang, the Red Gang and others. They could thus gain a monopoly over the entire opium market in Shanghai and the adjoining provinces. Huang thought this an excellent idea. Following a power struggle, Du took over the leadership of the Green Gang himself and incorporated the Canton-based triad the Three Harmonies into the Green Gang.

The merged triads were run by a troika consisting of Huang, Zhang and Du – Huang being the official head. In reality, however, Du, in the course of a few years, had become the actual head of the Green Gang, which was incontestably Shanghai's leading gangster organization. From around 1910 Du was the strongman of Shanghai. All coolies, shipyard and dock workers, postal and bank officials and many other workers in the Shanghai area were under the control of the Green Gang. Shanghai's numerous brothels and the extensive opium trade were entirely controlled by Du Yuesheng.

New alliances, such as the connection between Du and the newly-wed couple, Soong Ailing and H.H. Kung, were formed in Shanghai in this period. Du controlled the entire criminal underworld in Shanghai while the Kung family was well ensconced in the city's financial and money world. If the two sides joined forces, together they could run Shanghai's economy.

Finally there was Du's friend, Chiang Kai-shek. He was born in a city not far from Shanghai and was one year older than Du. Chiang and Du became friends in Shanghai, where in their youth they became acquainted with all the shady sides of the city's underworld together.

In 1908 Chiang Kai-shek had become a member of both Sun Yat-sen's Alliance Party and Du Yuesheng's Green Gang. He was a typical example of the fusion taking place at the time between the national political revolutionary members of the Alliance Party, forerunner of the Kuomintang, and the criminal gangsters of Shanghai's Green Gang. During the rebellion in China in October 1911 Chiang was given command of the Shanghai units, composed of members of the Green Gang.

This then was the group of revolutionary dreamers, criminal gangsters, political conspirators, clever tycoons and crafty military strategists, who in the course of the following years were to assume power in China.

The revolutionary Chinese, Soong Qing Ling and Sun Yat-sen, Charles Soong, T.V. Soong, Soong Ailing and her husband H.H. Kung, the triad leaders Huang Jinrong, Zhang Xiaolin and Du Yuesheng as well as Chiang Kai-shek, who later married the third Soong sister, Meiling, lived alongside Shanghai's large foreign business community. On the face of it, they were two completely different worlds, which did not mix socially. The Chinese, for example, were not admitted to the fashionable old Shanghai Club and the triad world was completely closed to Shanghai's foreign inhabitants. Nevertheless there was a certain symbiosis between these population groups as both had an interest in setting in motion the wheels of political and economic change in Chinese society.

During the early years of the new republic under the rule of Yuan Shikai, it was still uncertain what direction the hidden nationalist forces would take.

Shanghai

Vilhelm and Kirsten knew no more about the Chinese world of secret societies than the other Shanghailanders. They had as yet no knowledge of the main players of the future, many of whom lived within the protective framework of Shanghai's International Settlement and the French Concession. Shanghai's foreign businessmen and their families were used to living in a small, isolated enclave in a country that was often in turmoil and racked by civil war. History had shown that the two foreign sections would not be involved in hostilities if the inhabitants and their home countries made it clear that they were prepared to defend themselves against attacking forces.

When revolutionary forces took over Shanghai's Chinese sections in November 1911, the Shanghai Municipal Council mobilized the Shanghai Volunteer Corps (S.V.C.) to protect the foreign sections against all invading forces, no matter whether they were revolutionaries from the south or imperial loyalists from the north. The fact that the S.V.C. was on the alert had the intended effect on the Chinese. They kept away from the foreign sections and the Shanghai-lander volunteers did not fight.

Figure 50: Like most foreign businessmen in Shanghai, Vilhelm also served in the Shanghai Volunteer Corps (S.V.C.) for several years. Here he is (centre) with his unit, around 1915.

Europe was far away. However, the Danes in Shanghai, besides joining the Shanghai Volunteer Corps, also took part in efforts to maintain a defence in Denmark so that the country could retain its independence in a coming war. A number of leading Danes in Shanghai, including Laurits Andersen, Vilhelm Meyer, William Reedtz Funder as well as Captain J.J. Bahnson and Sophus Black, both of Great Northern, gave their support to the Danish Defence Collection of 1913. The request for contributions, addressed to 'Our Countrymen in Eastern Asia' yielded the sum of 2,653 Danish kroner, which was sent home to Denmark.

In 1913, however, civil war came closer to Shanghai. In July Yuan Shikai's Peking forces fought against rebels from Jiangsu province in direct proximity to the International Settlement. The Consular Corps declared the international parts of Shanghai neutral and the Volunteer Corps was mobilized once again. Regular European protective troops from British, German and Italian warships at anchor in the Whangpoo River landed in Shanghai in order to protect the area.

These were anxious times and Kirsten was expecting her second baby. In the heat of the Shanghai summer she gave birth to a daughter on 29 July 1913.

Bombs were falling nearby and the sound of machine-gun fire could be heard
as she was in labour at home on Avenue Road. Mary MacLeod was again present to assist at the delivery. She soothed Kirsten whenever stray bullets whistled
past in the garden. The little girl was christened Rose-Marie Meyer.

Peking

While Shanghai was the most important city in China when it came to trade
and economics, political power had been based in Peking since 1644 when the
Manchu Qing dynasty had taken over from the Ming dynasty in Nanjing.

Vilhelm had visited Peking several times. It was truly an amazing city with its
city walls and towers and all the temples and palaces. The city consisted of a
northern section, which the Europeans called the City of Tartars or the inner
city, and a southern section, the Chinese city, also called the outer city. The two
sections each had their own city wall, although they shared a common wall
where they were contiguous. Within the Tartar City lay the Imperial Palace, the
Forbidden City, to which only the imperial family and their officials and servants were admitted.

Figure 51: When the Manchus made an end of the Ming dynasty in 1644, the seat of the
empire was moved from Nanjing to Peking. This photograph taken in the early part of this
century shows the low houses of the city and their characteristic curving roofs.

Peking, as the seat of government, was the city of residence for foreign diplomats. But as mentioned earlier, few countries were allowed to establish legations, all of which were located in the inner city close to the Forbidden City.
Peking was not included in China's early trading treaties with the Western powers and no foreign businessmen had been allowed to settle in Peking as they
had in the large ports. It was not until the 1890s that the doors were opened a
fraction. This was primarily owing to pressure from foreign diplomats in Peking,
wishing to buy Western goods.

The first foreigner allowed to open a shop in the capital of China was the Dane Peter A. Kierulff. In 1859 he had gone to China at the age of 21, settling in Peking in 1874. Kierulff's Store rapidly became a profitable business and its clientele included not only foreign diplomats, but also Manchu princes of the imperial family and Mongolian princes who, accompanied by their concubines, went shopping for exotic foreign goods at the Danish merchant's shop.

After the Boxer Rebellion was put down in the summer of 1900, the 11 countries represented in Peking (Great Britain, France, Germany, Italy, Austria, Spain, the Netherlands, Belgium, Russia, the United States and Japan) had agreed that for security reasons their legations should all lie close together in a particular area. All Chinese buildings within the area were razed to the ground and a wall was built around the entire area. The Legation Quarter had its own administration and all the streets were given foreign-sounding names such as Legation Street, Marco Polo Street, Rue Meiji, Rue Hart and Rue du Club.

When Denmark entered a bilateral agreement in 1863 with the imperial regime in Peking, the question of establishing an independent Danish representation in Peking did not arise. According to the terms of the agreement, Danish diplomats were allowed to visit China, but the protection of Danish interests had been in the hands of the Russian Legation in Peking since 1874. As a consequence of Great Northern's activities in China starting in 1870, the importance of the Russian Legation's role as liaison to Copenhagen had steadily increased throughout the 1880s and 1890s.

E.A.C.'s activities in China, beginning in the year 1900, led to a renewal of the Danish wish to strengthen diplomatic ties with China. The initial step was taken in 1908, when Copenhagen decided to station a Danish legation secretary in Peking to serve in the Russian Legation. The Foreign Ministry in Copenhagen chose 36-year-old Count Preben Ahlefeldt-Laurvig, who had done service in England and the United States, and who in addition was married to a Russian. The couple took up residence in Peking in 1908.

After a few years, however, Copenhagen wished to establish an independent legation in Peking, headed by Count Ahlefeldt. Although the Great Northern Telegraph Company and the East Asiatic Company were willing to finance a significant portion of the expenses, the proposal met with opposition in the Danish Parliament. The Social Democrat Hans Nielsen couldn't understand how the government could support the idea of the thousand-year-old Kingdom of Denmark joining forces with the Great Northern and East Asiatic Company so as to form a joint-stock company with the purpose of hiring a minister to Peking.

Hans Nielsen emphasized that his opposition to the proposed arrangement was not directed against the designated minister, Count Ahlefeldt-Laurvig, as he had been informed 'that this nobleman, as opposed to so many others, was an excellent representative of Denmark'. The Conservative Party also opposed the idea that government responsibilities should be paid for by private companies.

In the report of March 1912 a majority of the members of the Danish Parliament agreed that this was a government matter, which had to be 'resolved in a manner most worthy of the state and most satisfactory to all interests con-

Figure 52: Count Preben Ahlefeldt-Laurvig (1872–1946) was sent to Peking in 1908 as Denmark's first permanent diplomatic official in China. During the early years he served as the legation secretary at the Russian Legation where this photo was taken in 1911. In 1912 Denmark secured its own legation in Peking and Count Ahlefeldt was appointed Danish minister. He was sent to Warsaw in 1920 and then to London where he was the Danish envoy from 1921–38. His son Kai Ahlefeldt-Laurvig married Vilhelm and Kirsten's eldest daughter Thea in 1932.

cerned by not only appointing the proposed Danish diplomatic representative, but also by assuming all expenses incurred'. In April the king in council confirmed the appointment of Count Preben Ahlefeldt-Laurvig as Danish minister to Peking also accredited to Tokyo. There was no space within the Legation Quarter itself for the new Royal Danish Legation in Peking, which was therefore initially established outside its walls, near Hataman Street, not far from the Imperial Palace.

As honorary Danish vice-consul in Shanghai in the period 1905–10, Vilhelm had become well acquainted with the other Danish consular agents in China. In 1908 he had met the new Danish legation secretary in Peking and the two Danes had quickly become friends. They met whenever Vilhelm went to Peking, which he did on a regular basis.

Andersen, Meyer & Co. Expands

Vilhelm and Kirsten's early years in China together were marked by great political upheaval. The young Danish couple also witnessed the success of the Shanghai foreign community in distancing itself from the revolutionary hostilities. The city's two foreign sections continued to be a political safe haven, where refugees of all denominations and nationalities could escape the violence of the warring Chinese factions. In the sanctuary of Shanghai there was room for everyone, whether they were political dissidents, artists, intellectuals or writers. The Shanghai Municipal Council in the International Settlement constituted a representative oligarchy consisting of foreign businessmen with a very high degree of autonomy in relation to both the Consular Corps of Shanghai and the Chinese authorities.

In the early years of the republic, trade in the city increased. It was not only the foreign business community that benefited: Chinese businessmen also reaped rewards from the boom. Many Chinese from both the well-established comprador families and the newly arrived merchant families were now participating in building up Shanghai's rapidly growing economy, not only within the banking system, but also in the fields of trade, industry and shipping.

For Vilhelm, these developments meant the opportunity to expand Andersen, Meyer & Co. further. One of Vilhelm's main areas of focus at this time was the textile sector, primarily imports of textiles from Manchester in England. When A. M. & Co. had taken over Sale & Co. in 1908, it had not only acquired a number of excellent employees, who remained with Vilhelm Meyer for many years, but also the firm's numerous Chinese 'chops', i.e. go-betweens with access to the vast Chinese market. Vilhelm, however, pursued a policy of caution. He imported no more than he could sell. When the boom came to an end around the time of the revolution of 1911, A. M. & Co. was not left with piles of textiles that could not be sold, as were a number of other Shanghai importers. Meyer's comprador, Mr Joh, was among the best in the business.

Engineering orders also increased during this period. The joint venture with Fearon, Daniel & Co. initiated in 1907 was based on a simple business model. F.D. & Co. was in charge of all buying of machinery in the United States through their office in New York, while A. M. & Co. was in charge of sales in China. The two firms did not pay each other a commission, but shared the total profits. The business went well for several years, but then Fearon, Daniel & Co. suffered heavy losses and in 1914 had to shut down operations in Shanghai entirely.

The Engineering Department, however, had become an important part of A. M. & Co. This was primarily due to the fact that in 1911 Vilhelm had succeeded in becoming the sole agent for General Electric Company, not only for Shanghai, but for all of China. The Americans in G.E. liked the talented and charming businessman from Denmark, who was able to link American suppliers with Chinese buyers so profitably. Despite the fact that Fearon, Daniel & Co. had to close down, Vilhelm continued expanding his Engineering Department, hiring a number of foreign engineers.

Figure 53: This print of Kirsten was made in 1912, based on a drawing by Erick Struckmann.

Finally, A. M. & Co. concentrated on importing a number of different product lines. In the early years various finished products were the prime import. Vilhelm later decided to concentrate imports within the area of building materials, particularly iron, steel and glass.

Vilhelm had established his first American business connections when he was in New York in 1906. When war broke out in Europe in 1914 it was clear to him that imports from Europe would be drastically reduced. If Western technology were to be introduced into China on an even larger scale in the form of machinery, the main suppliers would have to be American firms. For Vilhelm there was no mistaking the signs. His business ties with American firms would have to be strengthened.

NINE

The New York Corporation, 1915

The United States and China

When Vilhelm went to the United States for the first time in 1906 he had been impressed by the big, dynamic country and its rapidly expanding economy. This was a truly golden age of rapid growth for both the population and production. Vilhelm noticed, too, that as America began to play an important economic and political role globally, the American political debate was increasingly focusing on U.S. relations with the outside world.

In relation to China, American foreign policy was still based on the Open Door concept, formulated in 1899–1900 by Secretary of State John Hay. This policy advocated respect for the territorial integrity and independence of China, combined with the belief that China should treat all foreign companies even-handedly. Furthermore, the Republican William H. Taft, who had won the presidential election in 1908, had enthusiastically supported the idea of 'dollar diplomacy', which meant that the United States should promote its foreign interests by economic means and let diplomacy work for trade.

Figure 54: Willard Straight (1880–1918) married Dorothy Whitney, daughter of the wealthy Wall Street banker and future navy secretary, William C. Whitney. With his financial and business talents and excellent financial connections in New York, young Straight was a factor in ensuring American participation in the industrial export boom to China that followed in the wake of China's transition into a republic. Straight was one of the prime movers behind the scheme to transform Andersen, Meyer & Co. into an American corporation in 1915.

The American administration therefore backed the attempt in 1909 by American financiers and their colleagues from a number of European countries to work out agreements with the imperial government in Peking concerning loans to develop China's agriculture and industry. The plan was to set up an international banking consortium in order to channel the necessary capital to China.

One of the main players in these negotiations was 29-year-old Willard Straight of New York. He had travelled to China in 1901, working for several years in the Imperial Maritime Customs Service. During the Russo-Japanese War he had gone to Korea, becoming a correspondent for Reuters. He then entered the American Foreign Service and was appointed American Consul-General in Mukden (Shenyang) in 1906. After a year in the State Department in Washington D.C., he accepted in 1909 the job of agent for a number of different American banking groups interested in granting a loan to the Chinese government. The group was extended to include bankers from other countries and the goal was to develop railways in Manchuria.

However, the transfer of power in China in 1912 and the American presidential election of the same year, when the Democratic candidate Woodrow Wilson unseated the Republican Taft, put a temporary stop to these American activities in China. The Wilson administration wanted the United States to compete and not to co-operate with other Western countries and the new government in Washington therefore withdrew from the consortium negotiations, which to Straight's great regret were henceforth left in the hands of the Europeans.

In 1912 Straight returned to New York where he served as an expert in Far Eastern affairs in the large banking firm of J.P. Morgan & Co. on Wall Street. Here he had the opportunity to raise capital for promising investment projects in China, accepting the stipulations of the new administration, which insisted that such activities must be handled directly between firms in the two countries.

Straight was convinced that US firms could take part in the development of China and that on the whole the US economy would benefit from increased industrial export to the developing countries of the Far East. He was active in a number of export organizations and in 1914 he took the initiative to found the Association of American Exporters in New York. He renovated an old, two-storey building at Hanover Place near Wall Street, transforming it into a club house where members could meet to make contacts and exchange notes on the export trade, particularly experiences pertaining to the Far East. In the London of those days 'the Indies' was synonymous with all foreign trade and Straight called the new society and its building India House, based on the British model. In 1914, in collaboration with his wife Dorothy, he began the publication of the weekly journal, *The New Republic*.

A friend of Straight's, Edward B. Bruce, an American lawyer of the same age, had also began his career in the Far East. In 1907 he had gone to Manila as a lawyer for the American Philippine Railroad Company. The following year he had started out on his own in Manila, founding his own firm, Pacific Commercial Company.

Willard Straight was two years younger than Vilhelm Meyer. They knew each other well from China and Straight believed that Meyer, who already had a number of good suppliers in the United States, would be able to find buyers all over China. Bruce had a similar firm in Manila and an office in New York on Broad Street just like A. M. & Co. In 1914 a promising association between the three young businessmen based in New York, Shanghai and Manila respectively was to come into being. There was a fourth player, too – the somewhat older Galen L. Stone. He was a financier in the renowned Boston firm of Hayden, Stone & Partners, which also had an office on Broad Street in New York.

Figure 55: Galen L. Stone was a partner of Hayden, Stone & Company in Boston, Massachusetts. He became one of the principal stockholders of A. M. & Co., Ltd in 1915 and the first chairman of the board, from 1915 to 1923.

It was clear to Vilhelm that if Andersen, Meyer & Co. were seriously to embark on Sino–American trade, he would have to raise a substantial amount of additional capital. The most sensible solution seemed, in association with the three Americans mentioned above, to transform A. M. & Co. into an American corporation with business headquarters in New York.

Father and Son Meet in New York

The Washington and Peking governments both wanted to strengthen business relations between the two countries. The opening of the Panama Canal in 1914, significantly shortening the sea route between the eastern ports of the United States and China, heralded a new era. On the governmental level, steps were taken for an official Chinese delegation to visit the United States. Chang Chen Hsun, the minister for business and agriculture in the Yuan Shikai government, was to head a trade delegation in June 1915, consisting of approximately 20 Chinese businessmen from various provinces. The delegation was to go to New York and Washington D.C. and elsewhere, in order to discuss possibilities for American export and investments in China. This visit was an excellent opportunity for Vilhelm to go to New York and become actively involved in the trade of the future. At the same time he could decide on the best way to transform Andersen, Meyer & Co. into an American corporation.

The Shanghai representative in the Chinese trade delegation was the 23-year-old businessman James Lee (also called Li Lu-hsioung), from an influential family in Ningbo. Lee and Vilhelm were friends and the two agreed that Vilhelm should join the delegation in the United States in order to build up contacts for the new corporation, both among American suppliers and buyers in China.

In March 1915 Vilhelm wrote to Louis Meyer, his 72-year-old father in Copenhagen, telling him that he would be going to New York with Kirsten, partly to recover from an illness and partly to do some important business. He proposed that his father join them there in May. This idea was received less than enthusiastically by Vilhelm's siblings in Copenhagen, since they doubted that their father could manage such a trip. War had broken out in Europe and even though the United States was not (yet) at war with Germany, German submarines rendered any voyage across the Atlantic extremely hazardous.

Nevertheless the white-haired old merchant with his characteristic bushy sideburns had a great desire to go to America and be reunited with his youngest son, whom he had not seen for seven years. Since Vilhelm and Kirsten could not go to Europe because of the war, Louis considered New York an excellent place to meet. His daughter, Olga Hvidt, was willing to accompany him on the voyage and Louis Meyer decided to go.

On 25 April 1915 Louis and Olga left Copenhagen on the Scandinavia–America Line's steamship, the *Hellig Olav*. The trip, which also included a train ride across America to California and back, took two months in all. Throughout the entire journey Louis Meyer wrote down his impressions and experiences. The notes, sent home to the family in Copenhagen along the way, also contain a number of greetings to friends and acquaintances such as this little greeting to Kirsten's mother: 'If any of you see Mrs Bramsen, please thank her for the idea of the leggings, it was brilliant, since they afford excellent warmth to the feet.'

Denmark and Norway were neutral during the war. This was clearly expressed on board the *Hellig Olav*, with large printed posters issuing the following instructions: 'This ship is a neutral ship and passengers are therefore requested not to discuss politics.' 'Very sensible', noted the old merchant.

The *Hellig Olav* made it across the Atlantic without incident or act of war, docking in New York on 6 May 1915. But the war was in full swing and the following day news came that the English passenger ship the *Lusitania* had been sunk without warning in the Atlantic Ocean by a German submarine. A total of 1,153 passengers went down with the ship, including 128 Americans. In the United States the desire to go to war with Germany increased.

Figure 56: Louis Meyer (1843–1929) joined his youngest son, Vilhelm, in New York in the summer of 1915. Here the old merchant is shown crossing the Atlantic on board the *Hellig Olav.*

When Louis Meyer was about to go ashore in New York, the immigration doctor was in doubt as to whether foreigners over the age of 70 should be allowed to enter America. He was quickly convinced, however, that the old merchant was in fine form. Louis had no trouble with customs, in spite of all the cigars he always brought with him everywhere.

Louis and Olga were welcomed on the wharf by David and Harriet Dessau. David was the brother of Hartvig Dessau, married to Vilhelm's and Olga's oldest sister Anna. As mentioned above, it was David's firm on Broad Street, Melchior, Armstrong & Dessau, that provided Andersen, Meyer & Co. with office space. A few days later Vilhelm and Kirsten arrived, having left Thea and Rose-Marie behind in Shanghai. They had sailed to the West Coast and from there had gone by train to New York. There was great joy at the reunion. Louis provides the following comments:

> Vilhelm was satisfied with 1915 – and rightly so – despite his illness. Still a bit weak in the knees, though, although lively and agreeable, extremely preoccupied with the possible results of his visit here.
>
> Right after lunch Vilhelm went down to Wall Street to discuss business affairs with the Hong Kong Bank. At dinner at the hotel in the evening Vilhelm was 20 minutes late because of business appointments.

The following week was a busy whirl of Louis' visits to museums, Vilhelm's business meetings and the whole family's attendance at dinners and concerts. Developments in the war in Europe were also discussed.

Figure 57: It was in Manhattan in 1915 that Vilhelm raised the necessary capital to expand his Shanghai business. This was done by transforming the firm into an American corporation, Andersen, Meyer & Company, Ltd He was also successful in becoming the agent of a number of American firms interested in exporting to China.

Kirsten impressed her father-in-law by inviting the family to a charity concert where *Carmen* was performed. The American singer, Miss Farorar who had the title role, sang the American national anthem before the fourth act. Louis enjoyed this evening:

> She had an American flag in her hand and sang extraordinarily beautifully. The audience remained standing, she was called out three times and finally said that she would now sing it once more, but then everyone should join in. It sounded magnificent. Vilhelm's voice sounded brilliant in the large room. Ladies all décolleté. Gentlemen in evening dress. Jewels and feathers galore.

On another occasion they had dinner with the Dessau family, who lived near the Hudson River. From their windows 67 warships could be seen in full illumination. After dinner the guests took charge of the entertainment themselves and Louis noted with pleasure that Vilhelm sang and that 'his voice was very strong and was a great success'.

During his stay in New York Vilhelm met with several directors of the General Electric Company, especially with Maurice A. Oudin, manager of G.E.'s Foreign Department. On their recommendation Vilhelm and the Edison Company, which manufactured electric lamps, concluded an advantageous contract making A. M. & Co. their sole agent in China.

After a two-week stay in New York, Louis and Olga continued on their tour of America. Vilhelm and Kirsten wanted to go to California with them, but everyone agreed that Vilhelm should put his business affairs in New York first.

After a successful journey by train, father and daughter returned to New York on 5 June. They were met by Kirsten and Harriet. Vilhelm wasn't there, for he was involved in important discussions with the Chinese trade delegation. He had already done some business and Louis noted with his practical merchant's eye that his son 'had earned his travel expenses and then some – and they're not small!'

Vilhelm wanted to introduce his elderly father to the head of the delegation, Chang Chen Hsun, minister for trade and agriculture, who was accompanied by China's minister of culture. According to Louis' notes, this took place in the following manner:

> Vilhelm is so well acquainted with all of them that he went into their salon unannounced – and was warmly received by the two gentlemen. The oldest (74 years old) in a Chinese costume – most of them speak only Chinese. The old man is an important merchant – and very sharp. I was introduced to him. It was only a brief exchange, but he asked Vilhelm via the interpreter whether he would get the offer Vilhelm had promised him of a large steam plough for his country estates – he's estimated to be worth approx. 100 million gold dollars – *kein Spass* [no joke] – and is in China what Morgan is in America. He said a few words to the other gentleman, who fetched his portrait, which he presented to me with a deep bow. Vilhelm had told me in advance that he would undoubtedly say it was his good fortune to meet me. I was then supposed to answer that the good fortune was no less mine, etc. Now when he presented me with his portrait he said 'whether he might presume to have the extreme good fortune of giving it to me'. I replied that the good fortune was entirely mine in receiving it and we both bowed deeply to each other. Then Vilhelm slapped him on the back and said that *he* didn't have the extreme good fortune of owning his portrait. He was immediately given one with the same ceremony. The whole thing was great fun and very interesting.

Over the weekend Vilhelm and Kirsten went to Long Island to visit Willard Straight and his wife, Dorothy, the daughter of the well-known Wall Street financier, William C. Whitney. Louis was impressed by his son's acquaintance with Straight who, according to Louis' notes, was 'the right-hand man of J.P. Morgan, the millionaire, and married to a lady who is good for roughly 30 million dollars'.

When the two couples were together they talked of many things other than business. Like Vilhelm, Willard Straight was an excellent singer, particularly fond of singing Kipling's songs to the accompaniment of his guitar. Willard was also a fine draughtsman and painter and showed Kirsten his numerous drawings from his time in China, Korea and Manchuria. Finally, all four were interested in Chinese art and antiques.

Louis noted that Vilhelm's affairs in New York were going well:

> Vilhelm just dropped by – extremely pleased – justifiably so – with his mail from Shanghai and is to meet the president of the largest dynamite company in America, who travelled for a whole day from their headquarters to their offices

Figure 58: Chang Chien Hsun, head of the Chinese trade delegation to the United States in June 1915 and China's minister of agriculture and trade, delighted Vilhelm's old father, Louis Meyer, by presenting him with this signed portrait.

here in order to conclude a contract for their principal agency in China. The boss here had said to him – after receiving information from General Electric and the Steel Trust – that he could probably count on his conditions being met, since otherwise the president wouldn't have come.

Vilhelm got his contract with Hercules Company, which would supply dynamite to Chinese mining companies.

Louis' stay in the United States was drawing to an end and he felt that it was now his turn to give a dinner party for the family. It was an expensive one and old Louis is still remembered in the family for his remarks about it: 'I don't remember what the dinner cost and yet I'll never forget it!'

The following day Louis and Olga left New York on board the *Oscar II* of the Scandinavia-America Line and two weeks later the ship docked in Copenhagen harbour where Louis' large family were all there to welcome them. Grandfather's trip to America had been a great success.

Vilhelm and Kirsten accompanied the Chinese trade delegation from New York to Washington D.C. where Robert Lansing, the secretary of state, hosted a large dinner. The delegation was also received at the White House by President Woodrow Wilson. After meeting the president, Vilhelm urged James Lee, his friend from Shanghai, to let himself be photographed in his elegant American suit. As the two were strolling down Fifth Avenue in New York a few weeks later, they saw the portrait exhibited in a photo shop with the information that this was a photograph of a Chinese prince. Since China had now become a republic, Lee entered the shop to inform the owner of the studio that he was not a prince at all, but a modern businessman.

Taking Stock

The Chinese trade delegation returned to China, but Vilhelm and Kirsten remained in New York for a few crucial weeks. Vilhelm had established a number of excellent business contacts with both Americans and Chinese. Now he had to raise the necessary capital.

Vilhelm had become acquainted with the New York financial and business world from his base on Wall Street, the home of the New York Stock Exchange. The area around Wall Street, Broad Street and Pearl Street was the hub of the New York financial district, packed with banking firms, industrial enterprises and lawyers' offices. The first skyscrapers had begun to shoot up and the whole atmosphere was humming with economic growth and enterprise. The war in Europe was still far away, even though the German sinking of the *Lusitania* showed that the war was not limited to European soil.

Vilhelm joined Willard Straight's new association, India House, and felt very much at home in Manhattan and his office on Broad Street. His main task in this period was to convince Edward Bruce, the Manila-based lawyer and the two financiers, Willard Straight and Galen L. Stone, of the solidity of the firm of Andersen, Meyer & Co. and of the Chinese market's great business potential. He wished to make clear to them that transforming the firm into an American corporation and investing fresh development capital in the undertaking would be a highly profitable venture. He therefore drew up an extensive report on his ten-year-old firm.

The report of 14 June 1915, which happened to be Vilhelm's 37th birthday, consisted of 26 typewritten pages. After a brief description of the firm's development since its beginnings in 1905, he discussed the firm's three departments, which at the time of writing dealt with piece-goods, general imports and engineering.

The Piece Goods Department, under the management of the Englishman Ernest Anthony Measor, was primarily involved in textile imports from Manchester in England. The department was extremely profitable and future opportunities were excellent in view of the vastness of the Chinese market. The firm's chief suppliers in Manchester were prepared to offer finance 2 per cent cheaper than the banks and to send an expert to Shanghai on half pay, A. M. & Co. contributing the other half.

Figure 59: Li Lu-hsioung, who later called himself James Hsioung Lee, was one of Vilhelm's oldest Chinese business friends in Shanghai. It was Li's idea that Vilhelm should join the Chinese trade delegation in New York in 1915. In Washington, urged by Vilhelm, Li allowed himself to be photographed in a cutaway coat after the Chinese delegation had visited President Wilson in the White House. This painting, based on the photo, was done later.

The General Import Department was under the management of another Englishman, A. Eveleigh, who had been in the employ of the firm since 1906. Eveleigh, born in China, spoke fluent English, Chinese, Russian, French and German and had an excellent knowledge of the department's chief commodities: iron, steel, glass and other building material. After the outbreak of the war in Europe, the purchase of iron and steel had been transferred from Belgium and England to the United States where U.S. Steel Corporation had become the firm's new main supplier. This was another market in China with a vast potential, since all the most important buyers were among A. M. & Co.'s customers.

A. M. & Co. was also involved in the production of paper, having taken over the general management of Shanghai Paper and Pulp Mill. One of the products was 'joss' paper, a very thin, yellow paper used all over China to burn as offerings to the dead. Another product was tissue paper for packing and finally there was paper for the rapidly increasing manufacture of books and newspapers. For this purpose, A. M. & Co. imported paper primarily from Sweden, Norway and Austria, since the paper produced in Shanghai was not yet competitive. New products such as telegraph roll paper and railway tickets were also in the offing.

Electric fittings from the United States were another import. Vilhelm believed that if once you were the supplier of electric chords and plugs, you could easily branch out into the building industry, importing building materials such as steel doors and windows, roofing materials and complete steel construction buildings in large quantities. He pointed out that there was a rising interest in office and factory buildings built in the Western style. And looking further into the future, there was also the large and growing demand for steel products for the construction of railways and bridges.

The third department, the Engineering Department, was probably the most interesting one. Developments in this area had been so rapid that it had been necessary to invest the firm's capital in this department at the expense of the more general import business mentioned above.

Vilhelm describes the management aspects that had to be considered when moving into the wide open contracting market. One consideration was that of the selection of directors. Several of the well-established foreign contracting firms had engineers serving as administrative directors. While these men were undoubtedly competent to be in charge of the technical end of large projects, they were not trained to manage the business end. There were thus numerous examples of heavy losses. Vilhelm wrote in his report:

> The manner in which I have developed my business has been different. First of all I have personally taken entire charge of the business end of the department, leaving to the engineers only the technical part. I have made it our business not to ignore the small engineering business, but have used this small business to get in touch with all the various manufacturing and engineering institutions, railways, etc. all over China. I have engaged competent engineers from America and Europe and have let each of them handle such lines as they understand thoroughly and no more lines than they can give their full attention to.
>
> Our principal line has been the handling of the agency for the General Electric Company. As to the manner in which we have handled the agency, I can do no better than to refer you to this Company. The growth of their business has been, and is, very big, year by year. We have erected complete the light plant in Mukden. One of our engineers has been in charge since the erection and is in charge still. The plant has doubled itself on its own earnings, and not a single supply has been bought by them except what has been sold through us. We are selling them now regularly about 3,000 taels' worth of supplies a month, and could sell them a great deal more if I was prepared to give them credit for bigger amounts than I do now, namely about 20,000 taels at any one time. It would be perfectly safe to increase this credit very considerably, as all payments are guaranteed by the central government under an acknowledged guarantee lodged with the American minister in Peking. My financial resources, however, have not permitted me to give them more credit than I have already done.

The main line of the Engineering Department was thus to act as the agency handling the wide-ranging commissions of the General Electric Company. The light plant in Mukden (Shenyang), was followed by plants in Changchun and Wenzhou. G.E. machinery was now also supplied to power plants in Fuzhou and Amoy (Xiamen), and new projects were under way in Shanghai and Jilin.

According to Vilhelm's report, the electric import and contracting business automatically entailed an increase in the sales of other articles, since the demand for installations and appliances such as lamps, electric fans, lifts and electric motors was steadily increasing. New means of transport, such as cars, trains, trams and motorboats, needed electric equipment and motors, and the communications industry needed articles for telephones and the telegraphic network.

In many fields competition was fierce. At the beginning of 1914 the import of electric lamps into China was almost entirely in the hands of the Germans. However, through a highly dynamic but costly campaign, A. M. & Co. succeeded in securing 60 per cent of the market for G.E. lamps. This success was to a large extent due to the fact that G.E. had established a lamp factory in Japan, giving the company a competitive advantage in relation to other lamp manufacturers. In his report Vilhelm was highly optimistic:

> From the sales of the first three months of this year, we expect to sell in China about half a million lamps this year, which would be about 75 per cent of the total trade. We have secured the contracts from all the leading light plants in the country, including the last two contracts from the Shanghai Municipal Council. We have also secured contracts from the biggest railroad companies in the country. We carry a big stock of lamps and I consider that this is a line, which can be considered quite a regular daily business from which a regular very considerable income can be counted. We earn about 5 cents a lamp, and as the electric trade in China increases this sale will automatically increase. In order to thoroughly handle the sale of all kinds of supplies and fittings, I have established in Shanghai a construction department in charge of foreign engineers, where we already now employ a big staff of Chinese fitters, and undertake complete installations from the very smallest to the very biggest.

This promising co-operation in the selling of lamps continued when two years later G.E. decided to move its lamp production for the Chinese market to China. In 1917 the China General Edison Co. Inc., a G.E. subsidiary, started manufacturing the first incandescent lamps in China. Production began in a small factory on Nanking Road where the company trained Chinese workers in the art of bulb-blowing and filament-winding.

Vilhelm also stressed the promising opportunities in the Chinese telephone and telegraph administration where he had rather good contacts, since many of the key positions were occupied by Danes whom he knew well. In Hankou the firm had bid for the contract to establish the city's new telephone system.

Andersen, Meyer & Co. had also specialized in machinery for the manufacture of textiles, including cotton mills produced by Saco-Lowell Shops near Boston. This was a promising market as well.

Furthermore, Vilhelm handled the agency of a number of American firms in the railway sector, both in terms of rolling stock and track supplies and supplying raw materials from the United States to the Chinese railway factories.

The opening of mines was highlighted in the report as an area of increasing importance. Although there were as yet no clear rules pertaining to ownership or corporate organization, this was nevertheless an area in China with a huge potential and where direct co-operation between the Chinese owners and the contractors was of vital importance. In general, a great effort had to be made to ensure a good and trusting relationship with Chinese businessmen, as Vilhelm pointed out:

Figure 60: On the trip to the United States in 1915, Kirsten was photographed in San Francisco.

It is essential in all these dealings to let the Chinese feel that they will partake in the profits accruing from such an undertaking, and it is advisable, I consider, that they should do so. To get into close co-operation with the Chinese in these matters, it is necessary that they should feel that they absolutely trust the people they are dealing with. This they do not do, except after years of acquaintance with the people involved, or without being able to ascertain through their own people that the foreigner in question is entirely to be relied upon. I take it upon myself to state that my firm in this regard has a name, which could not be improved upon. From the very day I started my business I have made it an absolute point never to disappoint a Chinese who trusted us with supplying him the material he needed in engineering lines, where they had to rely upon us entirely to give them the right thing at the right price.

In the report Vilhelm also describes the work of the firm's ten engineers. A few of the engineers were from American firms, which paid part of their salaries. They were typically stationed on location at the factory or light plant for a certain period. Others were on loan to take charge of running Chinese enterprises. The Chinese government's Bureau of Printing & Engraving in Peking, for example, was managed by one of the firm's engineers. In addition Andersen, Meyer & Co. had established branches in a number of ports ensuring the continuing build-up of the firm's markets.

Vilhelm also stressed the importance of having good employees, who were thoroughly conversant with Chinese business methods and practices. A new man was rarely of any direct use during his first year in China. The extensive technical library provided for the use of the staff was also mentioned.

Vilhelm also deemed it vital to have able Chinese staff on the management level. For many years Vilhelm's chief secretary had been B.C. Wan, one of the first Chinese to graduate from Cornell University in New York. Not only did this education give Wan the necessary technical know-how; it also gave him invaluable access to the many Chinese graduates of Cornell and other American universities now holding leading positions within the Chinese administration and business community. With Wan in this position it was no longer necessary to have an independent comprador as go-between to the Chinese buyers. Wan's salary was linked to the department's profitability, so that high profits meant a bonus for him.

Incorporating the Company

Vilhelm's report convinced Straight, Stone and Bruce. On 2 July 1915, two weeks after the completion of the report, Vilhelm Meyer, Willard Straight and Galen Stone went to the New York State Registrar of Companies to register their new corporation, Andersen, Meyer & Co. Limited.

The share capital was set at $350,000, $250,000 of which being preferred stock and $100,000 common stock. The capital was divided into 35,000 shares at $100. Stone and Straight signed up in the first phase for 1,000 and 300 preferred stock while Vilhelm Meyer took over the 1,000 common stock. The difference between the two types of shares meant that the dividend on the preferred stock, 6 per cent of its nominal value, should always be paid in advance of the dividend on the common stock, also 6 per cent. In other words, the first $15,000 of the annual profits would always go to the two American shareholders. The next $6,000 would go to Vilhelm Meyer and if the company's profits exceeded $21,000, this amount was to be shared according to the three stockholders' share units, regardless of the type of stock. Vilhelm's $100,000 of the share capital was put up in the form of real estate – A. M. & Co.'s office buildings in Shanghai – while Stone and Straight invested cash in the new company.

In addition to the three gentlemen above, the board of directors consisted of Edward B. Bruce, the Manila-based lawyer, and James R. Knapp of New York. Stone was chairman of the board, Meyer was the president of the company,

Figure 61: Once A. M. & Co. had been turned into an American corporation, Vilhelm was able to expand his business. Here he is shown with the closest members of his staff in Shanghai, circa 1915.

Bruce the vice-president and Knapp the secretary. A. M. & Co. Ltd shared the address and offices of Bruce's Pacific Commercial Company in the newly-erected office building at 50 Broad Street in Manhattan.

Vilhelm Meyer returned to China from New York a happy man. Everything had gone well during his stay there. He had negotiated a number of agency contracts with American firms and also made contact with various influential Chinese businessmen and politicians. His firm was now transformed into an American corporation with freshly raised capital from Straight and Stone. Strong links had now been forged between himself in Shanghai, Bruce in Manila and Straight, Stone and Knapp in New York.

Vilhelm was in his element. Although he was no longer the sole owner of Andersen, Meyer & Co., he had created the financial basis for the rapid future development of his firm. As president and general manager of the new corporation, he could continue to run his enterprise according to the business principles that he had followed since starting out on his own in 1905.

Vilhelm felt great confidence in the future on his return to Shanghai in August 1915. He also saw opportunities in Singapore and on the Malacca peninsula (Malaya), where rubber production on the large rubber-tree plantations looked highly promising. Vilhelm and E.A. Measor, the manager of A. M. & Co.'s piece-goods department, established a new company, Meyer & Measor, with offices at 97 Robinson Road in Singapore. The firm, which invested in rubber export, acquired large storage rooms in Singapore and set up a pur-

Figure 62: During its early years the firm of A. M. & Co. imported a large number of Western articles to China. One of these was White Horse whisky as shown in this advertisement. Later the import line was changed, primarily comprising industrial and transport-sector products.

chasing department in Malaya. Measor moved to Singapore to take charge of the daily management of the new export firm.

The Manchu Palace in Peking

Vilhelm went to Peking in October 1915, staying at the newly erected Hôtel de Pékin. He had learnt from experience the importance of being on the good side of the Chinese authorities and the necessity of knowing the right people in Peking when carrying out big projects. This was more than ever the case after he had become president of a company backed by solid American capital. He was therefore interested in finding a house for his visits to the capital. The house he was looking for would also have to be suitable as a base for business trips to Northern China.

In Peking Vilhelm met Sophus Black, his old Danish friend, who had arrived in Shanghai in 1902, just as he himself had done. Black had been stationed there by Great Northern, had served in the company's telegraph offices in Shanghai and Tianjin, and had been the manager of the company telegraph station in Peking since 1907. The two friends met at the Peking Club, the club for foreigners, located in the Legation Quarter. Vilhelm told him that he was looking for a house. He couldn't do business with the Chinese at the hotel since they always ended up playing mah-jong, the ancient Chinese board game, which generally developed into quite a noisy affair.

Sophus Black knew of the very house. For several years Great Northern had rented a palatial compound from a Manchu prince, who had returned to

Figure 63: As the only building of Danish origin on The Bund (no. 7), the headquarters of the Great Northern Telegraph Company was an impressive structure. Here it is displaying the Danish flag flanked by a British and an American flag to show that the British Eastern Extension and the American Commercial Pacific also had their telegraph offices in the building. In 1922 Great Northern moved to a new building around the corner. Today the old building on The Bund has been renovated and taken over by the Bangkok Bank.

Mukden after the revolution. The Danish Mess, as the residential compound was called, was located a few hundred yards north of the Hôtel de Pékin and the Legation Quarter, close to the Imperial Palace. This compound, consisting of several houses in the typical Peking *si he yuan* [courtyard] style, was the residence of Great Northern's five Danish employees. The Mess was in the main house and their rooms in the other buildings. The Danish flag was flying at the outer gate. The young Danish telegraph operators, it seemed, found living conditions too primitive here. There were only earth floors and no bathrooms. It was freezing cold in winter and several telegraph operators were plagued by illness, undoubtedly due to the poor living conditions.

Vilhelm was welcome to take over the lease, but Black, who was going to be married a few weeks later, would like to remain in his present residence. This was a fairly small building on a hill and had been formerly used as a dressing room area for Chinese actors performing at the palace.

Vilhelm was immediately interested and they went to look at the Danish Mess, built in the beautiful, old Manchu style. A small dark alley, a *hutong*, led up to the large, outer gate with its porter's lodge and carriage yard. It was impossible to look into the compound area as the view directly within the gate was blocked by a grey wall. This was the traditional 'spirit wall' designed to keep out the evil spirits. Through a round moon gate you entered a flagstone courtyard surrounded by four buildings. In the courtyard and in the other small courtyards further on there were bronze statues and small pine-trees while flowerpots overflowing with fragrant flowers hung from the roofs. The buildings were connected by paved passages under elaborately ornamented pitched roofs supported by red columns. The ceilings of the passages protecting the verandas in front of the buildings were decorated with brightly coloured paintings of flowers, animals and landscapes.

The main house consisted of three large rooms – a dining room, hall, and living room – and several guest rooms at the back. Behind the main building lay an old Chinese garden with a beautiful old covered well and an artificial terrace of stone grottos. Sophus Black's house was further on in the compound and the remaining buildings served as the kitchen and servants' quarters.

Vilhelm was enchanted by the picturesque houses and immediately decided to take over the lease. Naturally Black and his future bride could remain.

Two famous Danes had recently visited Peking as Black's guests in the Danish Mess and had recorded their reactions. The city made a deep impression on the famous Danish actor, Johannes Poulsen, his stay in Peking being the climax of his long journey. He wrote in his diary of his arrival in the city in June 1915:

> The train ran along a huge city wall ornamented with colossal Chinese towers as we approached Peking. I have never seen anything like it. This was the vast thousand-year-old Chinese Empire. We arrived at a station. Henningsen and Black were there to greet me. We drove to the club in the Legation Quarter where we had a gin sling and then continued on to the Danish Mess. It was lovely in Peking – bright, clear air, wonderfully odd Chinese streets. Henningsen went to the office. I went to Black's house, saw his collections. He and the other Danes were living in the most magnificent Chinese house with paper window panes, an old Chinese palace.

Figure 64: At the end of the nineteenth century, the Great Northern Telegraph Company set up a telegraph station in Beijing. The young Danish telegraph operators lived in the Danish Mess located in Da Yuan Fu Hutong behind the Peking Hotel. Prior to the establishment of the Danish Legation in 1912, the Danish Mess was the gathering point for the small Danish community in Beijing and for visiting Danes. The Danish flag showed visitors the way.

The 34-year-old Johannes Poulsen was fascinated by the Chinese antiques he saw in the home of his hosts and particularly those in the home of the Norwegian General Munthe, mentioned above. Munthe lived with his wife in a building almost entirely rebuilt in the Norwegian style. As President Yuan Shi-kai's aide-de-camp and the Chinese government's liaison to the foreign legations, Munthe was now one of the most influential foreigners in Peking. Johannes Poulsen enjoyed his stay in the Manchu palace, although the excursions to the surrounding countryside could sometimes be tiring:

> I was tired of riding – traversing Peking's long, wide, hard-packed earthern streets was especially bad. Went to dinner at the Danish Mess in the evening. Afterwards on the veranda in front of Black's rooms, I sang for them and told Hans Christian Andersen's story 'The Rags'.

Two years earlier, Johannes V. Jensen, the Danish author and future Nobel prize-winner (1944), had stayed with Black. In his *Introduktion til vor Tidsalder* [Introduction to Our Time] he wrote:

> I was given a room near the gate. The first night I didn't close my door as the stove smelled of soot and from the bed I could look directly onto the street. The walls were as thin as paper, they were made of paper-covered wooden screens, every sound penetrated, footsteps, talk, strange cries near by and far away a Babel of voices, a hollow thud as of horses on a threshing floor passing outside on the hard packed road, crowds of people in blue tunics passing into the light of the gateway. In the middle of all this I fell asleep, my candle burning on the table and my head more or less out on the street.
>
> A long-robed creature holding a torch stood over me later that night and blew out the candle. The night watchman. Strange, long cries sounded, people still thronging by. A thick sound as of layer rustling upon layer, the inhabitants of Peking, who did not seem to go to bed at night.

Vilhelm quickly settled the formalities of the lease and at once set about renovating the buildings. If his father had been among the first to have running water and electricity in Copenhagen in 1891, Vilhelm would be among the first to have such modern conveniences installed in Peking.

Figure 65: In 1915 Vilhelm rented a compound in Peking. Having served as the Great Northern Danish telegraph operators' residence for several years, the compound was normally referred to as the Danish Mess. The main house, an old Manchu palace, is shown here.

In December Sophus and Minna Black were united in matrimony by the Danish minister, Count Ahlefeldt-Laurvig. They took up residence in the little house on the hill. Mrs Black wrote later about the renovation of the old Manchu houses:

> Vilhelm Meyer was quick on the uptake and it didn't take long before the young people moved out and the workers moved in. They put in wooden floors all over,

first in our house. They installed three bathrooms in the big house with hot and cold water, etc. In our house there wasn't room for fixed installations in the bathroom so an oven was built in the garden for our hot water.

When the workers were almost finished, Mrs Meyer came up to see to the furnishings. Chesterfield chairs and chintz sofas were sent from Shanghai – porcelain, glasses, silverware, etc. There was a great deal to consider since it was to be a home – Kirsten and Vilhelm Meyer's home – where they should feel just as comfortable as in their daily residence in Shanghai.

The living room looked lovely. It was very pleasant, too, whenever we came down for a drink to meet their friends or just sat around together chatting.

Those were certainly working days for Meyer, but they had old friends here, too. The children had their nurse with them from the beginning – then their governess, and I'm sure they had a pleasant time. They were sweet, indeed.

Vilhelm and Kirsten grew very fond of their second home, where they stayed whenever they were in town. They often gave parties both for Vilhelm's business associates and for their own friends. Kirsten sometimes had her friend Mary MacLeod along and the two ladies took their easels and went off on sketching trips around the ancient imperial city.

The three families, Ahlefeldt-Laurvig, Black and Meyer, got along well. As the Danish minister to Peking, Preben Ahlefeldt-Laurvig and his wife Mary wished to create a pleasant setting at the legation for Peking's Danish community. In this they were absolutely successful. Minna Black wrote in her memoirs:

> It was a pleasure to go there. Count and Countess Ahlefeldt were a magnificent couple at the legation for the Danish community. Not only when they gave their receptions, when it was an old custom that the bride of the year poured out the tea and the bachelors helped her serve it round. At their dinner parties they made sure that we always met the right people – both Europeans and Chinese – artists and legation people – and then we could sit around afterwards, chatting or playing a hand of bridge.

Darduse – the Laughing Buddha

The Ahlefeldt, Black and Meyer families shared a common interest – Chinese antiques. General Munthe was a special source of inspiration as he was an expert and had an excellent collection. In the vast isolated empire, which dated back several thousand years, there was a seemingly inexhaustible supply of objets d'art from former times – porcelain, glass, bronze vases, paintings, clay figurines, ancestral portraits and fine silk brocades. For centuries Chinese mythology and the Buddhist religion from India had been a source of inspiration for works of art in all shapes and sizes. Some of the best-known deities were Kuan Ti, the Chinese god of war and Kuan Yin, the goddess of mercy, not to mention all the many forms of the Buddha.

In Shanghai Vilhelm and Kirsten had often visited the city's curio dealers, and the new home in Peking whetted their appetite. They made many purchases for their two homes over the years and part of their beautiful collection is now on view at the National Museum in Copenhagen. Their daughter Anette, born in 1917, wrote about her father's interest in Chinese antiques in her book *Mist on the Window Panes* (Ricard 1959):

Figure 66: Sophus Black (1882–1960) arrived in Shanghai in 1902, the same year as Vilhelm. Black worked for Great Northern and later became the manager of the company's tele-graph station in Peking. Sophus and Minna Black are photographed here at the Danish Mess, shortly after their wedding in 1915.

Papa had not been long in China before he had caught the fever so common among foreigners out here: the curio-collecting fever. By now he knew well the many pitfalls awaiting the collector and the more he collected, the more he realized how little in fact he knew, and it was seldom he bought anything quickly. He would often have things standing on his writing desk – either at home or at his office – for weeks on end before he decided if he liked them well enough to keep. Then the dealer would call again and the bargaining would begin in earnest, and in the case of a more valuable piece it would easily go on for days or even weeks. It was all part of the game.

This bargaining was a battle of wits in which the Chinese delighted and which had been developed to a fine art over the centuries. Papa delighted in it too. The game had certain rules: to lie is an art and no shame, but to expose the liar, for instance by calling his bluff too crudely and so causing him to 'lose face' was shameful and not to be forgiven. When the rules were adhered to, the battle would rage back and forth. Each side would start with outrageous bids, and there would be protestations, head-shakings and talk of ruin and starving children. In point of fact, the dealer would usually get more personal satisfaction by selling with a small profit after long bargaining than otherwise. He would blame him-

Figure 67: The Danish Legation was located in a narrow lane entered by passing through a large, red gate. In her handwritten memoirs, Minna Black described the Legation and the residence of the minister in the following terms: 'We cross a courtyard where on the right we can see the trees in the garden and a large goldfish pond – on the left a small house where the doorkeeper and perhaps some of the servants used to live. We are now standing at the huge door leading into the hall. It's very big and just in front of us is a great mirror in a beautifully carved frame – the frame is large and magnificent. The spacious sitting room we entered had white French Empire furniture upholstered in yellow silk, a special shade of yellow, which we always said was suitable for the Imperial Palace. At the back of the room was a deep alcove completely covered in yellow silk with the loveliest embroidered brocade.'

The legation hall is shown here with its portraits of the Danish King Christian X and Queen Alexandrine. In front of the screen at left, guarding the entrance, sits the beaming Darduse.

self for a fool if the deal went through too fast and he got a higher price than he had expected, because what might he not have got had he raised the price in the first place?

Sophus Black was especially fond of the Buddha with the huge belly, called Laughing Buddha or Happy Buddha in tourist language. His official Chinese names are Milofo and Maitreya but he is also popularly known as Da-du-shen (Big Belly God). This is the name by which he is known in some Western countries, Darduse. He represents wealth and happiness and often sits at the entrance to a temple or a residence, beaming his broad smile.

Black felt a certain affinity with the happy Darduse. He and Darduse not only had a large belly and a happy smile in common, but also the characteristic large ear lobes, which according to Chinese tradition are the sign of the highest wis-

Figure 68: In China Darduse, the laughing Buddha, has always been the embodiment of happiness, abundance and joy. Johannes V. Jensen, the Danish author and later Nobel prize winner, who visited Peking in 1913, described in a later article Darduse's enjoyment of a successful wedding: 'He brayed at the top of his voice, danced in place like a rocking ball so that his earlobes, which resembled fat grapes, bounced up and down, he pawed at the earth and carried on in an unruly fashion like an impatient, snorting stallion, screeching and rearing up on his hind legs. The guests smiled at his pranks – this was Darduse's way. Darduse's laughter rang out like the grunting of a zebu. On the floor all around him danced the dogs of the house, the small Pekinese with their flat snouts and their eyes set far apart, barking like a bunch of silver gongs strewn all over the floor.' The porcelain figurine shown in the picture stood for many years on the mantlepiece of the Meyer family's library in Shanghai. (See figure 132).

dom. Black played up this resemblance and had several small bronze figurines of Darduse made which he presented to his friends.

Sophus Black had told Johannes V. Jensen about the happy and popular Darduse. The Danish author was particularly taken with the tale of the young couple who finally succeed in their aim of getting married, thanks to Darduse's clever intervention. He described the story a few years later in the Danish newspaper *Berlingske Tidende* and it later became his first play, *Darduse*, performed at the Royal Theatre in Copenhagen in 1937, with Johannes Poulsen as the obvious choice for the title role.

The Danish business people in China were fascinated by Darduse's legendary talent for business. As a marriage broker, Darduse was an expert at getting a commission from both sides. According to Johannes V. Jensen, the goal of every Chinese was to acquire economic profit. 'Darduse's celebrated sack was as stuffed as a pelican's bill before that wedding was over.'

Vilhelm felt that he was in tune with Darduse, who brought prosperity and happiness. Undoubtedly 1915 had proved to be a good year. By incorporating the company in New York, Vilhelm had created the necessary foundation for a wide-ranging business association between American firms and Chinese contracting parties. Based in Shanghai, Peking and New York, Vilhelm was now ready for big new projects.

TEN

War and Peace, 1916–1919

The War in Europe

In 1911 Kirsten had taken little Thea back to Denmark to visit her parents and her two sisters, Agga and Aagot. But she hadn't seen her younger brother Luis (also called Ib) since he had gone to Australia in 1908. Now, in 1916, she anxiously awaited news of her brother, fighting in the war in Europe.

Luis had not had an easy childhood. He wasn't interested in school and a stay at a boarding school in Hamburg had not increased his interest. In 1902, when he was only 16 years old, he had got a job on board a freighter plying Danish waters. He later went to Australia and New Zealand, where for several years he worked as an agricultural labourer.

At the outbreak of The Great War, great efforts were made in the British overseas possessions to recruit volunteers to fight against Germany. Luis was one of the first to join up with the Australian army in the Province of New South Wales. After fighting in the Battle of Gallipoli against the Turks in 1915, the Australian volunteers arrived in France in June 1916, to fight in one of the great battles of the war, the Battle of the Somme. The attack on the German positions started on 24 June with eight days of continuous shelling. On 1 July British forces attacked. By the end of the day, the British had lost more than 60,000 men. Luis was a private in a company positioned in mid-July across from the German lines. The new Australian forces were the target of German fire from the very first night. The Germans were using phosgene poison gases, and the new front soldiers had to get used to putting on their gas masks in a hurry.

Over the following weeks Luis experienced the hell of artillery shelling, attack and counter-attack. One of the Australian privates, a farmer from New South Wales, wrote the following account in his diary about the battles of 25 July:

> All day long the ground rocked and swayed backward and forwards from the concussion … like a well-built haystack … swaying about … Men were driven stark staring mad and more than one of them could be seen crying and sobbing like children, their nerves completely gone … We were all in a state of silliness and half-dazed, but still the Australians refused to give ground. Men were buried by the dozen, but were frantically dug out again, some dead and some alive.

The Australian soldiers did not have much protection in their trenches and a number of soldiers were rendered unfit for combat as a result of shellshock. During the course of a few weeks almost half of the 800 men in the Fourth Battalion were killed and there were not enough soldiers in the medical corps to carry the wounded behind the lines. Luis was one of the survivors.

After a short break behind the front line, the Australian soldiers were again sent in. The decimated battalions were now ordered to take the German trench

Figure 69: Kirsten's brother, Luis Ernst Grip Bramsen (1885–1916), died in the Battle of the Somme. He had joined the Australian forces as a volunteer. His name is written on the monument in Århus for Danes fallen in World War I, and on the wall of the large War Memorial in Canberra, Australia.

positions. At several points the lines between the Australians and Germans were only 100 yards apart. Any attempt to create an attack position closer to the Germans, however, was stopped by heavy German machine-gun fire. On 17 August the attempt was made in earnest and Luis was among the attacking Australian soldiers. This attempt was no more successful than the others. The Germans were firmly entrenched in their positions and Luis did not survive the attack. He was killed on the battlefield at Pozières on 19 August 1916.

In Shanghai Vilhelm and Kirsten read all about the war in Europe in the newspapers, including the dramatic Battle of the Somme, which lasted more than four months. During this period the entente forces succeeded in forcing their way 6 miles behind the German front lines. The losses on both sides were astronomical. The attacking forces lost 700,000 men while the Germans lost 600,000.

Then the telegram arrived from the family in Copenhagen with the sad news of Luis' death in France. Kirsten was devastated. He had been her only brother and as his elder sister she had felt a special responsibility for him throughout her childhood. Deep down she reproached her mother for a lack of love and understanding of this son who had had such trouble living up to his mother's social ambitions. He had gone to sea when he was 16 years old and at the early age of 30 his lonely life was now over – fighting a foreign foe in a foreign army on a foreign battlefield.

Civil War in China

Neither the United States nor China had as yet entered the war. Yuan Shikai wanted to prevent the new republic established after the fall of the empire from falling apart. He had been the emperor's military leader and it was difficult for him to let go of old traditions.

In 1915 Yuan Shikai arranged a 'popular vote', the results of which encouraged him to take the throne as emperor and thereby start a new dynasty in the long history of China. He actually managed to reign as emperor for three months, but the move caused such bitter resentment that in March 1916 he was forced to let himself be reinstated as president of the Chinese republic. He died two months later at the age of 56.

Once again the stage was set for a power struggle in China between a number of provincial generals and the supporters of Sun Yat-sen's Nationalist Party. For 12 years, from 1916 to 1928, the political scene in China was marked by a civil war, which came to involve a number of warring factions – Yuan Shikai's generals in Peking, the warlords in other parts of China and Sun Yat-sen's and Chiang Kai-shek's Kuomintang Nationalists in Canton. A new player, the Communists, entered the scene in 1921.

Shanghai was growing in this period as thousands of Chinese poured into the metropolis. In 1915 there were 620,000 Chinese living in the International Settlement alone. The number of foreigners in Shanghai was also on the increase, but the composition was changing. While formerly the British had been the dominant group, both in terms of numbers and influence, the Japanese were now pre-eminent when it came to population size. In 1915 out of a foreign population of 21,000, more than 7,000 were Japanese and 5,000 were British.

A. M. & Co. Expands

Although political conditions in China in this period were fairly chaotic, there continued to be a need for foreign firms capable of procuring the goods and engineering know-how so crucial to China's industrial development. In Shanghai Vilhelm demonstrated in several areas that he was on the cutting edge when it came to methods and principles of the execution of large projects.

As he made clear in his New York report in 1915, he placed special emphasis on being the co-ordinating link between buyer and seller. An American firm would deliver an entire factory or a complete power plant according to the specifications of the Chinese buyer, whether a private businessman or a public authority. Vilhelm Meyer would arrange the necessary communication and draft the proper contract. As a go-between, his speciality was a firm grasp of both the American conditions of delivery and the Chinese expectations of the finished product.

A fine example of this was the association with Saco-Lowell Shops, which produced complete cotton mills. This American firm traced its history back to the 1800s when American industrialists, wishing to free themselves of the stranglehold of textile imports from Manchester, England, had started their own textile factories, one of which was located at Lowell outside Boston and another in Biddeford, Maine on the Saco River. In addition to manufacturing textiles, the two factories developed machinery for the textile industry. In 1912 the two 'machine shops' merged, forming Saco-Lowell Shops, which in addition to concentrating on the American market, had also begun to look into the possibility of manufacturing machinery for foreign countries.

During his stay in the United States in 1915, Vilhelm had become the agent of Saco-Lowell. This was to prove of great significance for the American firm. In December 1915 two Chinese firms in Tianjin placed orders with A. M. & Co. for one cotton mill each. The orders were sent on to Saco-Lowell, marking the beginning of a wide-ranging export business to China.

In a book on Saco-Lowell's history, the following can be read about how A. M. & Co. operated as their agent in China:

> By the terms of this agreement Andersen, Meyer & Co. purchased machinery outright from Saco-Lowell, reselling it in China sufficient to cover shipping costs plus a commission. The value of this service was twofold. Saco-Lowell gained access to a market in which it was notoriously difficult to operate without knowledge of official and unofficial trade restrictions. At the same time Saco-Lowell was relieved of the financial burden of dealing directly with the Chinese mills.

This was the key to Vilhelm's growing success as a businessman in China. He understood both the extensive Chinese trade restrictions and the complex financial situation. Both the American suppliers and the Chinese buyers could see the advantage of letting the knowledgeable Danish entrepreneur act as their go-between.

Figure 70: The A. M. & Co. Company Trade Mark

In 1916 Vilhelm decided that A. M. & Co. should have a trademark on the company writing paper and on the machines manufactured in Shanghai and distributed to Chinese factories. He arranged a competition among the 300 or so employees and their families with a prize of $500 for the winner. A total of 40 suggestions came in. The participants' names were handed in anonymously, in sealed envelopes. The suggestions were hung up on a board and the employees cast their votes. Imagine everyone's surprise when it turned out that the wife of the General Manager had designed the winning trademark! Smiling, Vilhelm exclaimed that now he wouldn't have to pay the winner since it was all in the family! Kirsten took her revenge over the following years, however, for every time she bought anything that was not strictly necessary, she would smile sweetly at Vilhelm, saying it was only part of her prize money!

After registering A. M. & Co. as an American corporation in 1915, Vilhelm got busy opening a number of branches in China to serve as bases for the company's expansion into the large Chinese market. First came Tianjin (1915), Hankou and Jinan (1916), Hong Kong (1917), Mukden (Shenyang) (1919) and Canton (1920). New branches were later opened in Harbin (1925) and Qingdao (1929). The company also embarked on the export business, setting up a number of factories with this in mind, including a wool cleaners in Tianjin, a tannery in Hankou as well as factories manufacturing hairnets in Jinan and rugs in Kalgan (Zhangjiakou). The number of company employees and branches increased dramatically in this period.

The war in Europe made leading American business people eager to invest in new markets in Asia. This was particularly true of Stone, Straight and Bruce, who had great plans for taking part in the industrial development of the Asian Pacific countries. In addition to the international city of Shanghai, another perfect base for the three Americans' Pacific dream seemed to be Manila in the Philippines, which was under American sovereignty. As the director of Pacific Commercial Company in Manila, Bruce was especially qualified to bring in the Philippines.

In 1916 the three Americans founded a new company, Pacific Development Corporation, with a stock capital of US$ 5 million. This company, which was registered in New York in January 1917, was to be a holding company for activities in Manila and Shanghai. A number of Andersen, Meyer & Co.'s big American suppliers were among the main stockholders.

In 1917 the number of A. M. & Co.'s board members was raised from 5 to 11 and the share capital increased to $1 million. Later that year a number of shareholding transactions took place with the purpose of ensuring that the new holding company, Pacific Development Corporation, remained the sole shareholder of A. M. & Co. In compensation, A. M. & Co.'s shareholders, including Vilhelm, received shares in P.D.C., whose share capital was further increased to $10 million.

In December 1918 a new company was founded in Manila – Andersen, Meyer & Co. Ltd. Bruce was the president and the board included Meyer, Bruce and Stone. This was a sister company to A. M. & Co. of New York/Shanghai. The share capital of $2 million was gradually increased to $5 million over the following years.

The new corporate structure was now complete: a holding company in New York, Pacific Development Corporation, and three subsidiary companies, Andersen, Meyer & Co. of New York/Shanghai as well as Andersen, Meyer & Co. and Pacific Commercial Company, both of Manila. The business links between Straight, Stone, Meyer and Bruce of New York, Shanghai and Manila had been strengthened in earnest and the Pacific dream could now become a reality.

Family Life in Shanghai

In November 1917 Kirsten had her third daughter. The delivery again took place at home. Their Chinese servants had expected 'Master' and 'Missie' to be disappointed if a boy were still not forthcoming, but noted, somewhat to their surprise, that the new parents were delighted with their new daughter. The only one who was upset was 3-year-old Rose-Marie, who had been hoping for a little brother! At her christening a few weeks later the little girl was named Anette Kirsten Meyer.

The family residence on Avenue Road now housed many other inhabitants besides Vilhelm, Kirsten and their three daughters. The family had had an English nurse for many years, Miss Calder, who had entered the family's employ in connection with the birth of Thea in 1910. 'Nanny' was authoritarian when it came to such routines as washing faces and brushing teeth, but kind and entertaining too when she took the girls for walks. They often walked in beautiful Jessfield Park, near Avenue Road.

Many other foreigners also had Chinese 'amahs' or Japanese 'amahsans' to take care of their young children. When Rose-Marie was born in 1913, Kirsten hired a young Japanese nurse to help Nanny. 'Amahsan', as she was always called, remained with the family for over 20 years. She was a quiet, gentle presence, playing with the children and helping Kirsten perform all the daily domestic duties. It was always a source of hilarity when Amahsan marched around the living room in her Japanese kimono, singing Danish children's rhymes.

The house's Chinese staff was under the direction of Mr Liu, known as 'Number One Boy', who, in accordance with Kirsten's instructions, was in charge of the daily housekeeping. He was a fat, little man and always wore a silk cap on his closely cropped head. He knew everyone and everything.

One evening when Kirsten was newly-wed and expecting dinner guests, she noticed that the table was set with silverware that she had never seen before. It was not until several of the guests happily remarked that their silverware had been newly polished that she realized that the Chinese servants had their own network and it was perfectly common to borrow silverware etc. from each other. Number One Boy was an expert at this.

Number Two Boy, whose name was Chow, was intelligent and popular with the entire family. Tall and erect, he came from northern China. He could easily have become Number One in another family, but chose to remain with the Meyer family and in 1927 was promoted to Number One. The old head servant, who then retired, continued to live on the premises and was given the name 'Old Boy'.

One day when Chow was newly appointed, he had had a fight with the cook, who chased him around the table, wildly brandishing a kitchen knife. Mrs Meyer had come into the kitchen and immediately stopped the cook, resolutely taking the knife away from him. Chow had been devoted to the lady of the house ever since. Chow knew everything, too, listening to telephone conversations as if this were the most natural thing in the world. He always knew exactly where the various members of the family were to be found during the course of the day. He was efficient, discreet and helpful to all members of the Meyer family.

The kitchen was the cook's domain. As mentioned above, he was a very impulsive gentleman with a violent temper. At least once a year Kirsten would have to think of getting rid of him and would tell Chow to hire a new cook.

Figure 71: The Russian Revolution caused a large influx of Russian refugees to arrive in Shanghai. There were many artists among them, including the painter Jacoblev, who drew this portrait of the three sisters, Thea, Anette and Rose-Marie, in 1919.

And each time Chow would inform the lady of the house that he had now fired the old cook and hired a new cook. 'Is it the old cook?' asked Kirsten. 'Yes, Missie, old cook', replied Chow. 'All right, we'll try him', smiled Kirsten. In China no one must lose face.

In addition there was Number Three Boy, Liu, as well as a chauffeur and several others to help with the cleaning, washing and ironing. There were also a gardener and a tailor to give a hand as needed. Wages were not high, but it was part of the conditions of employment that any economies that the cook or Number One Boy made in connection with their purchases would be to their own benefit. When one of the Chinese servants fell ill, there was always a close relative to take his place, and when there were dinner parties, Number One Boy always saw to it that there was extra help in the kitchen, or wherever else it was needed.

Vilhelm's jovial charm and Kirsten's kind and mild manner made them well liked and respected by the numerous helpers in the home and contributed to the happy, pleasant atmosphere that invariably characterized the house on Avenue Road.

Vilhelm Meyer, Baritone

It was obvious to the members of the Shanghai foreign community that if they were to preserve their own Western traditions and culture in such foreign surroundings, they would have to make a special effort. Several amateur groups were formed for concerts, drama, ballet and opera.

Vilhelm had ample opportunity to cultivate his singing talent. It was the custom at private parties after dinner for some of the guests to oblige with a number, and whenever Vilhelm was among the guests he was always asked to sing a few songs in his beautiful baritone. He had an extensive repertoire, especially when it came to Danish and German songs. If there were no other Danes present, he would occasionally begin to improvise in the middle of a Danish song and, addressing Kirsten, sing about some of the guests present without their knowledge. On such occasions Kirsten would have difficulty keeping a straight face.

Vilhelm performed at larger functions, too. In 1912 a Russian lady pianist gave a concert at the Lyceum Theatre. Vilhelm took part in the concert and received the following review in the local German newspaper:

> To our knowledge this was the first time Mr Meyer has appeared before a Shanghai audience, but he took everyone by storm. Mr Meyer has a wonderful, mellow and pleasant voice and we very much hope that the German Concert Society will be able to prevail upon him to sing at one of the season's coming concerts.

Vilhelm performed in Ambroise Thomas' opera *Mignon* the same year. He sang the part of Lothario, the old man seeking his missing daughter. Vilhelm and the lovely soprano, Mrs Isenman, in the title role helped make the performance a huge success. Many able people, including a number of Vilhelm's and Kirsten's friends, organized the ambitious production and Mary MacLeod had designed the programme.

In 1913 Vilhelm sang at a concert given by Shanghai's City Orchestra at the town hall. The big Dane impressed the audience with his powerful rendition of 'Wotan's Farewell to Brunnhilde' from Wagner's *Valkyrie*, as well as more lyrical Nordic songs such as Grieg's 'Two Brown Eyes' and 'With a Primula Veris' and the Danish composer Hartmann's 'Fly, Bird, Fly'. Among the amateur musicians in the orchestra were Theodor Raaschou, the Danish Consul-General, on the violin, and Ernest Measor, one of Vilhelm's heads of department and future Singapore partner, on the cello.

The Great War put a temporary end to these amateur artistic endeavours. However, it was decided in 1917 to perform Puccini's opera *Tosca*, the proceeds of which were to go to the Allied War Funds. The allied countries' consuls in Shanghai gave the project their full support. The fact that Denmark was neutral during the War did not prevent Danes from taking part in the performance of *Tosca*. Once again Raaschou, the Consul-General, played the violin in the orchestra.

Tosca, written in 1900, had already enjoyed considerable success in Europe. But could opera amateurs handle such a demanding task? It was worth a try and the international community enthusiastically threw itself into the new undertaking. It was obvious that Mrs Isenman was a perfect choice for the role of Tosca. The role of her beloved Cavaradossi fell to the Dutch banker, Michel Speelman, and Vilhelm was given the baritone role of the wicked Scarpia, who is to blame for Cavaradossi's death, but who is himself killed by Tosca. Andersen, Meyer & Co. was in charge of all the lighting and several of the company's employees appeared in the opera.

Rehearsals took place in the autumn of 1917. But Speelman, the heroic tenor, caught cold and the opening night, which was supposed to have been in December, had to be postponed for several weeks. *Tosca* opened at the Olympic Theatre on 8 January 1918, despite the fact that Speelman had still not completely got his voice back. The opera proved to be a great success. The critics were full of praise, particularly for Mrs Isenman, who sang 'quite enchantingly', and for Vilhelm. Allowances were made for Speelman's voice not having fully recovered. Several critics, however, thought that the music was played a bit too loudly, drowning out the singers.

At lunch the next day a delighted Kirsten read the reviews aloud, first in the *China Press*:

> One of the truly grand successes of the performance was a magnificent character study of 'Scarpia', played by Mr V. Meyer. He played the part with a sure sense of character, and with regard to his singing, let it suffice to say that he has never been heard to greater advantage. It will be a very long time before Mr V. Meyer's 'Scarpia' is forgotten by the local opera lovers. It was masterful, convincing and tremendously vital.

The *Shanghai Times* wrote:

> But in my humble opinion the palm for the performance must be given to Mr Meyer. His fine voice is heard to great advantage in his part and his impressive stage presence is most noteworthy. His portrayal of the cruel and tyrannical character of the Agent of Police was a most masterful performance.

Figure 72: In 1918 the opera *Tosca* was performed in Shanghai, the profits going to the Allied War Fund. With his powerful baritone Vilhelm was the obvious choice to sing the role of Scarpia.

A third critic wrote:

> Mr V. Meyer, both in appearance, voice and depiction, made an ideal 'Scarpia'. He had evidently made a special study of his role as he was not only admirably suited to it, but acted it to perfection.

Figure 73: After the première of *Tosca* one of the critics wrote: 'Mr. V. Meyer in the role of the police agent Scarpia gave a very good interpretation and his singing was at all times excellent. He was evidently at home in his part and one felt quite sorry that his demise in the second act forbade further enjoyment of the voice in the last act.' In the picture Scarpia is being stabbed by the unhappy Tosca.

The head of A. M. & Co.'s accounting department, the Japanese Hara remarked after the performance that seeing Scarpia's eyes flare up in anger gave you an excellent idea of what the manager of Andersen, Meyer & Co. looked like if anything was wrong with the company books!

Vilhelm was well versed in European songs, but found inspiration in Chinese music, too. He was particularly fond of Peking Opera, whose most distinguished performer was Mei Lanfang. Once Mei Lanfang had come to dinner at the Meyer family. Anette has given the following description in her book, *Mist on the Window Panes* (Ricard 1959):

> He had come down from Peking to give a guest performance and we had been taken to see him act a few days before. Though we knew perfectly well that there were no actresses at the better theatres, and that men always took women's parts, it had been hard to believe that the strangely made up and gloriously dressed woman with the oddly high-pitched voice (whom we had watched with fascination and complete incomprehension) was really a man. But it was a man, if a small one, who came in, proudly announced by the Boy. To our surprise he was followed not only by his wife but by quite a number of other people as well. After having greeted Mama and Papa in the ceremonious Chinese fashion – of bowing and clasping his own hands – he casually and collectively introduced his followers, explaining that they were members of his family and as they had never dined at a foreign house, he had brought them along. He thought it would be a nice experience for them. Everyone smiled and bowed all round, and when Mama had a chance, she discreetly gestured to Number One.

Figure 74: A singer of opera himself, Vilhelm was fascinated by Chinese opera. He particularly enjoyed listening to young Mei Lanfang (1894–1961) with whom he became friends. Here Mei Lanfang is shown in a female role in a signed photo given to Vilhelm by the Chinese singer, later so renowned.

'Can do, Boy?' she murmured.
'Can do, Missie' he answered and glided out.
Dinner was delayed for a remarkably short time while a new leaf was put in and the table reset.

The End of the War

The war was drawing to a close in Europe. The United States had gone in on the side of the Allies in April 1917 and in August the Peking government joined the Allies, too. The immediate consequence of this was that German and Austrian territorial rights in China passed into the hands of the Chinese government and China's unpaid debt of compensation for the Boxer Rebellion to those countries was cancelled. China would also be allowed to participate in the coming peace conference.

The October Revolution took place in Russia and many White Russians arrived in Shanghai the following year.

At the peace negotiations in Versailles, the Allies resolved on 30 April 1919, although without the consent of the United States, that the German possessions in Shandong province in China were to be handed over to Japan. China's protests proved fruitless. The Chinese negotiators at Versailles presented a memorandum in which they demanded the annulment of the unequal treaties. None of the other delegates, however, took these views into consideration.

On 4 May 1919 a few hundred students staged a protest demonstration at Tiananmen Square in Peking. Arrests were made and within a very short time the anger felt by many Chinese led to the formation of the Fourth of May Movement, which in coming years was to become the national rallying ground for revolutionary Chinese. The new movement's objective was not only that China should free herself of the influence of foreign powers when it came to her own affairs. It also called on China to finally establish a modern republic, the goal of the rebellion of 1911 that had abolished the old, feudal imperial regime.

One of the numerous young revolutionaries taking active part in the Fourth of May Movement was Chen Duxiu, the dean of Peking University. Another was the 37-year-old author, Lu Xun, who, having settled in Shanghai, attacked traditional Confucianism and called for a liberated China. Liberation would also include women, who for thousands of years, by being subjected to the practice of foot-binding, among other things, had been deprived of any independent role in Chinese society. The drama A Doll's House by the Norwegian playwright Henrik Ibsen, had played an important role in this context. Just as Nora at the end of the play leaves her husband in order to go out into the world to seek her own destiny, so would the Chinese women take control of their own lives, according to the new way of thinking.

The Great War was over. The Treaty of Versailles had shown that very few countries paid any attention to Chinese wishes for greater independence and freedom from the shackles of foreign treaties. Conflicts of interest intensified and the basis for supporting a Communist form of government was created in this period. A number of young Chinese, inspired by the Fourth of May Movement of 1919, were later to become leading political figures in building up the People's Republic of China. Among these were 26-year-old Mao Zedong, 21-year-old Zhou Enlai and 14-year-old Deng Xiaoping.

Figure 75: In this advertisement from the *Official Guide for Travellers to the Orient, 1918/19*, published by the Japanese company Osaka Shosen Kaisha, one can see that most of the suppliers to Andersen, Meyer & Co. were American companies.

Although these Chinese regularly came to stay within the protective borders of Shanghai, the city's foreign business community knew nothing as yet of the revolutionary young Chinese and their theories, which in the course of time would transform the ancient empire into a Communist society.

Figure 76: Before his departure for Poland in 1920, Count Ahlefeldt-Laurvig, the Danish minister to Peking, stayed for several months in the Meyers' Manchu palace. The envoy is shown here with three officials of the Chinese Foreign Ministry. The little boy in the picture is Sophus and Minna Black's son, Christen.

ELEVEN

Expansion, 1920–1921

The Pacific Development Corporation

The war had brought the new superpower, the United States of America, on to the world stage in earnest. In Shanghai the American involvement in trade and industrialization had significantly increased and in New York, the new holding company, the Pacific Development Corporation, was in a highly expansive phase. An impressive office building was erected at 80 Wall Street and the new corporation moved in.

The American trio with whom Vilhelm had started operations in 1915, consisting of Stone, Straight and Bruce, was now reduced to two. Straight had joined the United States army when the United States had entered the war in 1917. At the end of the war in November 1918 Straight was in Paris, where he caught pneumonia and died within a few days. The intelligent, fascinating and versatile businessman was only 38 years old.

Business conditions in Shanghai were no longer as favourable in the post-war years as they had been in the past. Goods from Europe and America began to pour in and prices on a number of imported articles fell drastically. The board of the Pacific Development Corporation headed by Stone and Bruce nevertheless wished to expand, not only into the vast Chinese market, but throughout the entire world. In 1920 several members of the board went to China and the Philippines. In Peking they negotiated a loan of $5 million to the Chinese government with collateral in the year's tobacco and wine duties.

In view of P.D.C.'s vast Pacific dreams, it was vital to secure an area in Shanghai close by the Whangpoo River to be used as a loading port and storage facility for machinery and building materials. A. M. & Co. therefore purchased a large area on the river in the Yangshupu district in the northern section of the city. A port facility was erected, equipped with cranes and a number of big, concrete warehouses. There was also space for the corporation's large trucks, which would transport the goods to the rest of the country.

Other suppliers, too, were interested in delivering their shipments and storing them in the Yangshupu warehouses. On this basis A. M. & Co. founded a subsidiary company, Sun Chong Warehouse Company, which could be used by a number of firms for storage and transportation.

Vilhelm also built a number of big machine sheds in the Yangshupu area, where machinery and components could be fixed and tested. In time these activities were expanded into actual machine manufacture, which took place within the framework of the firm's machine shop. Later a window sash shop was also set up to manufacture steel-frame windows. AMCO windows were used in many of the new buildings shooting up in Shanghai.

Figure 77: The close co-operation between A. M. & Co. and G.E. is seen clearly in this picture of the machine shop in Yang-shupu, built in 1921.

The Meyer Family in Denmark

In the autumn of 1919 Kirsten was expecting her fourth child and the family agreed that she should take the three girls to Denmark for Christmas and have the baby in Denmark. Vilhelm would follow them in the spring of 1920 and for the first time the family would spend the summer holiday in Denmark together. Vilhelm hadn't been home since 1908 and Kirsten hadn't been there since 1911.

Kirsten and the girls stayed with Vilhelm's sister and brother-in-law, Jutta and Carl Zøylner, on their farm north of Copenhagen. There, on 5 February 1920, Kirsten gave birth to her fourth child, another daughter. The little girl was christened Marie-Louise.

Vilhelm was delighted when the telegram with the good news reached him in Shanghai. His Chinese friends, however, felt rather sorry for him since it wasn't a boy this time either! He immediately sent two telegrams, one to Kirsten and one to his brother, Ernst Meyer, in Copenhagen. To the latter he had merely written, 'Fill her room with roses'. Ernst felt that roses in February were altogether too extravagant so he bought one orchid, which he had delivered to Kirsten 'from Vilhelm'. Kirsten was somewhat taken aback since Vilhelm knew perfectly well that she did not like orchids. Ernst shamefacedly had to admit that he had not followed instructions.

Figure 78: In the summer of 1920 Vilhelm and Kirsten were reunited with Kirsten's two sisters, Agga and Aagot and their families. Svend Rohde, Gotfred Blom, Aagot Blom and Vilhem are shown standing. Agga Rohde is seated next to Kirsten, who has little Marie-Louise on her lap. The summer was a happy one for all the little cousins as they played together on the beach at Humlebæk.

In the spring Vilhelm joined the family in Denmark, where they rented the summer house 'Villa Narva' by the water, just north of Humlebæk. They also took an apartment in town. Vilhelm and Kirsten enjoyed this time spent reunited in Denmark, together with their four daughters. They paid visits to their parents. During the summer months Kirsten's parents moved to 'Villa Pam' in Humlebæk and Louis Meyer moved to 'Villa Padre' in Vedbæk. Many of Vilhelm's and Kirsten's sisters and brothers had married and had children, including William and Emilie Heering, who also had a summer house in Humlebæk.

Vilhelm and Kirsten agreed that when they returned to Shanghai they would take a Danish governess with them to help the two eldest girls keep up their Danish. One of the applicants was a young woman by the name of Gerda Nielsen, employed by Prince Harald and Princess Helene to take care of their children. She was now eager to go abroad. Kirsten liked the applicant and hired her in the summer of 1920. Miss Nielsen, as the children called their new governess, wrote to her mother in Copenhagen regularly about daily life in the Meyer family from 1920 to 1923.

New York

Once again Vilhelm turned his attention towards the United States. He wished to strengthen his ties with the Pacific Development Corporation as well as negotiate a number of new agency contracts for himself. He therefore decided that the family would spend the autumn in New York before returning to Shanghai early in 1921.

He left with Kirsten in August. They rented a large apartment in a modern building on 57th Street between 6th and 7th Avenues. The building was very close to Central Park, on the same block as the big, new concert hall, Carnegie Hall. Miss Nielsen, Nanny and Amahsan joined them with the children a few weeks later. They left Copenhagen on the *Frederik VIII*, arriving in New York in early October. In a letter to her mother, Gerda Nielsen described their arrival:

> At around 10 o'clock the quarantine officer came on board and we all filed past him, then came the passport officers who said we wouldn't be allowed to go ashore before they had seen the children's father! Well, fortunately Mr and Mrs Meyer were down on the dock to meet us so we were allowed to go ashore, but we had 34 pieces of luggage altogether, which had to go through customs! Mrs Meyer went home with the children and Amah while Mr Meyer, Nanny and I stayed with the luggage and we didn't get home until 4.30 p.m. The Meyers were enormously kind to me and I was put to bed after we had eaten.

The family spent the following months in the big city. For a few hours every morning Miss Nielsen would give lessons to Thea (10) and Rose-Marie (7). 'They know nothing', wrote Gerda Nielsen to her mother. 'Thea is sweet and tries. Rose-Marie is not sweet at all and very naughty, always trying to see how far she can go before I get really angry, but everything will hopefully work out all right.' In another letter she wrote:

> Thea, Rose-Marie and I were having tea together when we happened to talk about Denmark, about the departure. Thea suddenly says, 'You mustn't talk to us so much about the fatherland we love so much because then we'll just cry.' Which is exactly what she and I did a minute later! Well, I can usually manage to hear Denmark mentioned without bursting into tears. It was mostly the way she said it.

Nanny and Amahsan were in charge of Anette, who was 4, and Marie-Louise, who was always called Baby and who had not yet had her first birthday. In addition there were a Swedish cook and a Norwegian and an American housemaid. Gerda wrote:

> Baby is the loveliest child, happy and good ... Even though there are an awful lot of us to look after the children, 4 nippers can certainly take up most of one's time. Then Anette comes toddling up and says in her delightful Danish: 'Lil' me play wi' Miss Nielsen?' And then I have to be a dog or a doctor or whatever suits her best.

In her letters Gerda Nielsen gave a few brief glimpses of life in New York in 1920 and of the daily life of 'Mr and Mrs M.':

> The American women are dreadfully smart, but all very much alike. I find the men frightful, so uncivilized to look at, and I believe they work very hard. Mr Meyer does anyway, at the office at 9 in the morning, home again at 7 in the evening.

Miss Nielsen also noted that Mr and Mrs Meyer never read Danish newspapers, neither in New York nor in China, but that she herself was going to make sure that Danish newspapers would be sent to her regularly. And she liked her new job very much: 'No praise is too great for Mr and Mrs M. They are simply the nicest people I know – good to others and each other.'

The International General Electric Company

Every day Vilhelm went to his office at Pacific Development Corporation's new building on Wall Street and in the evening he and Kirsten went to concerts, the theatre, or took part in the social whirl. When the Meyer family entertained there was often – as in Shanghai – music and singing after dinner and Miss Nielsen, who could both sing and play the piano, was an active participant in these musical activities. Vilhelm also found time to take singing lessons with Klebansky, the Russian singer.

Figure 79: The corporate roots of the General Electric Company go back to 1878 when Thomas A. Edison (1847–1931) founded the Edison Electric Light Company. He was an ingenious inventor, first with his incandescent electric lamp and later in fields such as telephones, phonographs and dynamos.

Figure 80: Charles A. Coffin (1844–1926) began his business career as a shoe manufacturer in Lynn, Massachusetts. He later became head of the Thomson-Houston Company, founded in 1883. When this company merged with the Edison General Electric Companies in 1892 to form the General Electric Company, Coffin was elected president of the new company and Edison joined the G.E. board of direc-tors. For more than 20 years Coffin was an outstanding leader of a fast-growing and highly esteemed company. In 1913 Edwin N. Rice Jr. took over as president of G.E., while Coffin became chairman of the board.

During their stay in New York Vilhelm and Kirsten saw a great deal of Edward Bruce and his wife, Margaret, who had just moved back to New York from Manila. They now lived in a magnificent apartment, furnished completely in the Chinese style.

Vilhelm also kept in close contact with the General Electric Company, his main American supplier. Edwin W. Rice Jr had been president of G.E. since 1913. From 1914 to 1918 the foreign business of G.E. had increased threefold.

Figure 81: G.E. President, Charles A. Coffin, wanted the young and energetic Gerard Swope (1872–1957), from Western Electric Company to join G.E. in order to take over the international department. Swope agreed, but wanted a separate, though wholly G.E. owned, corporation. So in January 1919 Swope became president of the new International General Electric Company. Only three years later, in 1922, Swope succeeded Rice as president of G.E, a post he held until 1940 and again 1942–44. With a degree in electrical engineering from Massachusetts Institute of Technology, he had the technical background for the production, engineering and research operations of G.E. But he also developed remarkable skills as a suc-cessful businessman. Under Swope G.E. developed into a truly international company.

Figure 82: Owen D. Young (1874–1962), a lawyer from Boston, was hired by Coffin in 1913 as G.E. chief counsel and vice-president in charge of policy. In 1922 he succeeded Coffin as chairman of the board while Gerard Swope became president of G.E. Together Young and Swope became a formidable team. They managed to take General Electric through a seemingly limitless expansion period, followed by a prolonged and difficult depression leading up to World War II. They made G.E. into one of the biggest industrial complexes in the United States.

Figure 83: Anson W. Burchard (1865–1927), who had been Coffin's assistant, followed Swope as president of the International General Electric Company Ltd from 1922 to 1925, and was chairman of the board of I.G.E in 1922–27. He was also chairman of the board of Andersen, Meyer & Co. Ltd in 1923–27.

The export structure would therefore have to be developed and expanded, so in January 1919 the company's foreign department was changed into a new company, the International General Electric Company Ltd (I.G.E.). Maurice A. Oudin continued in the export business as vice-president of the new company.

G.E. had chosen Gerard Swope as the first president of I.G.E. Swope travelled extensively abroad during his early years with I.G.E. He reorganized the company's foreign offices, turning I.G.E. into a smooth-running organization.

Anson W. Burchard, one of the vice-presidents of G.E., was known to be a genius in financial matters. He had joined the General Electric Company as an engineer in 1902. Burchard had worked as assistant to C.A. Coffin, the first president of G.E., and was made a vice-president of the company in 1912 and a member of the board in 1917.

Vilhelm and Kirsten became close friends of Anson Burchard and Allene, his extremely wealthy wife. They lived in a house at 690 Park Avenue [which to-day houses the Italian Consulate General]. 'A delightful house', wrote Gerda Nielsen, 'completely in the French style with lots of old things, tapestries, chasubles, engravings, etc.'

The new subsidiary of G.E., the International General Electric Company, held its first general conference for its executive staff and officials from a number of associated companies in 21 countries. The meeting took place in October 1920, at Briarcliff Manor, New York. During the five-day meeting there was a general exchange of views on the many aspects of I.G.E's international business. The meeting was chaired by Gerard Swope, president of I.G.E., and opened with addresses from the chairman of the board of G.E. C.A. Coffin and the president of G.E. Edwin W. Rice, Jr.

The focus of the meeting was how to provide electricity and electrical appliances to all parts of the world. Among the participants was the manager of the I.G.E. office in Shanghai, W.M. States, who in his remarks underlined the necessity of having good agents 'with the agency for a large number of different kinds of apparatus, the machinery and all that goes with it'. He went on to explain why it was so important to have an agency like Andersen, Meyer & Co. in a country like China:

> For instance, a Chinese comes into Mr Meyer's office and wants to buy a cotton mill. He will say, 'I want buy a cotton mill, all same Mr Low'. 'How many spindles?' 'Alle same his. How much?' '200,000 taels.' 'Can do'. And Mr Meyer takes the contract for it. That means that everything that goes into that mill is left to the engineers of Andersen, Meyer & Company and handled in that way. We get the entire line of the motors and whatever General Electric equipment goes into it. If we were handling that direct, it would be a very hard proposition.

The meeting was the first of its kind. This was also the first time that the newcomer to G.E., the president of the newly formed I.G.E. Gerard Swope could explain the global aspects of the G.E. development strategy and underline the need to co-operate closely with the many associated companies abroad. In his speech he summarized his vision as follows:

> One of the biggest things the International Company offers, not only by this association but by its means of communication between the associated companies, is to exchange the best of one company with the best of another, and if we can in that way finally get each company to adopt the best methods of all the others, we will have in every country the best company and throughout the world a group of the best companies. I thank you.

After his speech everybody rose and applauded Mr Swope. Here was a man who could lead and inspire. Two years later he became the president of the entire General Electric Company.

Back to China

The Meyer family celebrated Christmas Eve in the Danish manner in the apartment on 57th Street. There was a big Christmas tree in the living room and Danish guests were invited to Christmas dinner. Miss Nielsen played the piano while the others sang Christmas carols around the tree. It was a happy occasion.

In early January the family left New York to return to China. The route went by train across Canada and by steamship from Vancouver to Shanghai. As usual, Vilhelm was surrounded by female travelling companions. In her book *Mist on the Window Panes*, Anette gives a description of what travelling with the whole family was like:

> Papa might jokingly make a fuss when he travelled with us – he said he felt like an Eastern potentate and grumbled that he missed having a male bodyguard around, to protect him from us all … but all the same, he took it with surprising calm and it did not really seem to worry him to travel with such a formidable company as we must have made: his wife, four daughters, a nurse, governess, Amahsan and often a young girl or two as well, whom Mama was chaperoning – and simply piles and piles of luggage.
>
> Only if we had to change trains on the way or if we all happened to arrive in good time before we were due to start, would he, usually so calm, get a bit fussed. He wandered restlessly around asking every uniformed man in sight whether this was the right platform? And was the train on time? And, though he knew perfectly well, when was it due to leave? Then he would compare the time of his watch with theirs and wind his up to be sure it was still going. After that, he started to count our mountain of luggage, invariably got mixed up and had to start again.
>
> In a customs shed he was hopeless and could never find the right keys, which annoyed the customs men and made them prone to open everything. Mama teased him when he searched frantically through his innumerable pockets for keys or tickets – 'Look at the efficient man, completely lost without his secretary,' and she would take over, asking him to keep out of the way please, and he would grumble and obediently wander off. Chewing his cigar, he would tramp up and down the platform, stopping for a chat with the peanut vendor and bookstall keeper, interested in the turnover and the intricacies of the trade, and buying masses of newspapers, detective stories and far too many nuts and sweets for us. In the meanwhile, Mama took charge of the luggage, smiled at the customs men and got everything over in no time.
>
> Sometimes Papa fussed us for a change. He had a terrible habit of arriving at the very last minute to catch an important train, or he would come running up the gangway of a steamer just as the last whistle blew. Waving his hat and beaming with pride, he would shout up to us leaning anxiously over the railings – 'Narrow shave that –wasn't it? But I made it!'

On the trip to Shanghai one gentleman joined the company – the 63-year-old Janus F. Oiesen, who was on his way to Peking to assume the position of

Danish envoy to China. Oiesen had been employed by the Chinese Customs Service for 43 years. His thorough knowledge of China and Chinese politicians was one of the reasons that the Danish government asked him to succeed Count Preben Ahlefeldt-Laurvig, now posted to Warsaw.

Figure 84: Whenever the Meyer family set out on a long voyage, it always meant an enormous entourage. Vilhelm was more often than not the only male. On a journey from New York to Shanghai in January 1921 the group were photographed at a train station in Canada. Vilhelm is shown standing next to Kirsten. Gerda Nielsen is behind them, tying a scarf in front of her mouth to protect herself from the cold wintry air. Amahsan is standing with the three eldest girls while Miss Calder, the nanny, is in front holding little 'Baby'.

The journey from New York to Shanghai on the other side of the world was a long one. Fortunately the old British empire had established a connection that was both fast and reliable. In 1889, the Canadian Pacific Railways (C.P.R.) had secured the imperial mail contract from the British government to serve as a link between eastern Canada and Hong Kong. Two years later the C.P.R. had established the Orient Service consisting of a train connection from Montreal to Vancouver followed by a connection by ship from Vancouver to the Far East. Three ships were built for this purpose, the *Empress of India,* the *Empress of Japan* and the *Empress of China.*

Before the War, the C.P.R. started building a new series of Empress liners at the Fairfields Shipyard in Scotland. The first ship, ready in 1913, was named the *Empress of Russia* and was followed by the *Empress of Asia.* They had both gone into war service, and in 1918 the *Empress of Russia* had been used to transport American troops to the war against Germany in Europe. The *Empress of Russia* was now back in service as a passenger and mail ship in the Pacific. It was a magnificent ship with all modern facilities, and the Meyer children looked forward to spending some time on board this ship.

Figure 85: The Meyers crossed the Pacific many times on the Canadian Pacific Railways liners. In 1921 the whole family went from Vancouver to Shanghai on board the *Empress of Russia*, shown here at the entrance to Vancouver.

The group first went by train from New York City to Montreal, where they spent the night at Hotel Windsor. The next day they all got on the train belonging to the Canadian Pacific Railway. In the evening they began their long journey across Canada, which took an entire week. Gerda found it difficult to write letters on the way because of the constant motion of the train. But she found that the scenery – Canada's snow-covered winter landscape – was simply magnificent.

On board the train, Mr and Mrs M. each had their own small compartment, while the four girls and Nanny shared two compartments. Gerda and Josefine shared a berth in a large sleeper compartment with 20 berths, 'men and women together'. The train crossed the beautiful Rocky Mountains and finally reached Vancouver on 12 January, where all the passengers going to the Far East were taken to the Hotel Vancouver. It was nice to get a real bath, wrote Gerda. In the evening Minister Oiesen invited the Meyers and Gerda to join him for dinner at a wonderful restaurant.

The next day the Danish travel group went onboard the *Empress of Russia*. As usual Gerda was a prolific letter writer. One of her letters, written in the writing saloon of the ship, begins in pencil. In the course of the letter she changes to ink with the following remark, which gives us a glimpse of the period: 'There – finally an inkwell free'.

However, it proved a rough voyage. After 12 days of stormy seas, Japan finally loomed on the horizon. The ship docked in Yokohama, Kobe and Nagasaki.

There was time for sightseeing in these ports, and Amahsan, who hadn't been home for several years, was given a month's holiday and took off, 'happy as a child'.

On 31 January 1921, 25 days after the family had left New York, the *Empress of Russia* docked in Shanghai. Gerda Nielsen could see the Danish flag on the top of the Great Northern building. It was flying from the E.A.C. ship *Chile*, too, as well as from one of Great Northern's cable ships lying at anchor in the harbour. Mary MacLeod, the family's faithful friend, was waiting on the wharf and saw to it that they all got home to Avenue Road. More than a year had passed since Kirsten had left Shanghai with her three daughters. She was back now, bringing her fourth daughter, little 'Baby', with her.

'Shanghai, the Liveliest Place on Earth'

Gerda Nielsen quickly grew accustomed to life in Shanghai, which she described regularly in her letters. She was delighted with the house, describing it as 'delightful, chock full of precious Chinese objects, yet tremendously cozy'. Concerning the daily routine on Avenue Road, she wrote that she took breakfast at around 8 am with Mr Meyer, Nanny and the eldest girls. Mrs Meyer always had her own breakfast sent up somewhat later. After a morning walk with her two pupils, Thea and Rose-Marie, Gerda gave them lessons in the library for three hours. Mr Meyer usually came home at 1 p.m. for lunch (always called 'tiffin' in the Far East). The meal consisted of four courses, namely soup, fish, meat and dessert. In the afternoons she once more took the two eldest for a walk to Jessfield Park, or into town. At 5 o'clock tea was served and dinner was at 8.

The girls had a hard time of it, linguistically speaking. The Chinese spoke Shanghainese among themselves and pidgin English with foreigners. The Meyer family spoke English a great deal because Miss Calder, the family's English nanny, didn't understand Danish. It was thus up to Gerda Nielsen to make the Danish lessons something special. In a letter to Gerda Nielsen's mother, dated '9th Mach', Thea, at 10, tried to express herself as well as she could:

> Dear Miss Nielsen's Mother,
>
> I hope you are well, this is in school but we are writing to you instead. We are going to a Fance-dress-party soon and on 11th Mach we are going to another party. Every day we go for a walk in a garden and play football it's great fun. I got 3 dollars and 30 cents for 4 weeks in school, not bad, eh. Miss Nielsen has got so thin that her skuhrt is falling off beecourse she plays footbohl.
>
> Sincerely Yours, Thea

At home, Vilhelm openly discussed business difficulties. There was a general, international economic recession at the time. It had also become clear by then that the Pacific Development Corporation's loan of $5 million to the Chinese government in Peking had been a huge mistake. Gerda Nielsen wrote: 'the Meyers are wonderful, delightful and nice, even though the business is going d— badly, but hopefully things will pick up again. Mr Meyer has such a frightful lot to do, but he never lets it show. He's just as calm as always.'

Figure 86: The house on Avenue Road had a magnificent, large garden, which the four sisters loved. Two Ming statues are shown in the picture taken in the summer of 1921. The statues were brought to Denmark in the late 1930s.

Gerda Nielsen also gave a description of the house:

> The house is not particularly impressive from the outside. Downstairs there's a fairly large hall, full of lovely old bronzes, the library (where we do lessons), with lots of priceless, old Chinese porcelains; a magnificent, folding screen has been placed on either side of the fireplace, painted on ivory inlaid in ebony. Shelves on both walls. A very large parlour with mahogany furniture upholstered in blue brocade, good pictures and ancient Chinese rugs on the walls. A large, comfortable, dining room also done up in dark blue with four lovely old temple bronze lanterns hanging from the ceiling. In addition we always have candles on the table at dinner. Outside the dining room and living room, a large veranda. Upstairs: three bathrooms, Mr and Mrs M.'s bedroom, Mrs M.'s enchanting dressing room, Thea's little bedroom, a very large night nursery for Nanny and the three little ones, a fine, large room for the day nursery, and the governess's room.

Whenever the Meyer daughters came to describe their childhood home in later life, their mother's dressing room always held a special place in their affections. It was a beautiful, large room, which was really more of a private sitting room for Kirsten than a dressing room. Yellow silk drapes hung at the French windows opening on the veranda, and there were beautiful, old yellow and blue Chinese rugs on the floors. Kirsten had a desk there so she could read or write to family and friends in Denmark, in peace and quiet. There were closets in the room, too, a few armchairs by the fire, a chaise longue where Kirsten would rest or read stories to the girls, and a small sofa where Vilhelm always used to have a drink and read the afternoon papers when he came home from the office. The colour scheme in Kirsten's room was bright while the furniture in their shared bedroom tended towards dark mahogany with full-length, wine-red curtains.

Figure 87: Thea was always the responsible big sister, here with Marie-Louise in 1921.

While Mr Oiesen was in Shanghai, the Danish community gave a big party in his honour. It was held at the French club, Cercle Sportif Français. A total of 110 Danes signed up for the banquet at which speeches were given and toasts proposed for Denmark's new man in Peking. Everyone danced until the wee hours. 'Oiesen was delighted and nice as ever, talked to all of us and actually danced!' wrote Gerda Nielsen.

Kirsten and Vilhelm gave two dinner parties for the new minister. Several of the Meyer's Chinese friends were invited to the second dinner, which took place on Oiesen's last day in Shanghai. Gerda Nielsen wrote the following about this event:

> Since the Chinese don't like to see ladies in décolleté we couldn't wear evening dresses. Meyer's right-hand man, the American Mr Rice and his wife, Mr Branston and Lilinau were here, in addition to the Chinese Mr Sy (eight years at Oxford, still dresses Chinese) and his wife, a lovely little thing in her late twenties. Then there was a young Chinese engineer in M.'s business, also Oxford educated, and an elderly Mr Fu and his fat wife, who didn't understand a word of English and occasionally had quiet laughing fits at the rest of us. The two married couples have the rank of mandarin and are very posh. Cook had been told Chinese would be present, so the dinner was a bit different than usual.

Gerda Nielsen also enjoyed the numerous musical events in Shanghai, both the private evenings of singing and the concerts in town. One day she witnessed Vilhelm Meyer perform at an afternoon concert at the town hall: 'It went

Figure 88: Janus Oiesen (1857–1928) was born on the island of Bornholm in Denmark. When he was 13 his family emigrated to the United States. As a 20-year-old Oiesen travelled to China where he was employed by the Chinese Maritime Customs Service. He worked in a number of ports in China and Korea. He was later appointed secretary general of the Chinese Customs Inspectorate in Peking and was granted the rank of mandarin in 1904. In 1921–23 he was the Danish minister to Peking. During his years as Danish diplomat, the Meyer Manchu palace functioned as the Danish Legation in Peking.

very well. Exclusively Wagner programme. He sang Wolfram's "Song to the Evening Star" from *Tannhäuser.* He was applauded enthusiastically. He has a really lovely voice, powerful and resounding.' There was no lack of diversions – masquerades, balls, concerts and banquets. Gerda Nielsen was invited out, too, and several evenings a week the Meyer family had dinner guests at home. Gerda described a dinner on Avenue Road in a letter:

> The table looked so lovely – a round table, large embroidered lace tablecloth in the middle, – a large, silver bowl centrepiece, containing nine dozen different coloured tulips – six two-armed silver candlesticks ablaze with candles – no other lighting in the room. The seagull-patterned dinner set, completely simple, fat-bellied wineglasses with just a narrow gold border on top. The walls and curtains dark blue. The boys in dark blue silk capes. A small fire in the fireplace. Eating in such surroundings is a pure, aesthetic delight. Well, the food was excellent, too, 5 courses and dessert.

Gerda was enthusiastic, but also conscious of the necessity of being on guard:

> I think Shanghai must be the liveliest place on earth, or else people here are just more restless than elsewhere, because they are always looking for something new going on. I am sometimes a bit afraid of being swallowed up in all the amusements, but as long as I am aware of the danger myself, I guess I'll be alright.

Figure 89: The sitting room in the house on Avenue Road was spacious. On the right is a portrait of Vilhelm's first comprador and his daughter. The home was renowned for its Chinese antiques, ranging from large bronze vessels to porcelain figurines and brocades.

The Danish Community

There were a good many Danes in China in the early 1920s – entrepreneurs, engineers, missionaries and employees of the Chinese service – 800 in all. The Shanghai Danish population was 400, ranking it fifth among the Western nations after England, Germany, the United States and France. The largest Danish firms in town were Great Northern and E.A.C. However, although Andersen, Meyer & Co. was no longer a Danish company, it employed a large number of Danes, including K.V. Aagesen, C.V. Jensen, U. Ulf-Hansen, Elias Gutter, V. Harth Olsen and Einar Park. Another Dane, Aage Corrit, started out at A. M. & Co. in 1918 and after opening his own engineering business built bridges spanning many of the largest rivers in China. The Danish engineer, Helge Fugl-Meyer, started out with Vilhelm Meyer in 1919. Later he became the head of the Whangpoo Conservative Board, finishing his career in Denmark as director of the Copenhagen Free Port, Ltd Edvard Trock, the electrical engineer, also began with A. M. & Co., working there until 1922 when he and his colleague, L. Larsen, established the Danish engineering and import firm of Larsen & Trock in Shanghai.

Shanghai had developed into a highly cosmopolitan city. However, the individual nationalities kept to themselves when it came to national clubs and as-

Figure 90: At the centre of the picture is a landscape painting of Lejre, Denmark, painted by Vilhelm Hammershøi, the Golden Age Danish painter. Kirsten's uncle, the dentist Dr Alfred Bramsen, supported the young Danish painter as early as the 1880s by buying a large number of his paintings.

sociations. Apart from the Danish Reading Society, which had been founded as a lending library as far back as 1885 by families associated with Great Northern, no other actual Danish societies had as yet been established. This would occur later. The Danish Tennis Club, however, served as a fixed meeting place for Danes. K.V. Aagesen from A. M. & Co. was for many years the chairman of the club. The members of the club congregated at the Shanghai Race Course, where the Danish club had its own tennis courts. The annual tournaments and distribution of prizes always attracted a great deal of interest.

There were many excellent opportunities for taking part in sporting or other outdoor events. Riding, sailing, hunting and houseboat excursions along the many beautiful canals and lakes were among the Shanghailanders' most popular leisure activities. The Paper Hunt was a particular form of horseriding, in which a few riders rode on ahead as the 'fox', leaving a trail of small pieces of paper behind. All the other riders followed, forcing their way across a terrain riddled with streams and waterways. The horses were small, fast, fiery ponies from Mongolia. A large crowd always gathered at the finish, including many local Chinese, who would wonderingly watch the foreigners in their white pants and red jackets come charging through the mud and dirt in an effort to be the first to get in.

Figure 91: The Shanghai Race Course was popular with the inhabitants of Shanghai, foreigners as well as Chinese. In this picture taken in 1920 Captain Bahnson, the Shanghai director of Great Northern, is shown leading his horse Guldborg to a race. Eleven-year-old Christian Islef, the son of Great Northern's bookkeeper, J.P. Islef, is shown in front of Bahnson.

Another widespread form of weekend entertainment was going to the races at the Shanghai Race Course. Vilhelm owned a pony, which ran in many races, and which, when it occasionally won, yielded its owner a nice return.

If one took the train to Henli on the way to Suzhou, an area of lakes and canals, there were various water sports to join in or just watch. These included boat races, for which Great Northern could muster a strong Danish team. Sailing dinghy competitions were another popular activity at Henli. Vilhelm and Kirsten were not particularly interested in sports, although Vilhelm did enjoy taking part in the sailing dinghy competitions. However, due to his size he was rarely among the winners and once he even succeeded in capsizing, much to everyone's delight. He preferred hunting parties and from time to time took a few days off to go hunting inland with friends.

Wei-Hai-Wei

The summer months in Shanghai were unbearably hot and humid and most of the city's foreign population tried to go north for the duration. Wei-Hai-Wei, a small coastal town in Shandong province, was one of the Shanghailanders' most popular resorts, particularly with the British. This was not only due to the pleasant summer climate, but also because it was under British sovereignty.

Figure 92: On the beach at Narcissus Bay at Wei-Hai-Wei stood five summerhouses. The last one, Cottage no. 5, belonged to the Meyer family. It was the only house with a red roof and was therefore generally referred to as 'Red Roof'.

Due to its excellent location, Wei-Hai-Wei had been in use as a naval base as early as the fourteenth century as a defence against pirates and attacks from Japan. When the British took over in 1898 the warship *H.M.S. Narcissus,* which was present on the occasion, gave a royal salute. In the bay, later called Narcissus Bay by the British, large Liugong Island provided excellent protection for ships anchoring there. The small, Chinese port of Ma-to on the coast, called Port Edward by the British, was used as an administrative centre. It had a government house, a church, etc. One mile away lay the Chinese village of Wei-Hai-Wei, surrounded by a city wall in the traditional style. This city of 4,000 constituted a small Chinese enclave in the British area, which was 190 square miles all in all, with a Chinese population of roughly 126,000.

In 1913 Vilhelm and Kirsten rented a house at Wei-Hai-Wei. They were given a long lease and the family spent all their summer holidays there until 1935. The house was generally the children's summer base from the end of June to the end of September. Vilhelm would normally spend a few weeks with the family in July.

As the house was the only one with a red roof, it was always referred to as Red Roof. Located directly on the beach along with four similar houses, its more official name was Bungalow no. 5. It consisted of seven rooms, four bathrooms and a separate building for the servants. Not very far from the house was a good well. There were no telephones, cars or motorboats yet – just lovely weather and beautiful beaches.

In 1921 the Meyer family spent the summer in Wei-Hai-Wei. Chow, two cooks and a coolie went on ahead to get the house ready in mid-June. Before being allowed to leave Shanghai for their holiday, however, Thea and Rose-Marie had to have their private examination in Danish and Geography. Vilhelm

Figure 93: Gerda Nielsen (1896–1980) was employed by the Meyer family as governess from 1920 to 1923. Her numerous letters to her mother in Denmark give a lively picture of daily life in the house on Avenue Road and of the Danish community in Shanghai.

and Kirsten were present on the occasion and Mrs Timm, whose husband was an employee of Great Northern, was the external examiner. It went well and Gerda Nielsen was glad that the girls as well as herself were praised. A few days later came the Natural History and History test:

> Rose-Marie spoke very well. Thea got a bit confused and ended up bursting into tears when I said I'd never seen a striped lion. Well, she is quite nervous, poor thing, while Rose-Marie just loves it and is almost cross when stopped.

The last test was Arithmetic, Religion and Singing:

> Thea unlucky in arithmetic again, did get a B though, whereas in all her other subjects she didn't get below an A. Mr M. and Mrs Timm did the marking, I had nothing to do with it, was thanked by the Meyers and was, of course, in seventh heaven.

The next group, consisting of Gerda, Nanny, and the four girls, could now leave for Wei-Hai-Wei on board the *Fengtien*. The voyage took two days. At the bay at Wei-Hai-Wei they were picked up by Chow in the family sampan, the Danish flag fluttering at the stern. The family's two local sampan men wore natty white hats, bound with red ribbons.

On a similar voyage to Wei-Hai-Wei a few years before, Chow, Amahsan, Rose-Marie and Anette had gone by ship from Shanghai. In the peaceful moonlit night the ship ran aground on a rock and began to sink. The situation rapidly grew chaotic as the Chinese deck passengers didn't want to leave their packages and possessions behind on the ship. Many jumped into the water and drowned. Chow went calmly below to Amahsan and the two little girls. He told Amahsan

Figure 94: Lyrical picture of the beach at Wei-Hai-Wei. The characteristic silhouette of Liugong Island is visible further out in the bay.

to dress the girls warmly. He himself heated some milk in a bottle for Anette. He then ushered the girls and Amahsan onto the deck and into a lifeboat. A Japanese freighter picked up all survivors, bringing them safely to Shanghai.

Gerda Nielsen quickly realized that Wei-Hai-Wei was a British naval base. Eight warships were anchored in the bay and during the course of the summer

Figure 95: Chow started out as a young servant in the Meyer family, and in time became Number One Boy, i.e. the person in charge of the entire staff. He was intelligent and helpful to everyone in the family. In this picture, taken by Gerda Nielsen, Chow is on the beach at Wei-Hai-Wei in front of the family's summerhouse. He later left China and became a businessman in California.

Figure 96: Gerda Nielsen loved experiencing the local street life of Wei-Hai-Wei. Here is a picture she took of an itinerant theatre group. Although the traditional Chinese pigtail was forbidden by the new republic of 1912, nevertheless it was still common 10 years after the abolition of the Chinese empire, as shown here.

she was invited to balls with the ships' officers either on Liugong Island or on board one of the ships. It was a real summer holiday – with swimming, and rowing in the sampan, or excursions inland in the donkey cart to see the temples, and hikes in the mountainous countryside. The children often spent time with other vacationing Shanghailander children. There were delightful picnics to the surrounding beaches, such as Dog's Nose Bay, Half Moon Bay, or Cats' Eyes Bay.

Gerda observed the daily life of Wei-Hai-Wei with interest:

This is much more the real China than Shanghai, little kids running around stark naked, almost all the men have pigtails, the land is divided into terribly small lots and cultivated in an incredibly primitive fashion, just like the sixteenth century at home. All the Chinese smile at you in a friendly way, a bit shyly. The women's feet are all frightfully bound up, literally smaller than my fist. However, you do see little girls under the age of 6 with natural feet, so hopefully that's over now.

The Chinese town is surrounded by a delightful old wall but inside it's so filthy and stinks so much that I got out again as fast as possible. The Chinese almost always dress the same, in dark, blue coolie cloth, when they have anything on at all. The women often wear red pants and blue jackets. You see the funniest vehicles and palanquins and carriages drawn by hinnies, frightfully stubborn beasts.

Figure 97: A day at the beach at Wei-Hai-Wei. Thea, Anette and Rose-Marie accompanied by Mrs Fox and Kirsten.

In mid-July Kirsten Meyer arrived with Mrs Fox, an English friend. Gerda Nielsen wrote that Mrs M. was as kind as ever and it was nice that she had come.

In August Vilhelm arrived. He was on his way to Peking on a business trip, but wanted to surprise the family by looking in on them at Wei-Hai-Wei. 'The children were of course beside themselves', wrote Gerda. In the evening Gerda dined with the Meyers and Mrs Fox. 'We had an awful lot of fun and both Mr and Mrs Meyer were in great spirits; they're so nice, and absolutely crazy about each other.'

In a private letter to her mother, Gerda brought up the subject of Vilhelm Meyer's celebrated reputation of being something of a ladies' man, which was occasionally the cause of gossip in the Danish community.

> The house is even livelier since Meyer has come for a short visit. He teases all of us and is terribly funny. Mrs M. is of course delighted. How she loves that man! Sometimes I'm afraid he's not worth it! He's a real charmer, but in my opinion he ought to be satisfied with his enchanting wife! He's often the subject of gossip – mixed with envy if you ask me!

The summer took its course. The big girls were again given lessons in the morning. Early in September Kirsten went to Peking to meet Vilhelm, accompanying him back to Shanghai.

Gerda Nielsen and the children returned in early October after a stay of more than three months at Wei-Hai-Wei. Vilhelm and Kirsten were on the wharf in Shanghai to greet them. Kirsten was wearing a mourning band since her father, Aage Bramsen, had died in Denmark. She was sorry she hadn't been able to attend his funeral, but waited a few days before telling the children the sad news. There was no reason to spoil their joy at seeing their home on Avenue Road again.

TWELVE

Years of Crisis, 1921–1923

The Chinese Communist Party

The International Settlement area of Shanghai was – and remained – a free city within the vast Chinese realm. If managed well, foreign firms could do very well for themselves. Others went bankrupt. The Shanghailanders, many of whom had lived there for two or three generations, took it for granted that their free city constituted their own little territory. Nevertheless, it was precisely the city's special status that involved it in the political showdown that was to characterize the China of the 1920s. Foreign residents were not the only ones to profit from the treaty rights in relation to the Chinese authorities. Chinese, too, who for political, economic or other reasons wished to 'leave' China, could find a place in Shanghai's International Settlement area.

It was the policy of the Soviet Union that the doctrine of Marxism should be spread to all countries. China with its masses was an excellent target for the Bolsheviks' new Communist ideology and the free city of Shanghai was well suited as a base for its dissemination to China. In April 1920 three Soviet agents arrived in Shanghai where they met with Sun Yat-sen and Chen Duxiu. In May Chen established a Communist cell in Shanghai. Shortly afterwards similar cells were set up in Peking by Li Dazhao, a librarian at Peking University, and in Changsha in Hunan province by Mao Zedong, Li's assistant at the library. A number of other cities followed suit. In the autumn of 1920 Communist activities in Shanghai intensified with the publication of the leaflet The Communist. Youthful supporters of the new movement, including 23-year-old Zhou Enlai and 15-year-old Deng Xiaoping, were sent to Paris to be schooled in Marxism.

In June 1920 the Dutchman Hendricus Sneevliet arrived in Peking. He had been sent by the Komintern in Moscow and used the cover name of G. Maring. He and Li Dazhao arranged that Maring would continue on to Shanghai for a secret meeting with the purpose of founding a Chinese Communist Party. In Shanghai he met with a Soviet agent and 13 Chinese representing around 50 Communists from the entire country. Ever since the protests in Peking the two-year-old Fourth of May Movement had appealed to many young Chinese wishing to fight both foreign imperialism and domestic feudalism. There was fertile soil for a Chinese Communist Party.

The secret meeting began on 1 July 1921 in Shanghai's French Concession, in a house in Rue Wantz. The participants were staying nearby at a girls' school, which was empty during the summer months. By holding the meeting in Shanghai, the group was protected against interference from the militias of warring Chinese provincial warlords and police units.

Figure 98: In his younger years Mao Zedong (1893–1976) benefited from Shanghai's international status. At a secret meeting in Shanghai in the summer of 1921 he was one of the founders of the Communist Party of China, which 28 years later would gain power over the whole of China.

Among those present was Mao Zedong, the 28-year-old school teacher from Changsha, who was particularly active in drafting the programme of the new party. On the fourth day a man came to the meeting place, making enquiries about an address. The participants were afraid they were under surveillance by both the French police and the triad leader, Du Yuesheng, whose headquarters was nearby. They therefore decided to move the meeting elsewhere, travelling by train to a town 60 miles south of Shanghai. Here they rented a boat and sailed out on to the lake where they proceeded to draw up the new party programme. The main points were: (a) the establishment of a free and sovereign China, which meant that the Soviet Union would have to give up Manchuria; (b) the cessation of all foreign exterritorial rights in China and (c) an end to China's repayment of the remainder of the compensation sum incurred in connection with the Boxer Rebellion. Chen Duxiu, in Canton at the time, was elected first secretary general of the party. At the annual meeting in Shanghai the following year party membership had risen to 123 and in 1923 membership had further increased to 432.

In this period were sown the seeds of the Chinese Communist Party, which during the course of the following decades was to constitute a greater and greater challenge to Sun Yat-sen's Nationalist Party and which after many years of fierce fighting would finally seize power over all of China, nationalizing all foreign businesses in China as well as a number of Chinese-owned firms.

Daily Life on Avenue Road

In Shanghai people were still unaware of the new political currents and life took its usual course. Although there was famine in Northern China and civil war in many of the provinces, the atmosphere was not bleak. In a letter to her mother, Gerda Nielsen captures the tone of their carefree existence: 'Don't be anxious if you hear of disturbances in China because there's terrible fighting just up the river and they mistreat each other dreadfully. But it has nothing to do with us.' The last sentence, 'it has nothing to do with us', was typical of many Shang-hailanders' attitude to political events in China. Many people felt that Shanghai's special status, as well as the presence of military units and warships from a number of Western countries, constituted a sufficient guarantee of retaining the city's status as a 'free city' outside Chinese jurisdiction. This assumption was to prove incorrect in the long run.

Figure 99: Nanking Road was one of the main thoroughfares of Shanghai with space for cars, trams, rickshaws and bicycles. This picture was taken in 1923.

The Meyer family celebrated Christmas Eve in Shanghai in the typical Danish fashion, with a Christmas tree with all the trimmings and presents. Kirsten was an expert decorator and the Christmas tree was trimmed in the Danish manner, although a few American decorations from New York were added, as well as small Chinese paper flowers from Peking. In the evening there was a dinner for Danish guests. The next day there was a large Christmas tiffin with the family's American friends, followed by Christmas dinner for their English circle.

There was a New Year's celebration, too, as well as a celebration at the Chinese New Year, which was not until February. Gerda Nielsen and some friends went to see the New Years' festivities in the Chinese section:

There was a huge crowd, pushing and shoving, only Chinese. We were the only foreigners. Lundquist speaks fluent Chinese and translated for us what people said. It wasn't very flattering: 'foreign devils', and a few Chinese girls said they couldn't understand that a 'foreign lady' (me!!) dared to go in there on such an evening. It looked lovely in there. The small streets with the open shops in all kinds of bright colours, lit by large, round lanterns with red Chinese characters. This covered up the dirt a little, which otherwise simply grins up at you in there, but there was a continual stream of the most dreadful beggars, both men and women, all the way into the middle of town, where the temple is. A Chinese cannot or dare not refuse a beggar then, or the evil spirits will get him! Dreadful women with dead or dying children in their arms, showing the most disgusting, running sores, etc. We forced our way to the temple and then went inside where it was swarming with Chinese burning joss-sticks and paper money for themselves and their dead. It looked enchanting with all the bright red candles and joss-sticks burning, the air grey with smoke and pictures of the different gods in deep shadow. In the large, main temple the effect is spoiled by an extremely sharp electric light in the middle of everything. On the way home we went through Foochow Road where all the teahouses are. Everywhere there were crowds of Chinese in their Sunday best, carrying neat little red packages and, just like children, having the time of their lives setting off fireworks. Everywhere there was a great bustle and a terrible racket!

The servants are completely mad these days. They stay up most of the night, eating and drinking so one tries to bother them as little as possible. It is the only time of the year that they really have any fun.

As mentioned above, music was an important element in the social life of the winter season. In the Monday Club the members took turns every Monday arranging musical evenings at which the performers would either sing or play a musical instrument. Both Vilhelm and Gerda Nielsen were performing members. Although Kirsten had grown up in a musical family, many of whom played a musical instrument, she herself had never seriously taken up singing or playing an instrument. But she was fond of music and delighted to be the hos-tess at musical evenings at home on Avenue Road. These evenings would some-times develop into veritable concerts, as was the case on 20 January 1922. Gerda Nielsen wrote:

We spent the whole day pottering about, getting things ready in the sitting rooms. The table, the sideboards, etc. were moved out of the dining room. Instead there were four large sofas and a lot of small armchairs and small chairs. Mrs M. thought rows and rows of chairs were so boring so instead we set up sitting rooms all over. We had around 100 seats that way. We dressed in our best and at 9.30 p.m. people began to arrive. A great many had arrived by 10 p.m. and then the concert began. It went absolutely beautifully. There were around 130 people, a number of the gentleman remained standing most of the time, or sat in the library, drinking and smoking.

Vilhelm opened the concert with an aria from 'Benvenuto Cellini'. Then a number of guests played or sang various pieces including Schubert and Debussy. A string quartet played a piece by Grieg and the Italian Maestro Mario Paci, Shanghai's most famous conductor and pianist, who had accompanied the evening's vocal soloists, concluded the concert with some piano pieces by Chopin. After the concert there was supper. Gerda had spent a most enjoyable evening:

It's hopeless trying to make a list of who was there for there were Danes, Swedes, Norwegians, English, Americans, Dutch, Italians and Frenchmen. I had a wonderful time circulating and talking to everybody. It was 1.30 in the morning when Mrs Meyer and I went upstairs and there were still a few gentlemen left.

The success was repeated a week later with a new programme and a new guest list. This time there were 160 guests!

Figure 100: The Manchu palace in Peking was an excellent spot for Vilhelm to negotiate with his American business associates. In September 1921 the future of Pacific Development Corporation was discussed. Vilhelm is shown here standing in the centre, Kirsten seated on the left with their American guests. At right are Sophus and Minna Black, who lived in one of the Manchu houses.

In February 1922 Prince Axel of Denmark visited Shanghai. He arrived on the E.A.C. ship, the *Asia,* to visit the city which Prince Valdemar, his father, had visited on board the *Valkyrien* in 1900. Since 33-year-old Prince Axel was attached to E.A.C., Vilhelm's and Kirsten's neighbour, Carl Johan Knipschildt of the E.A.C. Shanghai office, was his host during the visit. The Meyers, too, gave a big dinner party at home for Prince Axel on 5 February, little Marie-Louise's second birthday. A jazz band provided dance music after dinner. According to Gerda Nielsen's accounts, the evening was a huge success. Her frank impression of the guest of honour was the following: 'Prince Axel is extremely tall and thin with an ugly face and a typical Copenhagen accent – but he's terribly nice and very pleasant.'

Corporate Reconstruction

Vilhelm had gone to Peking several times in the autumn of 1921 for meetings with his American business partners. In 1919 he had been awarded a Danish order and in 1921 he and his American friends had received the highest Chinese order available to foreigners. This was the Chia Ho order, second class with sash. It was called the Order of the Golden Harvest, not without a certain irony inasmuch as Pacific Development Corporation's large loan of US$ 5 million, as mentioned above, had collateral in duties accruing from the annual tobacco and wine harvest. It was now clear, however, that this was a case of non-payment as neither interest nor repayment was forthcoming from the Chinese government. The crucial question was therefore what could be done to avoid a total disaster for the holding company.

Figure 101: In 1917, a branch of the General Electric Company, the China General Edison Co., Inc. established a small factory in Shanghai, which produced the first incandescent lamps in China. Here is a picture showing the glass-blowing department after the factory had moved to Robinson Road, Shanghai, several years later.

In February 1922 Vilhelm went again to Peking to discuss the situation with his partners, especially Edward Bruce, the president of P.D.C. Together they negotiated with representatives of the Chinese government. In view of P.D.C.'s precarious situation, the visiting Americans and Vilhelm decided that certain corporate reconstructions would have to take place in New York. The two A. M. & Co. companies, in Manila and Shanghai/New York respectively, would have to be merged so as to form a single stock company registered in Manila and additionally registered in New York.

The lawyer Lionel F. Schaub and 10 other New York businessmen, including Bruce, were on the board of the New York company. Schaub represented P.D.C., the sole shareholder. The board decided at a meeting in March to recommend the liquidation of the company. An extraordinary board meeting was held on 14 March at the P.D.C. headquarters on Wall Street, at which the liquidation of the seven-year-old corporation was officially resolved.

A few days later the company Andersen, Meyer & Co., Ltd, founded in Manila in 1918, was additionally registered in New York at the address 80 Wall Street. The board of the company was influenced greatly by Edward Bruce, who was its chariman, and by his former affiliation with P.D.C. Vilhelm was given a seat on the board.

Vilhelm did not take part in the New York meetings. His position as the firm's general manager remained unchallenged despite the new corporate structure. However, the structure had become more complex than when he was his own master in Shanghai. He was now employed as the general manager in Shanghai of a Philippine corporation, Andersen, Meyer & Co. Ltd, also registered in New York, whose share capital was owned by the American holding company Pacific Development Corporation. The corporation risked bankruptcy if the Chinese government in Peking did not start repaying the large loan of US$ 5 million.

Vilhelm wondered how long P.D.C. could survive without receiving repayment on the loan. For the time being, however, he had no option other than to continue his work in China, so he kept on building factories, railways and bridges and importing machinery and motors.

Holiday

Even though the situation was critical, Vilhelm and Kirsten also found time for a brief holiday.

At Easter 1922 they invited some friends on a houseboat tour, beginning and ending in the picturesque city of Suzhou, not very far from Shanghai.

In addition to Vilhelm, Kirsten, Thea and Rose-Marie, and of course Gerda Nielsen, there were 12 Danish and English friends along on the tour. They took the train from Shanghai to Suzhou where they boarded three houseboats and a motorboat. Vilhelm and Kirsten had their own houseboat, the *Tom*, and had borrowed the other boats for the excursion. The boats were punted through Suzhou's old canals which were overhung with characteristic arched stone bridges. The tour continued to the city of Mutu. Occasionally the houseboats, none of which had a motor, were drawn by the motorboat. Gerda wrote with great enthusiasm about the whole tour. Here is a brief glimpse of Mutu:

> It was the most picturesque sight, sailing through the narrow canals, often so narrow that getting through seemed absolutely impossible. Houses on both sides, we looked directly into the poor rooms only illuminated by an oil lamp or a miserable kerosene lamp, packed with Chinese, crowding round the windows and doors to look at us.

The next day they continued on to large Lake Tahu, where they went for long hikes in the mountains, admired the sunset on the lake and took pleasure in

Figure 102: When one wanted to get away from the hustle and bustle of the Shanghai business world, nothing could beat a houseboat voyage up-country by way of the numerous canals and lakes. The Meyer family's houseboat *Tom* was also popular when there was a regatta on the river, as shown in the picture.

the lovely, sunny Easter weather. Every evening they all met for dinner on the Meyer's houseboat, enjoying the lush scenery, so different from flat, everyday Shanghai. As Gerda wrote in her letters to Denmark: 'It was really lovely to get away from Shanghai for a bit and hike until I drop instead of always dancing until I drop.'

In June the school year was drawing to a close. Once again there were exams for Miss Nielsen's two pupils, who did very well. They concluded with the Danish national anthem and everyone was deeply moved. It was 14 June, Vilhelm's 44th birthday, and there was a big dinner party at home. After dinner there were songs and music as usual. Later that evening the guests threw themselves into the more entertaining part of the singers' repertoire. Arias from *Faust* and *Carmen* were sung, the British Captain Campbell taking the part of Carmen with a red rose in his hair and a fan. Vilhelm did the toreador, wrapped in a tablecloth.

A few days later Gerda and the girls went up to Wei-Hai-Wei. There were quiet days on the beach, excursions into the surrounding area and dinner-dances on board the British men-of-war. Kirsten and Mrs Fox followed a few weeks later.

Vilhelm also managed to spend a few weeks at Wei-Hai-Wei, arriving by ship from Shanghai with four English friends, who like him had all come to spend their holiday with their families on the coast. Vilhelm had bought a motorboat, a complete novelty in China. He had brought it with him on the ship from Shanghai. Imagine everyone's surprise when the five paterfamilias roared up the coast in the motorboat! The MacLeod family, too, was on holiday on Narcissus Bay. Everyone was in good spirits, revelling in the lovely weather. Gerda Nielsen described Vilhelm Meyer as 'a schoolboy who has finally got his longed-for holiday'.

Vilhelm had to go up to Peking. However, due to internal strife between the provincial warlords, it was no longer possible to cross Shandong province by train. Instead Vilhelm had to take a ship to Tianjin and then go by train to Peking, where P.D.C.'s precarious situation was still the central point of the negotiations.

Vilhelm was to return to Shanghai directly, but had arranged for Kirsten, Gerda Nielsen, Thea and Rose-Marie to join him in Peking in order to visit the numerous points of interest in the Chinese capital. Arriving at Tianjin by ship, the female party stayed with Sophus and Minna Black, who had moved there. The next day they took the train to Peking where they stayed at the Manchu house.

The ladies had a lovely time in Peking, visiting temples, the Forbidden City, the Summer Palace, the Great Wall and the Ming tombs. On 26 September, King Christian X's birthday, Vilhelm, Kirsten and Gerda Nielsen attended a Danish dinner at the Hôtel de Pékin followed by a large evening party at the Danish Legation given by their old friend, Oiesen, the minister.

The Crisis Worsens

The Meyer family was back in Shanghai in October. P.D.C.'s crisis now made itself felt in Shanghai and Vilhelm had to cut back on the A. M. & Co. staff.

Vilhelm and Kirsten went to Manila to meet with Bruce and discuss the bleak prospects for the future. Discussions in Manila made it clear that P.D.C. would probably have to declare bankruptcy and that the future of A. M. & Co. hung by a single thread. Vilhelm had to accept the fact that his shares in P.D.C. were worth nothing. It was clear to him that he and his partners in New York were in very deep water and that he would have to go to New York himself if the subsidiary A. M. & Co. were to have any chance of survival.

On the way back from Manila, Vilhelm and Kirsten visited A. M. & Co.'s branch in Hong Kong, in existence for five years, and the branch in Canton, in existence for two years. The two branches were growing nicely, supplying Canton and important Guangdong province primarily with large power plants and locomotives. The Hong Kong office was located on impressive Des Voeux Road.

In Canton A. M. & Co.'s offices were on Shamian Island in a building that the firm had bought a few years before. The island, linked to Canton by a small bridge, had replaced the foreign 'factories' formerly located near Shamian. Fascinated, Vilhelm and Kirsten strolled around the island, admiring the way the European and American commercial firms had set themselves up in magnificent, large buildings. It was strange to think that over a hundred years ago this very city of Canton had been the destination of Peder Lassen, Kirsten's great-great-grandfather, on his long voyages to the Orient for the Danish Asiatic

Company. In the Pearl River the large Chinamen had lain at anchor near Whampoa and Danes Islands, ready to return to Europe laden with silks and porcelain.

Returning to Shanghai, Vilhelm made preparations for a long absence. He went by ship to Vancouver in November, reaching New York in early December 1922. P.D.C.'s bankruptcy was now a fact and Vilhelm's task was to transfer back to Andersen, Meyer & Co. his former agency contracts with a number of American firms.

Over the next three months Vilhelm worked at high pressure to achieve his goal. His primary contacts were his old partners, International General Electric, Saco-Lowell Shops and Baldwin Locomotive Works. As a rule an agent like Vilhelm was faced with the paradox that if things went well the suppliers would take over the business themselves, dispensing with the go-between, who merely increased costs, and contracting directly with the buyers. This had not occurred in Vilhelm's case, however. His thorough understanding of Chinese conditions made him a clever businessman and a good financier. It was said in Shanghai that only the president of A. M. & Co. and the president of Hong Kong and Shanghai Banking Corporation truly understood the complexities of currency and exchange conditions. All his business associates had complete confidence in Vilhelm personally, and his former business connections in the United States had no qualms in backing him now. They all agreed to support the continuation of Andersen, Meyer & Co. in Shanghai.

Vilhelm Meyer Weathers the Storm

Vilhelm was thus successful in re-establishing a number of agency contracts. However, it was also clear to the American suppliers that the board of directors would have to consist of new people and that they themselves would have to play a more active role. Edward Bruce left the board of directors of A. M. & Co. and General Electric acquired a greater influence on the affairs of the re-established A. M. & Co. G.E. had made some important changes in the top management six months earlier. In June 1922 Gerard Swope, the president of International General Electric, succeeded Edwin W. Rice Jr as president of General Electric, a position he held for the next 18 years. Anson Burchard, Vilhelm's close friend in G.E., succeeded Swope as president of I.G.E. and chairman of its board.

In early 1923 Burchard became the new chairman of the board of Andersen, Meyer & Co. The other major suppliers had their own board members. While Galen Stone continued on the board of A. M. & Co., Edward Bruce had had enough of the harsh realities of business life. With the collapse of the Pacific Development Corporation, his Pacific dreams were over. He chose instead to become a painter and in the following years lived in different places, including France and Italy.

Vilhelm left New York on 8 March 1923. Just as in 1915 he was highly pleased with the outcome of his trip. In the eight intervening years he had built up a large business. Grandiose schemes, in particular Bruce's concept of Pacific Development, as well as the general economic crisis following the World

Figure 103: It was always a festive occasion for the girls when their father came to Wei-Hai-Wei. There were Danish flags on the family's boat and the sampan man wore a large V.M. on his straw hat, as shown in the picture. Anette is in the centre together with a friend and little Marie-Louise.

War had almost put an end to everything he had built up in Shanghai since 1906. But he had managed to weather the storm by re-establishing and strengthening his business connections in the United States. Although the parent company Pacific Development Corporation had ceased to exist, Vilhelm was deeply relieved that he had pulled through the crisis and would be able to ensure the survival of his old firm.

At home on Avenue Road life had followed its usual course, but without the head of the family even Christmas had been dull. It cheered everyone up a great deal when a telegram arrived in late January stating briefly, 'All plans successful'. Gerda Nielsen wrote home: 'So everything has apparently turned out well. Indeed, he has worked awfully hard.' Vilhelm was on his way home. After crossing Canada by train he sailed to Japan where Kirsten had gone to welcome her enterprising husband. On board ship they made plans for the years to come. Gerda Nielsen had to return to Denmark, but they agreed that their prime concern was to consolidate A. M. & Co. and continue to keep the whole family together in Shanghai.

Vilhelm and Kirsten docked in Shanghai on 24 March 1923, and were welcomed by four happy daughters – their father had been gone for over four

Figure 104: All her life Kirsten and her four daughters stood in a row whenever they were to be photographed. Here are all the female members of the family at Wei-Hai-Wei in 1922.

months. His luggage was full of clothes and presents for everyone. Kirsten was given some lovely dresses. 'He has excellent taste, you have to grant him that', wrote Gerda.

Gerda Nielsen went back to Denmark in May. She had been with the Meyer family for more than two and a half years and had become part of the family. She had been a good teacher to the two eldest girls and also a great help to Kirsten in daily life. Her beautiful singing voice, excellent piano playing and lovely smile made her highly popular among the Shanghailanders, old and young alike. A number of farewell dinners were given in her honour with songs and speeches. Saying goodbye to Mrs Meyer was particularly difficult for Gerda, for 'when all is said and done, she is the one I like best of all of them'. Nevertheless Miss Nielsen returned to Denmark where she later married.

The Meyer daughters again spent the summer holiday in Wei-Hai-Wei, where Kirsten and Vilhelm also spent some time, then a few weeks in Peking, and then it was time for Thea and Rose-Marie, now 13 and 10, to return to Shanghai to attend the English School. In their letters to Miss Nielsen in Denmark they tell about their new school, as shown in these few lines written by Rose-Marie:

Dear Miss Neilsen!

I am very sorry that I didn't write you before but we have been so ekcited about going to a reel school. It's so much fun wenn there are many children, there are 18 in my klass but there are not enuff teechers for our teecher is very ill so Form I teacher has to mind two classes.

Figure 105: Kirsten and Vilhelm in front of 'Red Roof' at Wei-Hai-Wei. Summer, 1922.

The two girls did well in school and their parents were happy that they were able to keep them at home for another year.

A Danish Architect Comes to Visit

In 1923 the Danish architect, Steen Eiler Rasmussen, then a 25-year-old student of architecture, was given the opportunity to go the Far East on an E.A.C. ship. He later described his experiences in his book, *Rejse i Kina* [Travel in China], published in 1958, which also contains several sketches and watercolours.

Arriving in Shanghai in September he wished to spend a few extra days in the fascinating city. But if he gave up his berth on the *M/S Java* he could not be assured of passage on another E.A.C. vessel. He discussed his problem with Jessen, an E.A.C. engineer, and some Danish ladies he met at a tea party in town. They had the perfect solution:

> Now if I just did what they told me everything would be all right. For you see, talking to the general manager of E.A.C. yourself is no use. He is too high up. He needs a little prodding by someone he respects and doesn't want to cross. In short, the ladies agreed that I should pay a visit to Mrs Meyer tomorrow. I was so ignorant that I didn't know who Mrs Meyer was. It seems she is married to Vilhelm Meyer of the firm Andersen & Meyer. It's a very large firm, Andersen is no longer there and Meyer is considered one of the richest and most important Danes in China. And what's even more important, Mrs Meyer is incontestably the first lady of the Danish community. All I have to do is go there with Jessen, the engineer, and explain my case. Then she'll get interested and call the director of E.A.C., who will say, 'Yes, of course, when Mrs Meyer wishes it'.

Steen Eiler Rasmussen was not convinced that this was the proper procedure. He didn't know Mrs Meyer, but Jessen assured him that she was expecting his visit. It turned out that Jessen had recently taken one of Steen Eiler Rasmussen's trunks with him on the train from Peking to Shanghai. The trunk had contained a number of the drawings and water colours that the young student had made on his journey. As Jessen was examining the sketches more closely, a lady passenger in the carriage had become interested in the beautiful drawings. She turned out to be Mrs Meyer of Shanghai, who loved painting herself and who was very much taken by the young Dane's drawings. Jessen had promised Mrs Meyer that the young man would pay her a visit when he was in Shanghai later on. Steen Eiler Rasmusssen could see that he would have to go and meet the lady:

> I will not deny that the whole undertaking made me nervous. But Mrs Meyer made it easy for me. In such a situation it's wonderful to meet a woman of the world, incapable of doing or saying anything that is not precisely what the moment requires. Her self-confidence helps one get through it, carrying one into a conversation that is as far removed from the trivial as it is from the embarrassingly personal.
>
> It was a very hot morning. She came out to meet us in a loose, white dress of a very thin woollen material. She was the very picture of the decent, well-dressed European lady. She looked directly at me with bright, blue-green eyes as though she wanted to impress my appearance on her memory. She was kindly interested in hearing what I had seen and not seen in Peking and then got around to the question of how long I would be able to stay in Shanghai.
>
> I told her that unfortunately I had to leave the day after tomorrow. Was that really necessary? It was much too short a time and there was so much she would like to show me. I explained the case to her and she immediately said – as though it had been written into her lines – that if there were anything she could do to postpone my departure she would be happy to do so. She would call the director that very evening and let me know tomorrow.
>
> Then we talked of other things. We strolled around the large, beautiful home, looking at the paintings from Peking and the lovely Chinese antiques – marble, porcelain and much more. We had a pleasant time, had tea – it turned out to be quite a long visit.

Steen Eiler Rasmussen did actually manage to postpone his departure from Shanghai and Kirsten Meyer was able to show him some of the city's colourful temples and buildings. His travel book gives a vivid description of the throbbing pulse of Shanghai, as it appeared in 1923:

> It is customary for Europeans to speak of Shanghai as a dreadful place. This is said with a tired and depressed expression, which is supposed to indicate the torture of living in such barbarous conditions. The truth is that Shanghai is an unusually lively and interesting city where Chinese and Europeans mix in the most fantastic way. It is one of the business centres of world trade, a station where East meets West, just like Venice when it was at its zenith. Everything here is life and business, buying and selling at a furious pace. The city changes its physiognomy every 10 or 20 years. – There aren't many cities where so much construction is going on – with so much opulence and so little taste.
>
> Shanghai isn't beautiful, but there is an enchanting, oriental colour to the whole motley cosmopolitan life of the city. Nowhere else do they drive so incredibly fast in the streets. The rickshaws whizz around corners on one wheel and the coolie stops up so short at the tram stops that one gets a serious shock and almost falls out backwards. When driving in an automobile one often sees Chinese dash-ing out right in front of the car in order to cross the street. The explanation for this is that they know there is always an evil spirit at their heels, which is run over in this fashion. Sometimes the Chinese are, too.

Shanghai by Night

Steen Eiler Rasmussen was not the only Dane to visit Shanghai in 1923 and write about it later. Tom Kristensen, the Danish author, later gave a description of Shanghai's night life on Nanking Road at the establishment called the New World. Here it was possible to wander around on several floors, watching theatrical performances, listening to entertainers sing or read aloud, or to play billiards.

The 30-year-old Dane writes about his nocturnal expedition in the following terms:

> I stared into a current of faces and I stared myself sick, for they told me too much. It was as though they had been more exposed to existence than we. Black pockmarks had shot small furrows in their skin. Cataracts had stuck chalk in their pupils. Blindness lay like a layer of ice over their eyes. Life and all the evil spirits had ravaged them. The constant changing of the mask, the daily task of a Chinese, had worn their faces, which often brought to mind that of a monk or a seedy actor. Each head was concentrated depravity or elegance, its expression massive as the bust of an emperor from the time of the Roman decadence.
>
> There were many women. Shanghai, according to the Peking newspapers, is a city smoking with licentiousness and immorality and the women thus walk about freely. The amusement establishments and hotels are indecently alive with them. Many of those passing me in the face-filled dream into which China has precipitated me were beautiful. Their intriguing, almost naughty smiles coaxed honest sympathy from me. No Japanese childishness here, no sweet foolishness. No – a deep, indecent knowledge lurked in their dark glances. The Chinese woman promised more than the Japanese, but was silent about the paradisiacal state of innocence that every little Jap girl with her smile makes us stupid men believe she lives in.

I half-closed my eyes when I saw the faces of the Chinese girls. I tried to imagine that I had that little slanting fold in the corner of my eye. My eyes squinted as in the sun and by trying to look like them on the outside I hoped that part of their soul would wash up into my white body. I caught a little of them, a certain dark sweetness like the taste of rock candy – but then I had to laugh.

They looked like kids, they really did, with their black hair cut off just above their eyebrows. They looked like little girls who, before they're fully dressed, love to strut around in their little pants enjoying the lack of restriction that the dress will later curb. They were toddlers in silk and they walked free and undaunted, their small feet pointing straight ahead according to modern Chinese law, which says that women must have natural feet the better to go their own way.

Tom Kristensen drank in all the impressions. However, China was and remained another world, which could be difficult for a Westerner to understand. He went out into the rainy Shanghai night:

The traffic was heavy and in the wet street, where the lights of the automobiles swept across the puddles, small flames sparkled. Black shadows shot by on a swarming background of flames. All Nanking Road flickered.

I have often dreamt of something new, but here everything was so alien that even the hoarse croak of the car horns sounded like China. Nothing was familiar. The electric lights burst into Chinese characters. The cries wailed. I sought in vain for something familiar.

Russian Refugees

The Bolshevik advance in the new Soviet Union gave rise to a stream of Russian refugees leaving the country. Many Russians sought refuge in Shanghai, known for its acceptance of foreign immigrants. The growing Russian element in the population, however, turned certain concepts upside-down. No longer were all white inhabitants prosperous. The poor Russians, who had left everything they owned behind them in Russia, had to take whatever work and housing there was. Prostitution, which had always flourished in the city, now had a distinctly Russian flavour, greatly appreciated by the wealthy Chinese, too.

Voluntary relief work was organized in a number of areas so as to assist the large number of refugees. Vilhelm's former partner, Iwan Dolgorouckoff, was particularly active in assisting the numerous young Russian soldiers stranded in Shanghai. Kirsten was instrumental in helping the Russian women. In October 1923 she wrote in her large characteristic handwriting to Gerda Nielsen about this work:

Dear Miss Nielsen,

I am in my 'office' at King's Daughters. I have taken charge of the Russian Maternity Fund, or rather I am the one who founded it. Mrs Grosse had so much to do with all the refugees and was quite at a loss because they had a large bill at St Marie's Hospital that they couldn't pay. This was in July and then I got up a collection. People were marvellous, saying that since I was in charge I could have what I wanted. I got $1,500 and that's what we live on.

I give these women – ladies – an admission card to the Hospital with their name and a number on it. The names are bizarre and then I pay for them out of my

Figure 106: The British lawyer Ronald Neill MacLeod and his wife Mary were among Vilhelm and Kirsten's closest friends. Although Mary had more talent as an artist, Ronald drew excellent portraits. Here is one of his portraits of Kirsten drawn in 1925. Mary gave watercolour classes and Kirsten, who loved to draw and paint, was one of her pupils. They often went on painting excursions into the countryside.

fund, $2 a day and $10 for the operating room. The sisters there are so nice and you can imagine how delighted they are, knowing that their bill will be paid. In addition I pay for the milk that is given to them and their children and if they have several children, I pay for them, too.

I do the same thing here at King's Daughters. They let me use their Committee Room three times a week. I'm here Monday, Wednesday and Friday from 10 to 11 am so I don't have to have them at home at all hours and there's a nice Russian lady here, who acts as the interpreter.

Many of those that come are quite decent, while others are so dreadfully poor and wretched that one can hardly feel sorry for them! Really complete animals and filthy, say the sisters at the hospital, quite beyond description.

I began asking them if they would like to work – knit, sew and crochet – and they are so happy to do it. So I give them wool (it's paid for by my fund) and I pay them what I think is fair for the work. They knit little socks, woollen sweaters, little sweaters and caps and I now have so much of it that I have to start giving them other things, sweaters for Vilhelm, men's socks, which I give to Dolgorouckoff! He has a home for soldiers, you know. I'm now getting my friends to give me work for them. They have started using other women, too, and I don't have the heart to say no.

Milk for the children is the costliest item. But I'll manage. And there are the races next week so I'll be able get someone to give me some extra money.

Vilhelm had pulled through the P.D.C. crisis, Kirsten had her hands full with her charity work and the four girls, aged 12, 10, 7 and 3, were enjoying their carefree existence in the home on Avenue Road. But outside the protective garden walls and Shanghai's international limits the struggle for political power in China was raging.

Thirteen

A New Corporation in Delaware, 1923–1926

Political Alliances

The political situation in China in the early 1920s continued to be characterized by the internal power struggle between the warlords. Sun Yat-sen lived in Canton, where he had founded the Kuomintang Party. General Chen Jiongming was the dominant warlord in the surrounding province of Guangdong. He had been one of those who had risen up against the imperial government in 1911 and had now joined his military units to Sun's political forces. Sun Yat-sen's plan was to make a joint advance on the north from Canton in a large-scale campaign. In time a Northern Expedition might lead to the unification of China. General Chen, however, had no real intention of co-operating with Sun. He turned against him and had his men fire on Sun's house. In the dark of night Sun Yat-sen and his young wife, Soong Qing Ling, managed to escape from Canton.

During the next few weeks Sun remained hidden on a ship, the *Yung Feng*. Although Chiang Kai-shek was not impressed by the intellectual K.M.T. party leader, whom he considered to be something of a dreamer, he could see that in the Kuomintang Party Sun had the popular, political support necessary to unite the country. Chiang therefore joined Sun on the *Yung Feng*, where the two agreed to use Shanghai as the springboard for their future political aspirations. Under cover of the city's special international status, together they would set up the necessary network of political, economic and military players and prepare to seize power over the whole of China. Chiang Kai-shek's position as Sun Yat-sen's possible successor was thus strengthened.

In Moscow Lenin was aware that ties to China would have to be given high priority. Late in 1922 the Russian Adolf Joffe was sent to China to decide which of the many warring factions the Soviets should back. After a visit to Peking, Joffe realized that this was not the place to establish any form of co-operation.

He went to Shanghai in January 1923 and had several meetings with Sun Yat-sen, who had moved with Soong Qing Ling into a house in Rue Molière in the French Concession. The prime question for the Soviet strategists was whether Moscow should support the Kuomintang, which was supported by a reasonable percentage of the population, or the newly founded Chinese Comunist Party, whose doctrines were closer to Moscow, but which was still a relatively unknown party in China. They decided to back the K.M.T. to begin with, while opposing a merger of the K.M.T. and C.C.P. In Moscow's opinion the Chinese Communists should have the chance to develop their new party.

On 26 January 1923, Sun and Joffe signed a joint resolution concerning future co-operation between the Soviet Union and the Kuomintang. The Soviets would renounce the territorial concessions that Tsarist Russia had forced upon Imperial China. In addition to the written declaration, Joffe further promised that Moscow would provide advisors and financial aid to the Kuomintang in its struggle to take control of all of China. Sun's political position was hereby strengthened. The warlords in Yunnan and Jiangxi gave him their support and they were able to bring their joint forces to bear against General Chen in Canton, who was forced to relinquish his power base. Sun Yat-sen was able to return to Canton.

Figure 107: In 1925 the young, ambitious officer Chiang Kai-shek (1887–1974) became the successor of Sun Yat-sen (1866–1925), the founder of the Nationalist Party.

In June 1923 China's Communist Party held its Third Party Congress. It was established at the meeting, which took place in Canton, that the guiding political force of the Chinese revolution was the Kuomintang. Members of the C.C.P. were allowed to join the Kuomintang on an individual basis so that there would be no rivalry between the two parties.

In August Chiang Kai-chek left for Moscow where he spent a few months. His stay in the Soviet capital was to have great significance for his subsequent political career. He learned a great deal about the Soviet police and military and made arrangements for large arms deliveries to the K.M.T. He was, however, completely disillusioned when it came to Communist doctrine. It appeared that he didn't thrive in the colourless Soviet society, nor was he blind to the power struggle taking place in the Kremlin, particularly between Stalin and Trotsky. He believed that in the long run Moscow would betray the Kuomintang in favour of China's Communist Party and that Soviet promises to support the K.M.T. were therefore not to be trusted.

In October 1923 the Russians sent Mickael Grusenberg, a 39-year-old Lithuanian, to Canton. Under the cover name of Borodin he was to be Moscow's liaison officer to the K.M.T. Young Zhou Enlai, just returned from a stay in Paris, was to serve as his secretary. The disillusioned Chiang Kai-shek returned from Moscow in November while Borodin was trying to persuade the K.M.T. to let itself be guided by the Soviets. Sun asked Chiang to come to Canton and help build up the K.M.T.

In January 1924 the K.M.T. held its first National Party Congress. The meeting took place in Canton and it was resolved to establish a close co-operation between the K.M.T. and the C.C.P.. The Congress marked the establishment of an alliance between the leading revolutionary forces in China, an alliance which was to last for the next four years. Among those that took part in the conference were the K.M.T. leaders, Sun Yat-sen and Chiang Kai-shek, and the C.C.P. leaders, Mao Zedong and Li Dazhou. Sun was made the official head of the K.M.T. government, which was formed at the Congress.

Sun and Chiang were aware that the K.M.T.'s military base would now have to be reinforced. On the basis of a resolution passed at the Party Congress, Chiang Kai-shek founded a military academy on Whampoa Island in Canton in May 1924. Chiang became the academy's commander as well as the chief-of-staff of the K.M.T. army. Zhou Enlai was one of the new cadets' instructors. He was made the head of Whampoa Academy's political department and was thus responsible for political schooling. The Soviet Union paid all costs in connection with the establishment of the Academy and sent large consignments of weapons to Whampoa.

The foundation of the new military academy strengthened Chiang's power base considerably. In addition to the inherited respect children show their parents, the teacher–student relationship has always been an essential element in Chinese society, a relationship based on loyalty and fidelity. There were 3,000 applications for 500 available places at the academy. Chiang could thus make sure that the greatest possible number of cadets were selected from the ranks of the Green Gang and was thus able to build up a loyal military machine at the grassroots.

Sun and Chiang were aware that they would have to build up a strong economic foundation for their political aspirations, too. They agreed that T.V. Soong, Sun's brother-in-law in Shanghai, was the right man for the job. A central bank was set up and T.V. Soong was appointed minister of finance in the K.M.T. government. Soong carried out drastic economic reforms in Guangdong province, ensuring the K.M.T. the necessary capital.

In November 1924 it became clear that Sun Yat-sen was seriously ill. Nevertheless he wished to go to Peking to discuss China's future with the warlords

Figure 108: Zhou Enlai (1898–1976) became the political leader of Huang-pu (Whampoa) Military Academy in Canton where he worked with Sun Yat-sen and Chiang Kai-shek. As a member of the Chinese Communist Party, he clashed with the Nationalist government as early as 1927.

from the northern part of the country. In December Sun collapsed during one such discussion and was immediately hospitalized in Peking. The doctors' diagnosis was that he had cancer of the liver and did not have long to live. He died on 12 March 1925 in Peking, surrounded by his closest friends from Shanghai, Qing Ling, his wife (who later turned out to be one of the few members of the K.M.T. circle never to lose faith in their revolutionary goals), her brother T.V. Soong and her sister, Soong Ailing with her husband H.H. Kung.

Sun Yat-sen lay in state for two weeks and over half a million Chinese filed past to say goodbye to the man who had been one of the prime movers in the overthrow of the antiquated, imperial regime. His coffin was temporarily placed near the ancient imperial Ming graves.

With the death of Sun, the stage was set for a new power struggle in China. And Chiang Kai-shek was waiting in the wings.

A. M. & Co. Is Registered in Delaware

While the Canton of 1923–24 was the centre of vast political and military upheavals, the situation in Shanghai at the time was more stable. In the Meyer family house on Avenue Road life took its peaceful course. As a businessman, Vilhelm followed political developments in China with great interest. The city had its own political life, too, with the annual Shanghai Municipal Council (S.M.C.) elections. Vilhelm had a seat on several of the Municipal Council's financial and cultural sub-committees. However, he was not a candidate for the S.M.C., which managed the daily life of the International Settlement. Over the years the Municipal Council's prime tasks had been to protect Shanghai's international status while ensuring the greatest possible scope for the business community. Legislation was kept to a minimum so as to give market forces free play.

A number of changes took place in this period within the ranks of the Danish envoys to China. In Peking the Danish minister, Janus Oiesen, was succeeded in 1924 by Henrik Kauffman. The Consul-General of Denmark in Shanghai, Theodor Raaschou, died the same year and was succeeded after 20 years of service by Svend Langkjær. Not until 1921 had Raaschou, who had employed Vilhelm Meyer as an unsalaried vice-consul in 1905–10, received extra staff, the new vice-consul, Hugo Hergel from the Danish Ministry for Foreign Affairs. He was succeeded by vice-consul Carl Brun in 1924.

The Danish Consulate General in Shanghai had moved in 1914 from Whangpoo Road near Garden Bridge to a large villa at Avenue Dubail 1 in the French Section. The Danish community gathered there on various occasions, including the large annual reception celebrating King Christian X's birthday on 26 September.

Vilhelm and Kirsten spent the summer of 1924 in Denmark with their children. They had rented Mikkelborg, a beautiful, waterfront summer residence built around a quadrangle, near the village of Nivå. From this base they could visit friends and family, who were either in Copenhagen or also spending the summer along the Øresund coast, the sound separating Denmark and Sweden.

After the holiday Thea and Rose-Marie moved to the farm, Eskemosegaard, near Birkerød where they were to stay with their aunt and uncle, Jutta and Carl Zøylner, and attend school in Birkerød. Vilhelm and Kirsten returned to China with the two younger girls. They brought Helene Carøe with them as the girls' governess, replacing Miss Calder, the girls' nanny, who had returned to England. Family life in Shanghai was very different without the two eldest girls. However, the family was to return to Denmark the following summer, via New York this time, where Vilhelm hoped to set up a new corporate structure.

Since 1922 A. M. & Co. had been registered in both Manila and New York State. Vilhelm felt it was now time to restore the structure he had originally worked so hard to set up in 1915, i.e. a purely American-registered corporation. During his stay in the United States in the early summer of 1925, Vilhelm was successful in setting up the new structure. He chose the state of Delaware as the domicile of A. M. & Co. rather than New York, since Delaware legislation offered a number of advantages to American companies with investments abroad. Wilmington, Delaware, therefore became the corporation's official domicile. Corporation Trust Company of America, which handled administrative tasks for a large number of American companies, agreed to take on the new corporation, too. The commercial head office would still be located in Manhattan,

Figure 109: Theodor Raaschou, the Danish Consul-General in Shanghai for many years, died in Shanghai in 1924. In this picture taken at the official funeral service Vilhelm is shown in the centre next to the bier. It was Raaschou who employed Vilhelm as honorary vice-consul at the Danish Consulate in 1906.

New York. The share capital of the new Delaware corporation was estimated at $11.5 million.

On 23 June 1925, Andersen, Meyer & Co. was registered. Although Ivan Andersen (Dolgorouckoff) had left the company almost 20 years before, Vilhelm retained the firm's original name, Andersen, Meyer & Co., as it had become almost a household name in China.

Anson W. Burchard of International General Electric was again made chairman of the new board of 11 members. Among the other members of the board were Vilhelm Meyer, Galen L. Stone, William de Krafft of Baldwin Locomotive Works, and Robert Herrick of Saco-Lowell Shops. Vilhelm Meyer was reinstated as president in Shanghai. His vice-presidents were Clifford H. French, W. Wright and Hugo Reiss, all of whom had been in the firm for many years. In addition Paul N. Forum, his old friend from E.A.C., accepted the position of head of the company's new office in New York. French, an American, had formerly been employed in the Ministry of Finance in Manila. He was a respected businessman and later became chairman of the American Chamber of Commerce in Shanghai.

Wright was Scottish. He had gone to Shanghai in 1910 as the representative of a Scottish firm to supervise the installation of elevators in Shanghai Club building on The Bund. He had joined Andersen, Meyer & Co. in 1911 and over

Figure 110: Even though Ivan Andersen (1875–1947), one of the co-founders of Andersen, Meyer & Co. in 1905 along with Vilhelm, left the firm after a few years, the two Danes remained friends for the rest of their lives in Shanghai. Although Andersen himself came from the small town of Lemvig in Denmark, his mother was a scion of the noble Russian house of Dolgoroucki. On this basis Ivan Andersen changed his name in 1913 to Iwan Dolgorouckoff. When thousands of White Russian refugees were pouring into Shanghai after the Russian Revolution of 1917, Dolgorouckoff played an active role in the relief work. When addressing Dolgorouckoff, the Russians used the title of *Knees* (prince), which pleased him immensely. In this picture taken in 1921, Dolgorouckoff, who remained a bachelor all his life, is shown in front of his house with his butler of many years.

Figure 111: Vilhelm Meyer's northern European appearance and German-sounding name made it easy for Shanghai's concert-goers to identify him with Wagner's vikings. In connection with a Wagner concert in April 1924, the newspaper *North China Daily News* printed this drawing with the comment that Vilhelm Meyer ought to appear in the concert that evening in the get-up shown in the picture, 'just like one of his ancestors'. The drawing was by Sapajou, the newspaper's well-known Russian cartoonist.

the following years had worked his way up in the firm, his advance interrupted only by the World War, at which he was one of the first British nationals in Shanghai to volunteer.

In the course of a mere 10 years A. M. & Co. had experienced a number of different corporate structures. In 1915 Vilhelm had founded an American corporation for the first time, with headquarters in New York. In the period 1918–22 the corporation had formed part of the holding company Pacific Development Corporation. In 1923 Vilhelm had salvaged his company from the P.D.C. bankruptcy and now in 1925 he was back on track with a purely American solution, the location of his official headquarters now being Wilmington, Delaware. The three-year-old Manila company was closed down and A. M. & Co. moved uptown from their offices in the Pacific Development Corporation building on Wall Street to 79 Madison Avenue. The last links with the vast, abortive Pacific schemes were severed.

Summer in Denmark

After the successful completion of his business transactions in New York and Delaware, Vilhelm took his entire family to Denmark. They spent the summer

Figure 112: Three of Vilhelm's long-time associates and vice-presidents are shown here, the American, Clifford H. French, the Scot, W. Wright and the Dane, Paul N. Forum. French and Wright (top) were in charge of the financial department and the sales department respectively. They lived in Shanghai whereas Forum (bottom left), was for many years head of the A. M. & Co. New York office. Forum was also in daily communication with the board of directors in New York. William de Krafft (bottom right), was treasurer at Baldwin Locomotive Works in Philadelphia. He was chairman of the board of A.M & Co. from 1927 to 1937.

of 1925 at Hotel Marienlyst in Elsinore. In New York they had hired Josephine, a young black girl, to accompany them to Denmark. Vilhelm had additionally rented an apartment in central Copenhagen. The daily changing of the guard was a great hit with the four girls, who now ranged in age from 5 to 14. The youngest, Marie-Louise, later described the girls' first meeting with the Royal Guards:

> On the first morning my mother sent us off for a walk. Four identically dressed little girls, lovely coal-black Josephine with her bright green turban and little Japanese Amahsan, wearing her colourful kimono and tripping along on her high-soled wooden sandals.
>
> Unsuspectingly, we followed the Royal Guards on their way to the Royal Palace with the same interest that a large crowd of Copenhageners followed us. Imagine my mother's astonishment when we returned home accompanied by two police officers! Somewhat embarrassed, but courteous and firm, they begged Mama to see to it that this walk did not become a daily event for they couldn't take it upon themselves to be responsible for keeping the curious people away from us and at the same time keep up with the Royal Guards. The next day we were sent off in two groups.

After the summer holiday Thea and Rose-Marie went back to Eskemosegaard while the rest of the family returned to Shanghai.

Vilhelm was in high spirits on his return. He was now ready to continue his contracting activities in China on his own terms. However, he was well aware that a great deal depended on the political situation, particularly since the power struggle between Sun Yat-sen's political heirs after his death was as yet unresolved. During the family's absence the events of the summer in China had revealed pockets of political unrest in many areas of the country.

Shanghai had hitherto avoided involvement in political and military confrontations, but in May 1925 events had taken a completely new turn. The Meyer family had left for the United States at the start of the unrest. On his return to Shanghai Vilhelm was filled in on the details of the summer's upheavals.

Power Struggle in China

In mid-May a Chinese factory worker had died in a Japanese textile factory in Shanghai as the result of an injury inflicted by a Japanese foreman. This led to a demonstration on 30 May in front of the Louza police station on Nanking Road, which was primarily staffed with police officers of British nationality, as were the other police stations in the city. The protesters, many of whom were radical students, carried banners with such slogans as 'Down with Imperialism', 'Abolish Exterritoriality' and 'Down with the Unequal Treaties'. When several demonstrators got too close to the police, the British assistant commissioner had given orders to fire. Twelve Chinese had been killed and even more wounded. The smouldering anger latent among the Chinese workers and students had flared up. The Chinese business community, too, had found the behaviour of the British police unjustifiable.

At a nocturnal meeting at which Du Yuesheng, the head of the Green Gang, had been present, it was decided to call a general strike to show the British

Shanghailanders that this form of police brutality was unacceptable. During the next few days everything had ground to a halt. More than 150,000 workers had gone on strike and for the first time Shanghai's Chinese population had made it clear that although the French Concession and the International Settlement were not officially under Chinese jurisdiction, nevertheless the real power lay with the Chinese population, which in terms of size was vastly superior to the foreigners.

Figure 113: Between 150 and 200 Shanghai Danes served in the S.V.C. over the years. Several of Vilhelm Meyer's Danish engineers joined the S.V.C., including Aage Corrit, Fugl-Meyer, L. Sommer and John Rainals. Vilhelm's close friend Sophus Black was also active in the S.V.C. while living in Shanghai. Pastor Eilert Morthensen of the Danish church did service as army chaplain and as a member of the Scandinavian Artillery Company. This picture taken in 1925 shows a section of the Danish platoon, which formed part of the Scandinavian Company.

Whenever there were disturbances in town the International Settlement's Municipal Council could always mobilize the Shanghai Volunteer Corps. This was done during the disturbances of May 1925, too. The corps, founded during the Taiping Rebellion in 1853 with a force of 100 men, had been placed under the Municipal Council in 1879. It now consisted of approximately 2,000 volunteers divided into a number of companies, in principle according to the soldiers' nationalities. The infantry thus consisted of the following companies: two American, five British, one Italian, one Portuguese, one German, one Austrian, four Russian, one international, one Jewish, one Chinese, one Japanese and one Filipino. The Scandinavian volunteers formed part of a Scandinavian machine-gun division and after 1924 made up a Scandinavian company, the 'C Company', which was later allotted light mountain guns and therefore changed its name to Light Gun Battery. In the Volunteer Corps there were also a field-gun battery, a company of engineers, two cavalry divisions, two machine-gun divisions, an

armoured car division, a company of interpreters with Chinese interpreters, as
well as a transport company and an intelligence company.

The 30 May Massacre committed by the Shanghai police had triggered off
protest demonstrations in many places in China, particularly in Canton where
Chiang Kai-shek's cadets had staged a demonstration in front of British and
French soldiers. On 23 June 1925, on the street directly across from Shamian
Island, foreign forces had opened fire on the Chinese. Fifty-two had been killed
and twice as many wounded. The street is called 23 June Street today (6 2 3 Lu,
meaning June 23 Street). This episode led to an extensive strike in the British
Crown Colony of Hong Kong, which was to last for more than a year and a
half. The strike clearly demonstrated the depth of Chinese dissatisfaction with
foreign conduct in China, particularly that of the British.

Figure 114: During the disturbances in Shanghai in the summer of 1925 the Scandinavian
Company was called up, too. The Scandinavian volunteers' orders were to cordon off the streets
within a given area and inspect traffic entering and leaving the bordering Zhabei district. A
Danish volunteer is shown here searching Chinese for hidden weapons.

On 1 July 1925 K.M.T. established a Nationalist government in Canton and
in August all K.M.T. military units were merged together to form the National
Revolutionary Army.

In Shanghai the foreign business community closely followed the new political developments, which were described in the English-language newspapers.
K.M.T. quickly split into a left wing, led by Wang Jingwei, and a right wing, led
by Chiang Kai-shek. In the ensuing power struggle Chiang Kai-shek emerged victorious, strongly supported by his Green Gang cronies in Shanghai, primarily
Du Yuesheng.

In March 1928 Chiang staged a coup in Canton. The pro-Communist leaders
of the Whampoa Academy and the Russian advisors were put under house

arrest. Chiang and his loyal K.M.T. partisans took over the real power in the K.M.T. and during the course of the following months Chiang succeeded in being elected formal head of the K.M.T.. As the highest political and military K.M.T. leader in Canton, Chiang had finally established the power-base necessary to launch the Northern Campaign, a prerequisite for the reunification of the vast Chinese realm.

Figure 115: The emblem of the Shanghai Volunteer Corps consisted of the International Settlement's coat of arms and the date '4 April 1854'. This was the day that Shanghai's Volunteer Corps had received its baptism of fire. The Danish flag (upper right), was one of the 16 flags in the emblem. The Settlement's special form of joint government, characterized by the inscription *Omnia juncta in uno* [all united into one], was one of the few examples of earlier international cooperation, and as such would later prove a source of inspiration when founding the United Nations.

After Chiang had seized power he again made peace with the C.C.P. His purpose in restoring the alliance between K.M.T. and C.C.P. was to ensure the continuation of Soviet aid, crucial to Chiang's political aspirations. Chiang was aware that both K.M.T. and C.C.P. owed a political debt to Sun Yat-sen, universally considered the Father of the Revolution. It was therefore essential for Chiang to become Sun's successor. Although his marriage offer to Soong Qing Ling, Sun's widow, was rejected, Chiang married Qing Ling's sister, Soong Mei-ling, the following year.

Peace Restored in Shanghai

Although Chiang Kai-shek had strong supporters within the Green Gang in Shanghai, the Shanghailanders were not greatly affected by the power struggle taking place in Canton. In Shanghai peace had been restored after the May disturbances. This was primarily owing to the fact that after many years of resistance, the Shanghai Municipal Council had finally agreed to allow Chinese to be elected to the Municipal Council. This had not been provided for in the original agreement, but pressure from the city's Chinese business leaders led to changes in this area.

A population census of Shanghai's International Settlement in 1925 showed that the population consisted of 30,000 foreigners and 810,000 Chinese. Over 95 per cent of the population was thus Chinese, but without any influence on the administration of the International Settlement. In the French Concession there lived 8,000 foreigners and 297,000 Chinese, corresponding to the distribution in the International Settlement. The French, however, had already allocated a seat on their Municipal Council to two Chinese in 1914. But there was the added difference that the French Municipal Council had a merely advisory function since the French Consul-General, acting on instructions from Paris, was the decision-making authority in the French colony. In the International

Figure 116: In 1925 A. M. & Co. built the American Club on Fuzhou Road. This was the first of the foreign clubs to open its doors to Chinese members. Today the building is the seat of Shanghai's Supreme People's Court.

Settlement, on the other hand, the Shanghai Municipal Council (S.M.C.), was the real decision-maker.

It was decided at Shanghai's annual Ratepayers' Meeting in April 1926 that the S.M.C. should be increased by three Chinese members. (The increase was carried into effect in 1928.) At a similar meeting the following year it was resolved that the parks located within the borders of the Settlement, including Jessfield Park and the park areas on The Bund, should henceforth be open to the Chinese. These decisions helped improve relations between foreigners and Chinese.

Upon his return in the early autumn of 1925 it was clear to Vilhelm that Andersen, Meyer & Co. was doing well. Business was on the increase and all over China the corporation's activities were continuously expanding. There was a great demand for power plants, factories, bridges, roads, machinery and motors, and A. M. & Co. was involved everywhere, building, supplying and delivering. American, European and Japanese factories and businesses in Shanghai were thriving side by side with Chinese firms. Leading Chinese businessmen and bankers had formed the Shanghai General Chamber of Commerce and Shanghai Bankers' Association, both of which had a great impact on economic developments in China.

Both Chinese and foreign business people saw the advantage of Shanghai's remaining an autonomous city. This would prevent its being dragged into the inevitable military conflicts that would ensue when Chiang Kai-shek began his march towards the North.

It is true that public order had been restored in Shanghai, but the 30 May Massacre had clearly shown that if the Shanghailanders were to remain in China's largest commercial centre, the old inequalities between the Chinese and the Shanghailanders would have to be abolished. Although very few Shanghailanders had as yet met Chiang Kai-shek and his political followers, it was nevertheless the general opinion in Shanghai that a strong leader was necessary to get the vast Chinese realm under control and that Chiang Kai-shek had both the ambition and the ability for the job. The main question, however, was whether in the long run Shanghai could retain its unique international status.

The Flying Danes

The Danes in Shanghai received a special visit in May 1926, when Captain A.P. Botved of the Danish Air Force arrived on a small plane from Copenhagen, which was on its way via the Middle East and Southeast Asia to Tokyo and back again to Denmark via Siberia. He was accompanied on the flight of 18,000

Figure 117: Danish diplomats dressed to the nines. Here Consul-General Langkjær and his assistant, Vice-Consul Brun, are waiting for the arrival of the Danish plane carrying Captain Botved and Second Officer Olsen.

miles by Michael Olsen, his mechanic. His sponsors included H.N. Andersen of E.A.C. During his stay in Shanghai, where Consul-General Svend Langkjær gave the Flying Danes a great deal of assistance, Botved wrote:

> Our excellent Consul-General, who in addition to being a diplomat is also a sportsman, had had around 100 Chinese workers, if I recall correctly, working for at least a week levelling the square prior to our arrival. Shanghai is the place where long-distance airmen usually smash their machines. At any rate Pelletier d'Oisi's crash last year was fresh in everyone's memory. He damaged his machine when landing because of the faultiness of the preparations. That wasn't going to happen to us, hence the prodigious amount of work. Actually the whole thing wasn't so prodigious in terms of money. As far I remember, each man was paid roughly only 50 cents a day in Danish money.

On a flight like this tremendous transitions can hardly be avoided. We came directly from very primitive conditions in Ninghai to Shanghai, where you find not only the longest bar in the world – at the Shanghai Club – but also inordinate luxury at the large, tip-top world-class hotels. As the guests of E.A.C. – E.A.C. is a very large firm indeed, but it meets its match here in one that's just as big: Great Northern – we lived like lords at Astor House. The largest Danish community in the Far East is in Shanghai, it's even bigger than the one in Bangkok – and what splendid people and what a reception they gave us.

The reception committee included Vilhelm and Kirsten Meyer, who gave a big welcoming party at home on Avenue Road. Anette and Marie-Louise presented the aviators with flowers on the landing field at Hongqiao. This event was immortalized in the Danish company Richs' photo series in Denmark. When Marie-Louise returned to Denmark the following year for her summer holiday, her cousin informed her that she was now famous, since she had appeared on a Richs photo!

Figure 118: When Captain Botved landed his two-seater aircraft in Shanghai in May 1926, Vilhelm and his daughters Anette and Marie-Louise were among the many Danes on the landing strip in Hongqiao to greet the two Danish aviators.

FOURTEEN

Troubled Times, 1926–1929

The October Massacre

In the late summer of 1926 the main topic of conversation in Shanghai was whether the city would be affected by Chiang Kai-shek's advance on the north, which had been launched in August.

The K.M.T. troops' primary objective was the large Yangtze River valley, 500 miles north of Canton. Inland, a force was moving northwest on the three cities of Wuchang, Hankou and Hanyang, collectively known as Wuhan. Chiang Kai-shek himself commanded a force advancing northeast towards Nanchang and Shanghai, where Chiang's main adversary, General Sun Chuanfang, was in command.

Wuhan was taken in September and the K.M.T. government then moved north from Canton to Hankou. The campaign produced results. Together K.M.T. and C.C.P. troops fought their way up through several provinces, including Hunan province, where the confrontation with the provincial landowners and generals was led by the young Communist, Mao Zedong. The advancing forces also took Hubei, Jiangxi and Fujian provinces.

In the autumn of 1926 Chiang Kai-shek was faced with a crucial choice. The alliance between the Kuomintang and C.C.P., which had been in existence more or less whole-heartedly since 1923, had now proved itself capable of achieving significant military objectives. In his battle against the Chinese provincial generals, Chiang would therefore have to draw on whatever military and political support he could get from C.C.P. for as long as possible. However, in the long run he regarded the Communists as his greatest and most dangerous rivals. It was therefore already vital for Chiang to weaken their power.

From his base in Nanchang Chiang Kai-shek communicated in secret with Du Yuesheng and Huang Jinrong, the heads of the Shanghai triads. The Shanghai Communists were planning to seize power in all of Shanghai, including the International Settlement and the French Concession. Chiang Kai-shek promised them that he would send a contingent of Whampoa cadets to support their venture. Instead Chiang Kai-shek saw to it that the provincial general, Sun Chuanfang, who had military control of the Shanghai area, was informed by the Green Gang of the impending rebellion.

The Communist insurrection in Shanghai in October 1926 failed. The rebels fell victim to a surprise attack by General Sun's forces and the Whampoa cadets did not come to their aid as promised. A large number of Communists and workers were killed, but nobody suspected Chiang Kai-shek and Shanghai's triad leaders of being behind the October Massacre.

The foreign Shanghailanders anxiously followed the conflicts raging just outside the International Settlement area.

A Nephew Pays a Visit

In November 1926 Caj Gericke, the son of Vilhelm's sister, Emma Gericke,
visited Vilhelm and Kirsten. He had secured a job as an electrician on board the
E.A.C. freighter *Afrika*, which was on a five-month voyage from Copenhagen to
Vladivostok and back. Throughout the entire journey 21-year-old Caj kept a
journal. His notes on Shanghai make no mention of the political unrest, which
had characterized the city the month before. Life in the International Settlement once again took its carefree course.

Figure 119: The Bund, 1928. In the centre of the picture is the Hong Kong and Shanghai
Banking Corporation's building, constructed in 1923. The tall edifice on the right with the
two small turrets housed the offices of the *North China Daily News*, the most important
foreign newspaper in Shanghai. The paper closed down in 1949.

Arriving in Shanghai on 19 November 1926, Caj immediately went ashore
to find a directory:

> I looked up Andersen and Meyer; it took up a few pages. I then discovered that
> he lived at 19 Avenue Road so I hired a motorcar to drive me out there.
> I rang the bell and a boy opened. I gave him my card and took off my coat.
> Then I went into the sitting room where Uncle Vilhelm was sitting and we went
> up to Aunt Kirsten's room. They were terribly kind and of course asked me to
> stay for dinner. It was almost 8 o'clock but they don't eat until 8.30. They were
> going out to dinner, but then I could go to the Carlton Cinema and afterwards to
> the Carlton Restaurant with Miss Carøe. Naturally I didn't refuse and I got $20!

When Aunt Kirsten went up to dress we went into my uncle's library and had two cocktails. His library was one of the most beautiful places I've ever seen – and it was insured for $75,000!

Then they drove off and Miss Carøe and I had dinner served by two boys. I don't remember what we had, but I had a glass of whiskey with it. When in the Orient ...!

Figure 120: Vilhelm Meyer, president and managing director of Andersen, Meyer & Co., Ltd, in his office at the firm's headquarters on Yuen Ming Yuen Road in Shanghai.

After the film the two young people went to the Carlton Restaurant to dance to a 12-piece jazz band. Gericke was back on his ship at 2 am and noted that the evening had cost $9. 'Everything is extremely expensive in Shanghai'. The next morning he took a rickshaw to Nanking Road to go shopping.

It was about 9 o'clock and the whole street was filled with cars and rickshaws full of businessmen and the traffic was directed with electric lights and some really huge Indians, who really terrified the coolies. They did look impressive and they all carried rifles on their backs.

The young Dane, who was easily impressed, continued on to Yuen Ming Yuen Road to visit the Andersen, Meyer & Co. office buildings. He was shown around by Mr Aagesen and was particularly impressed by the fact that the firm sold almost 400,000 lamps a month! He then went to town with Aunt Kirsten, his 10-year-old cousin Anette, and Miss Carøe. Back home on Avenue Road, Caj had a good chat with Kirsten 'in her magnificent room' and was shown around the entire house. 'I saw the children's night nursery, it was great, and their day nursery, Uncle Vilhelm's and Aunt Kirsten's bedroom and the sitting room. All the rooms were huge and beautifully furnished.'

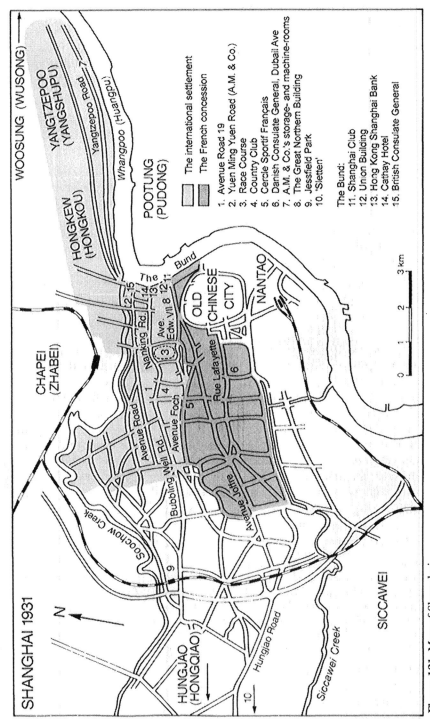

Figure 121: Map of Shanghai

At around 9 p.m. a number of Danish guests came to dinner. Vilhelm mixed the drinks himself and afterwards they went in to dinner.

> Uncle Vilhelm was very entertaining and we had a lot of fun. I don't know what we had to eat, but it tasted great. And the table was so beautiful with lovely crystal, beautiful plates with seagulls painted on them, and the boy always put the seagull so you saw it from the proper side and a really gorgeous tablecloth.

Young Gericke noted that dinner wasn't over until around 11 p.m.: 'They keep the strangest hours here'. After dinner the party went down to the Hotel Majestic.

> Miss Carøe had mentioned it as the biggest and loveliest of all the Shanghai hotels. She said that after a dinner party it was very common to go dancing at a restaurant. Uncle Vilhelm's home was the only place where there was occasionally dancing after dinner. Miss Carøe had described the Majestic as absolutely splendid and I wasn't disappointed. It was really gorgeous. A huge room, with a high ceiling and an enormous dance floor with lights down by the floor and up on the ceiling, and a fountain in the middle. On one side there was a 14-piece band, the best I've ever heard, and they played four or five tunes in a row after which they took a 5-minute break. And when they played, the lighting was very soft, changing with every tune, so sometimes it was red and sometimes green.
>
> We had a couple of drinks and sandwiches and left at 1.30 am. Their system of payment is very practical, but dangerous as they only sign a receipt for things and then they get a bill on the first of the month, not just in restaurants, but also for motorcars, etc.

Caj was driven back to his ship, which left for Japan the next morning.

A few weeks later on the way back to Europe the *Afrika* put in at Shanghai once more. It was 29 December 1926. Late in the afternoon Caj went to Yuen Ming Yuen Road to see his uncle. 'You would have thought I was visiting the king. I was handed a piece of paper where I had to fill out two lines: who I was and what I wanted. Then the boy tiptoes in with it and and only then can you go in.' But once inside Caj again found his uncle 'tremendously kind' and was delighted to be invited to dinner at the Meyer family home the same evening and to a fairly large ball the following evening.

Caj Gericke again spent several enjoyable days in Shanghai and the party at Uncle Vilhelm's and Aunt Kirsten's was a wonderful experience for the young sailor, who had to get along in his best English, since apart from himself there were only three other Danes among the guests. But everything went well.

> We had bouillon, lobster, some meat, plum pudding and ice cream and several kinds of wine and champagne. We were around 50 guests, both young and old, and the young ladies were all very smart and all danced unusually well. The plum pudding was served flaming!! And there were, I believe, 12 or 14 boys to do the serving. When we had eaten we danced in both rooms and there were four musicians playing. At 2 am it was over and Uncle Vilhelm's car took me home again. It was the best evening of the whole trip and I shall never forget it.

The next day the *Afrika* steamed out of the harbour heading south towards Hong Kong. The few days Caj Gericke spent with the family in Shanghai were influential in his decision to settle in Shanghai a little over four years later, in 1931.

The Shanghai Capitalists

As things developed, it was characteristic that not only foreign but also Chinese businessmen were drawn to Shanghai. The rapidly growing city had now clearly become China's commercial capital in terms of domestic as well as foreign trade. The city had already become a magnet in the final years of the empire. In particular, Chinese businessmen from the port of Ningbo in Zhejiang province south of Shanghai were to play a highly influential part in economic life.

These Chinese businessmen, the Shanghai capitalists, profited by the area's international status now that revolution and civil war had weakened the role of state and province in many areas of the country. In Shanghai a number of banks, including the Bank of China, were registered in the International Settlement so as to be free of the ambiguous and uncertain Chinese banking regulations.

Figure 122: Li Ming (1887–1966) was one of Vilhelm's close Chinese business friends. He was the director of the influential Chekiang Industrial Bank, which he later moved to Hong Kong after the Communists came to power in 1949.

Shanghai thus constituted a free city for the city's Chinese business community, too. They formed organizations, which were to play an important part in the economic and political future of the city. The Shanghai General Chamber of Commerce, founded in 1902, was their most important mouthpiece. More than 80 per cent of its members came from Zhejiang province. Another influential organization was the Shanghai Bankers' Association comprising a total of 22 banks, 14 of which were managed by bankers from Zhejiang. In addition there was the Chinese Ratepayers' Association, founded in 1921. The members of this organization, all of whom had businesses within the International Settlement and therefore paid rates, wanted Chinese representatives on the Municipal Council. As mentioned above, this was put into effect in 1928.

The Shanghai Stock Exchange, founded in 1921, also became an important element in commercial life. Vilhelm was one of the many Shanghailanders to buy stock in foreign and Chinese Shanghai businesses. He closely followed developments on the stock market and had an excellent feeling for the right time to buy and sell.

One typical representative of the influential Chinese in Shanghai was Li Ming, born in Zhejiang province in 1887. Prior to the revolution of 1911 he had received a commercial education at a university in Japan and had then become affiliated with the Chekiang Provincial and Industrial Bank. He assumed the position of head of the bank's Shanghai branch and in 1923 helped transform it into a privately owned bank, Chekiang Industrial Bank Ltd, of which he became the director. Li Ming was also chairman of the board of the Bank of China and sat on the boards of a great number of other banking, investment and insurance firms. In 1926–34 and 1946–49 he was chairman of the Shanghai Bankers' Association.

Li Ming and Vilhelm Meyer became close friends, also seeing each other socially. They both had an excellent grasp of China's trade and economy and were on the board of a number of financial companies, including the Yangtze Trust Company and International Investment Trust Company of China Ltd, along with Vilhem's old friend, Michel Speelman, now president of the International Savings Society. Vilhelm and Speelman were also on the boards of the International Assurance Co. Ltd, the Far East Insurance Co. Ltd, and the American Oriental Banking Corporation.

The interplay between the Chinese Shanghai capitalists and the foreign business community was an important element in the economic development of the metropolis. The Chinese were fully aware that their own investment opportunities were dependent on the presence of foreign firms. On the other hand they were also conscious of the risk of greater and greater foreign influence and competition at the expense of their own manœuvrability. Both parties followed the political power struggle with great interest, particularly the relationship between Kuomintang and China's Communist Party. And both parties were firmly convinced that Shanghai's international status would continue to guarantee that their economic transactions would remain untouched by the military and political conflicts unfolding around them.

In her book *Mist on the Window Panes*, Vilhelm's daughter Anette gives the following description of her father's relationship with the Chinese businessmen with whom he negotiated:

> My father had liked the Chinese from the very first and got on well with them. He had early learnt that all transactions must be done their way, even when their notions of truth and honesty might appear to differ from Western ideas. On the

Figure 123: Michel Speelman was one of Vilhelm's closest friends in Shanghai. It was Speelman who helped Vilhelm find employment at the Russo–Chinese Bank in 1902. The two friends also met on the opera stage. In the 1918 performance of *Tosca*, Speelman sang the role of Cavaradossi to Vilhelm's Scarpia. During World War II Michel Speelman was chairman of the Committee for the Assistance of European Jewish Refugees in Shanghai.

other hand, when once agreement was reached, the spoken word was enough for both parties and there was seldom any need for paper contracts or signatures. He was never known to break his word, which is why the Chinese trusted him implicitly, and he had many Chinese friends, who quite apart from anything else were impressed by the very size of him. They also admired the fact that, though he gladly joined in the celebrations previous to which no important deal could be made, they could never manage, even by united efforts, to drink him under the table ... Neither did he ever show signs of impatience as the sometimes slow and round-about way of coming to an agreement might have tempted him to.

Unrest in Shanghai

In December 1926 the long-awaited split within the ranks of the Kuomintang took place. In Hankou, K.M.T. forces came under the leadership of Wang Jing-wei. In Nanchang and later in Nanjing, the K.M.T. was led by Chiang Kai-shek, whose right-wing nationalism became more and more apparent. It was Chiang Kai-shek's wing that would dominate the K.M.T.

When the British Concession areas in Hankou and Jiujiang fell to K.M.T. troops in a surprise attack, London was forced to accept the fact that the old British rights in these two inland cities had come to an end. This made it all the more crucial for the British to maintain the treaty rights in the important coastal cities, but primarily in Shanghai. Some 20,000 British troops were dispatched to strengthen Great Britain's military presence in the strategically important port. Consquently, 42 warships from Great Britain, the United States, Japan, France, Italy and Portugal lay at anchor in the harbour and more ships were on the way. Holland and Spain also sent ships.

Nerves were frayed in Shanghai's foreign population. If this enormous display of military force were not successful in keeping K.M.T. forces away from the International Settlement, heavy fighting between Chinese and foreign forces would result and the city would be transformed into a battlefield. Many Shanghailanders decided to send the women and children out of the city.

Vilhelm and Kirsten therefore found it advisable for Anette and Marie-Louise to go back to Denmark where Thea and Rose-Marie were already. They themselves would remain in Shanghai. It was the first time since 1920 that there were no children in the house on Avenue Road. It was a very difficult decision. In January 1927 Helene Carøe accompanied the two girls on the trip back to Denmark via India and the Middle East on board the E.A.C. ship *Malaya*. The voyage took several months.

The Hour of Truth

After General Sun's October Massacre, Zhou Enlai had arrived in Shanghai to help build up Communist cadres. Slogans such as 'Abolish the Unequal Treaties' and 'Give All Foreign Territory back to China' clearly expressed the growing Chinese oppositon to the special status applying to Shanghai's two foreign sections.

Zhou Enlai was behind the next revolt in Shanghai, beginning on 19 February 1927 as a general strike. Chiang Kai-shek's troops did not come to their aid this time either. Students and workers demonstrating in the international section were turned out of the area by the police and thus handed over to the northern forces, which immediately beheaded the rebels, displaying their heads on poles as a warning to other troublemakers.

Over the following weeks the two groups fought each other: Shangai's Communists against General Sun's Peking forces – Chinese against Chinese. In the unequal battle the Communists put their trust in the K.M.T. troops approaching the city. But when these were 20 miles away, Chiang Kai-shek ordered a halt. Chiang realized that he now had to make a crucial decision. Should he enter Shang-hai in the name of the revolution and put a final end to the foreign presence and domination or should he keep the city out of the great military showdown?

It was Chiang Kai-shek's brother-in-law, the K.M.T. government's Harvard-educated minister of finance, T.V. Soong, who made Chiang realize that Shanghai might be taken without a military confrontation with the well-armed foreign troops and numerous battleships anchored in the river. T.V. Soong convinced Chiang that clever diplomacy in dealing with the Shanghailanders and cunning extortion when it came to Shanghai's rich Chinese businessmen would produce

Figure 124: Chiang Kai-shek married Meiling, the youngest of the Soong sisters, in 1927. From 1928 to 1949 Chiang Kai-shek and Soong Meiling were China's presidential couple. Afterwards they went to Formosa (today Taiwan) where Chiang Kai-shek was president until his death in 1975. He was succeeded by a son from his first marriage, Chiang Chingkuo, president of Taiwan from 1975 to 1988.

much better results for Chiang in the long run. The decision to spare the financially powerful Shanghai was thus made jointly by the military strategist Chiang Kai-shek and his financial expert T.V. Soong.

They now wished to find allies in Shanghai primarily among Chinese businessmen and bankers. They also needed an obliging attitude among the foreign business community, which ultimately could have no interest in a Communist takeover of the whole Shanghai area. The French were quickly sworn in; the triad leader, Huang Jinrong, saw to that.

It was also crucial to ensure contact with the leaders of the International Settlement. In late February Chiang's crony, Du Yuesheng, head of the Green Gang, had met with the head of the Shanghai Municipal Council, the American businessman, Stirling Fessenden. Du told Fessenden that all signs now indicated that the Communists would seize power over all of Shanghai. Chiang's K.M.T. troops, however, were prepared to fight the Communists and thus ensure the continuation of foreign rights in Shanghai. But Du had one condition: units of Chiang's troops would have to be allowed to pass through the two foreign sections on their advance on the north.

Fessenden put Du's plans before the Shanghai Municipal Council. Although the Municipal Council had never before allowed Chinese troops to set foot in the International Settlement, they nevertheless agreed that this concession would now have to be granted. The Council members realized that the alternative was a Communist takeover of Shanghai and thus the end of the International Settlement.

Figure 125: H.H. Kung married Ailing, the eldest of the three Soong sisters, in 1914. He was minister of industry in 1928–31 (see letter to Vilhelm Meyer, Fig. 143). In 1933 he succeeded his brother-in-law, T.V. Soong, as minister of finance but did not inspire the same confidence in the Shanghai Chinese business community as did Soong. Vilhelm Meyer was in regular contact with both H.H. Kung and T.V. Soong, both of whom spent a great deal of time in Shanghai.

The alliance that was established in this period was a strange one. Stalin did not support China's Communist Party but instead Chiang Kai-shek's Kuomintang Party, which for its part was seeking to co-operate with representatives of the capitalistic, Western powers in Shanghai.

Zhou Enlai, the head of the C.C.P. in Shanghai and Chiang's former colleague at the Whampoa Academy, was totally unaware of Chiang's schemes. On 21 March the Communists in Shanghai, under the leadership of Zhou Enlai, again staged a general strike in the entire city. Electric power and telephone connections were cut off. This time the Communists were successful in beating General Sun's troops, which retreated to the north.

The K.M.T. troops and Chiang Kai-shek now moved into the Shanghai area from the south. Chiang met with his old friends from the Green Gang. They had trained a civilian force of 1,000 men, which was to be brought into action against the workers. Shanghai's Chinese business community, many of whom were members of Shanghai General Chamber of Commerce, were requested to provide financial assistance. They realized that what they were up against was extortion, but were prepared to pay for the retention of Shanghai's special international status and were thus able to raise a total of US$ 50 million within a few days.

The hour of truth came on 12 April when Chiang struck at the Communists. Members of the Green Gang wearing white armbands, in conjunction with Whampoa cadets from the K.M.T. forces, attacked a number of C.C.P. offices in Shanghai's Chinese section. More than 700 Communist leaders were taken

Figure 126: T.V. Soong or Soong Tzuwen (1894–1971) was the eldest son of the Soong family. He was the Nationalist government's minister of finance (1928–33) and was able to establish the necessary connections to Shanghai's Chinese and foreign business community. Soong abolished the ancient Chinese currency, the tael, and introduced the Chinese silver dollar, the yuan. As minister of foreign affairs, Soong was successful in making the United States and Britain rescind the old 'unequal treaties' in 1943.

prisoner or shot. Zhou Enlai was one of the few who escaped. In his novel, La Condition Humaine the French author André Malraux described the hopeless situation of the Communists during those battles in Shanghai.

Chiang Kai-shek was able to move the Kuomintang headquarters to Nanjing six days later. Shanghai now became the place where Chiang Kai-shek could replenish the new government's depleted coffers. Chiang and his triad cronies, Du Yuesheng and Huang Jinrong, were now able to put further pressure on the Chinese business community to pay large sums to the K.M.T. All means were used. The kidnapping of reluctant Chinese bank directors or their children, detention and confiscation became the order of the day. The situation developed into a veritable gangster and terror regime. The Green Gang was not only able to operate in the Chinese sections of Shanghai. They could also – in contrast to the K.M.T. soldiers – operate in the French Concession and the International Settlement. The French Consul-General chose to co-operate with the Green Gang. Since Huang Jinrong was the head of the French Security Police, the French authorities were able to provide their citizens with an effective form of protection.

Du Yuesheng was given a seat on the board of a large number of institutions including the Shanghai Stock Exchange, the Shanghai Bankers' Association, the Shanghai Chamber of Commerce and the Bank of China. Du was also installed in the Municipal Council in the French Concession.

The Communists, however, had not lost heart. The lesson they learned from recent events was that in future the workers and peasants would have to be the driving force in a confrontation with the Nationalists. On 1 August 1927, a number of C.C.P. leaders including Zhou Enlai staged a revolt in Nanchang in Jiangxi province against K.M.T. troops. It was this date that was later considered to be the founding date of the Red Army. The Nationalist Army, however, was clearly superior and a few weeks later Mao Zedong withdrew the remaining C.C.P. forces up into the Jinggang mountains where the Communists would consolidate in coming months.

In December 1927 Chiang Kai-shek was married to Meiling, the youngest of the three Soong sisters. It was a fashionable wedding, which took place in Shanghai with a huge reception at the Hotel Majestic. Chiang had thus become the brother-in-law of the deceased Sun Yat-sen, even though Sun's widow, Soong Qing Ling, who was in Wuhan, totally dissociated herself from Chiang and his brutal policies toward the C.C.P.

Chiang now held the fortunes of the Shanghai Chinese in an iron grip and was subsequently able to continue his campaign towards the north. K.M.T. troops took Peking in June 1928 and Chiang could see the outlines of the goal he had set himself long ago – a united China. On 10 October 1928, the 17th anniversary of the revolution against the old empire, Chiang Kai-shek officially named his Nanjing government the Nationalist Government of China. One of his brothers-in-law, T.V. Soong, was made minister of finance while another brother-in-law, H.H. Kung, who was married to Soong Ailing, was made minister for industry, commerce and labour in the new government. C.T. Wang was appointed foreign minister.

Although Chiang Kai-shek had gained a power-base against both the Communists and the left wing of the K.M.T. itself, he had to face the fact that the revolutionary bases established by Communist forces with their stronghold in the Jinggang mountains constituted a potential threat to his plans of creating a Nationalist China. He would have to keep an eye on them and strike when the threat became too great. In the meantime, however, the Nanjing government could concentrate on building up a new administration in China.

Shanghai's foreigners were again able to heave a sigh of relief. Once more they had been allowed to continue their highly unusual form of government.

The Danish Community in Shanghai

The outside world followed developments with bated breath. This was also true of Danes inside and outside of China. The Danish envoy to Peking, Minister Henrik Kauffmann, was considering what position the Danish government should take at such time as the Nanjing government in its demands for the termination of the 'Unequal Treaties' would turn its attention to the Danish–Chinese treaty signed by Waldemar Raasløff way back in 1863. It was particularly the principles of Danish exterritoriality and fixed tariffs that the Chinese would no longer honour.

The expected notice arrived on 1 July 1928 signed by the foreign minister, C.T. Wang. In Nanjing, Kauffmann then negotiated a new trade and friendship

Figure 127: Jesper Jespersen Bahnson (1875–1962) was trained as an officer of the engineers and called himself Captain Bahnson all his life. In 1900 he was offered a job with the Great Northern Telegraph Company. He went to Shanghai in 1904 where he later served as the Far Eastern manager of Great Northern until 1933. Bahnson was one of the leading Danes in Shanghai and did a great deal of work for the various Danish societies including as chairman of the Danish Society.

treaty between Denmark and China effective as of 1 January 1930. A solution had been arrived at, that was in keeping with the times.

Ever since Vilhelm's arrival in Shanghai in 1902 the number of Danes in China had been steadily increasing. A census in 1926 showed that there were roughly 800 Danish citizens in China, 400 of whom lived in Shanghai, i.e. four times as many as 25 years before. Of the roughly 200 Danes in Manchuria, 120 were missionaries. The remaining 200 Danes lived primarily in Tianjin/Peking, Hankou, Canton and Xiamen (Amoy).

The distribution of the 400 Danes in Shanghai was approx. 200 men, 100 women and 100 children. Great Northern continued to have the greatest number of employees and their families in Shanghai, around 120 in total.

The city's club life was particularly wide-ranging. The individual nationalities had their own clubs, too, and the Danes had a large number of their own. The oldest was the Danish Book Club, founded in 1885 by employees of Great Northern Telegraph Company with the purpose of establishing a library of Danish books. The club was located in the Great Northern building on Avenue Edward VII.

The Danish Tennis Club, whose courts were located close to the Shanghai Race Course, was started in 1906. Vilhelm Meyer was a member, but never one of the winners of the annual tournaments. For many years the chairman of the club was the engineer K.V. Aagesen of A. M. & Co.

Another club of great importance was the Danish Charity Society of Shanghai, founded in 1923. The foreign citizens living in the International Settlement only paid real estate taxes, the city's social costs being kept at a minimum. Danes who went bankrupt in Shanghai were therefore left to their own devices if other Danes didn't come to their aid. The first chairman of the Charity Society was Captain J.J. Bahnson, who was succeeded by Vilhelm Meyer in 1925.

Figure 128: Laurits Andersen (1849–1928) went to Shanghai as a machinist in 1879 on one of Great Northern's cable ships. In 1890 he entered the cigarette business where he made a fortune. He later sold his business to the British American Tobacco Company. Andersen, who was unmarried, bequeathed part of his fortune to a special foundation managed by the Danish Charity Society of Shanghai. In the picture Laurits Andersen is shown receiving the Order of Dannebrog (Commander), from Consul-General Langkjær in 1927. In 1995 the Laurits Andersen Fund in Denmark and Fudan University in Shanghai entered upon a scholarship agreement. The Fund now sends two students per year – as Andersen scholars – from Denmark to Shanghai to study Chinese at Fudan University.

The Danish Charity Society provided loans and financial assistance to 'needy Danes in Shanghai', disbursing several thousand dollars a year. However, when the Danish Consulate General also began referring 'stranded sailors' to the Society, the board felt that a fairer distribution of activities should be found. Vilhelm, who was acquainted with consular affairs, discussed the case with Consul-General Langkjær, and got all parties to agree to the following arrangement: In principle, sailors were to be given assistance by the Consulate General, which could, however, recommend that the Charity Society lend a hand. The board of the Society would then reach a decision in each individual case. Danes in distress that were not sailors were to be referred to the Charity Society, which would then reach a decision in each individual case. If the Society did not feel in a position to help, the party in question would be referred to the Consulate General.

When the very wealthy Shanghai businessman, Laurits Andersen, died in 1929, part of his legacy was a foundation for the endowment of Danes in China. The task of helping to manage the foundation was entrusted to the Charity Society. Vilhelm felt that as chairman he would be able to do his bit when it came to helping Danes who had gone broke in Shanghai's ruthless environment. He was on the board for several years along with his good friend and neighbour, C.J. Knipschildt, his former business partner, Iwan Dolgorouckoff, and his friend of many years, Captain J.J. Bahnson. When Vilhelm succeeded Bahnson as chairman of the Danish Society, (to be discussed below), Bahnson again assumed the post of chairman of the Charity Society.

Figure 129: The large Danish community in Shanghai met every year on 26 September, King Christian X's birthday. Vilhelm is shown here on that festive day in 1927 in the garden of the Consulate General at Avenue Dubail where, accompanied by a British military band, he entertained the guests with some popular Danish songs.

The Danish Church opened in a chapel at the French cemetery in Pahsienjao near Avenue Joffre. The first Danish clergyman was Pastor Eilert Morthensen, who was succeeded by Pastor N.H. Søe in 1930. Kirsten was a member of the Parish Council for several years and a frequent churchgoer.

In 1925 The Danish School Association of Shanghai was established. The purpose of the Association as stated in the bylaws was 'to work for the preservation of Danish language and culture among Danes in China'. The membership of the Association reached 100 within the first few years, including of course Vilhelm and Kirsten Meyer. The main task of the Association was to establish a Danish school in Shanghai that would take in children from the first grade upwards. In 1927 they succeeded in establishing the Danish school with its first eight pupils. The school, under the direction of a clergyman of the Danish National Church, consisted primarily of a day-school, which provided Danish children with a formal Danish education. The number of day-school pupils increased within the next few years from 8 to 25 pupils in five classes. Anette and Marie-Louise Meyer attended the school for two years, from 1929 to 1931. In addition there was a Saturday school in which around 50 children, including the day-school pupils, could receive instruction in Danish language and culture.

During its first year, the school was given a room at the Danish Consulate General on Avenue Dubail to be used as a classroom. The school could also use

Figure 130: Shortly after his arrival in Shanghai, Vilhelm became a member of the prestigious Shanghai Club. The elegant club building was located at The Bund no. 3. The club was famed far and wide for having the longest bar in the world – 33 yards. This segment of a very large drawing by Sapajou, Shanghai's famous Russian cartoonist, shows a number of club members. Vilhelm Meyer, his hat set at a rakish angle, towers over the others. The gentleman with the pointed noise (upper left) is the then British Consul-General, Sidney Barton, whose son, Hugh Barton, married Rose-Marie in 1937.

the Consulate dining room in the morning. Obviously such an arrangement could not continue and everybody was delighted when in 1929 they managed to find suitable premises in the American Masonic Lodge, on Route Dufour in the French Concession. As mentioned above, a Danish clergyman was in charge of the day-to-day running of the school. The teachers were volunteers from the

Danish community, for example the two Danish teachers, Mrs Jordan, married to K.E. Jordan of the Chinese Customs Service, and Gudrun Trock, married to the businessman Edvard Trock. In addition the Consul-General gave a daily morning lesson in arithmetic the first year. His colleague Vice-Consul Carl Brun taught Danish history in the Saturday school.

On the initiative of the chairmen of the four Danish societies (the Danish Book Club, the Danish Tennis Club, the Danish Charity Society and the Danish School Association), an umbrella association was formed in 1929 in Shanghai, namely the Danish Society in China. It was to be in charge of all common objectives and interests and the board was also supposed to represent the Danish community to the outside world. Captain J.J. Bahnson was elected chairman. Vilhelm became deputy chairman and in 1931 assumed the post of chairman. C.J. Knipschildt, Arne Eskelund, Knud Rothe, Chief Pilot S.P. Jørgensen and the A. M. & Co. engineers K.V. Aagesen and Elias Gutter were among the active board members. The annual general assembly was held at the Palace Hotel located on The Bund.

The first task of the Danish Society was to plan the royal visit in March 1930, which we shall hear more about in the following chapter. In addition the Danish Society arranged the annual party on the king's birthday, 26 September, at which congratulatory telegrams were sent by Great Northern to Amalienborg, the Danish Royal Palace in Copenhagen.

In addition to the Danish associations, Vilhelm was also a member of the old, illustrious Shanghai Club. This was probably the most prestigious club in the Far East – with a highly British stamp. The club building on The Bund, which in 1910 had replaced the old building of the 1860s, had a bar, a restaurant and clubrooms on the ground floor while on the upper storeys there were rooms that the members could rent. Several members, typically well-established bachelors, used the Shanghai Club as their address for many years. The bar room was world famous due to its 33-yard-long bar, also known as the 'longest bar in the world'. This was where the Shanghai business elite would meet – only men were allowed to be members – for lunch or a drink after a hard day at the office.

Vilhelm was also a member of the British Country Club where the entire Meyer family enjoyed the tennis courts and other sports facilities. As president of a large American corporation, Vilhelm was also a member of the American Club, whose magnificent club building on Foochow Road had been built by A. M. & Co. Incidentally, this was the only national club also open to the Chinese. In New York Vilhelm was a member of India House founded by his friend William Straight in 1914 and in London he was a member of Thatched House Club.

After the disturbances of the summer of 1927, Vilhelm and Kirsten went by train across Siberia to Denmark to see their four daughters. When it was time to return to Shanghai after the summer holiday, Vilhelm and Kirsten still deemed it best to leave all four girls in Europe. The two eldest were sent to a boarding school in Switzerland and it was now the turn of the two youngest to live at Eskemosegaard and go to school in Birkerød.

Figure 131: Henrik von Kauffmann (1888–1963) was Denmark's minister to China from 1924–32. He helped draw up the Danish–Chinese treaty of 1928. Kauffmann is shown here during a visit to Shanghai, together with Thea.

In the summer of 1928 Kirsten returned to Denmark with Amahsan. After the establishment of the Nationalist government in Nanjing, the political situation was once more under control and Vilhelm and Kirsten wished to gather the family again in Shanghai after the summer holiday. Apart from Rose-Marie, who remained at the Brillamont School in Switzerland, the girls returned to Shanghai with their mother in October 1928. As a replacement for Miss Carøe, Kirsten had brought along a French governess, Renée (whose last name is unfortunately unknown to the author), who was primarily supposed to help the children with their French.

The Danish community in Shanghai celebrated a real Danish wedding in December 1928. The vice-consul, Carl Brun, was married to Karin Dalberg, daughter of King Christian X's chief-of-staff, Colonel Oluf Dalberg. The wedding was held in the Danish church, which was packed with Danes, the consular corps and many Chinese officials. Pastor Eilert Morthensen wed the couple. Anette and Marie-Louise were dressed in beautiful bridesmaids' dresses and the Danish Minister to Peking Henrik Kauffmann led the bride up the aisle. He was on his way back to Peking from Nanjing, where he had completed negotiations concerning the new Sino–Danish treaty. Afterwards there was a big reception in the Consulate General on Avenue Dubail, where French gendarmes regulated the heavy wedding traffic.

Figure 132: In the house on Avenue Road the library was furnished with a beautiful, long porcelain folding screen along the wall. A white figurine of Darduse stands on the chimney piece.

Paradise or Hell?

After the establishment of the Nationalist government in Nanjing, peace was again restored on the political front. But a great deal had changed in the course of recent years. Shanghai was no longer a paradise. The alliances between the Nationalist government in Nanjing and the Green Gang in Shanghai had changed life in China's largest city in a great many areas. Gangster rule, prostitution, kidnapping and opium had become part of everyday life.

Shanghai was now a huge metropolis attracting Chinese from all regions of the country like a magnet. With a total population of 3.5 million, it was now one of the biggest cities in the world. The port was the sixth largest in the world and the city's banks financed 90 per cent of China's foreign trade. Shanghai had become an industrial power-house, commanding alone 40 per cent of China's total workforce within the industrial sector. It was a city where the poorest coolies lived in clay huts while the richest, both Chinese and foreigners, lived in opulent villas within the protective borders of the two international sections. Young foreigners wishing to get a share of Shanghai's delights still came to the metropolis, but the risk of a débâcle had increased over the years.

Figure 133: The dining room was panelled in dark wood in a mixture of European and Chinese styles. A portrait of Kirsten's father, Aage Bramsen, is hanging above the fireplace.

Aage Henriksen, a young Dane who went to China to work in Peking in 1929, gave a salutary warning in his 1931 travel book *Dagligt liv i Peking* [Daily Life in Peking] of the dangers confronting young Europeans and Japanese in Shanghai.

There is something in the air that tells you something is going on here and there were more than a few sensational rumours of the wild, hectic life they live here. How often on board did I hear tales of human shipwreck in this Sodom and Gomorrah of the Orient – small, sad tales of human lives that people are so quick to 'put in their place'. The school that the 'young people' sent out here have to survive is often a hard one. It's a trial and tribulation to him whose character isn't strong enough to pass the test: he will be lost, wrecked, to use the *terminus technicus*. The young man comes out here alone, alien, in his early twenties or perhaps not even 20 yet. He longs for home and friends. In the beginning he writes long letters home about all the new things he sees and experiences, but little by little all the new things become everyday fare, there isn't nearly so much to write about any more. He begins to feel lonely. This is the indescribable atmosphere of East Asia, perhaps particularly of Shanghai, under the influence of which you need only spend one single, melancholy evening to discover what loneliness is – and loneliness in the Far East is worse than anywhere else on earth.

The young man has the firm intention of saving money. Who knows, perhaps he's secretly engaged back home – so there he sits in his spare time, like a constant tin soldier, in his room, probably not a particularly comfortable room. He reads, writes, sleeps – but during the hot, humid Shanghai summer evenings sleep is often a rare commodity, the books are about things that suddenly seem so remote, the hours drag by so slowly – and then in this psychologically critical state the proper moment always comes for him to go to the club with his mates for the first time – by accident. There he has his first drink followed by others. His blood flows more quickly, the evening is sultry, heavy with the atmosphere unique to the big cities of the East. Shanghai's 'air' has its effect. He is introduced to young ladies – there are lots of American girls there. Many of them only go out there to find husbands, or to be kept and lead the carefree, pampered, lazy life that foreign women lead in the Far East. Coldly superior, merciless, they go to work. Other women, less scheming but no less dangerous, come from elsewhere. What an incredible number of Russian women there are in Shanghai! Many of them live in beautiful houses, arrange dancing evenings and drinking parties. And the young man needn't pay, just sign a 'chit' – that's how it's done everywhere, shops, hotels, even the chauffeurs. Naturally he has to go by car whenever he goes out with his 'girl', all the others do, those that are a little older with the larger salaries. And if he wants to be included he has to do as the others. He invites people to small excursions. If you have a drink somewhere, well, the car is waiting just outside. You become open-handed in the Far East – particularly when you only have to sign your name in the chauffeur's book afterwards. And then comes the first of the month when the bill is presented. Then the young man opens his eyes for a moment to the fact that 'many rivulets make a river'. However, he's already forgotten by the second. Hopelessness again enfolds him and he again grasps at the only thing, which makes life bearable for him here – whisky, women and cars – even though his entire salary is spent on it.

Gradually the young man works up a debt and one fine day when his leave is approaching, his debt has grown to a few thousand dollars. It is no longer a question of signing chits, the courteous readiness with which the Orient receives its young has stopped a long time ago. All the open arms opened 'especially' for him are no longer there. Kindness, helpfulness, friendship – everything his dollars procured for him are gone with the wind. Rumours about his financial situation have spread; incredibly but inevitably, everyone knows. So he goes to his boss, who pays of course, but going home on leave now is naturally out of the question. The voyage and the sorely needed holiday are dropped – the debt must be worked off. Perhaps he gets sick in addition, the climate goes hand in hand with the rest of Shanghai, which only exists to ruin his health. His little fiancée finds somebody else, she's tired of waiting and then he himself may find a Chinese girl, first as a housekeeper, just not to be alone. Finally he marries her; she bears him half-blood children, the poor half-castes, for the most part despised by the East and not really accepted by the West either. At the age of 40 he's a beaten man, who no longer longs for anything; his pale, unhealthy haggard face with its lifeless eyes bears witness to this – Shanghai now has another pair of dead eyes.

Vilhelm, who was now 49, could recognize many of Shanghai's dangerous elements in this description, but could also note with a certain inner satisfaction that he himself had got through the 27 years he had spent in Shanghai in one piece. The city had changed a great deal and was now a giant commercial and industrial centre with a mighty pulse and powerful social, political and ethnic tensions.

Reunited in Shanghai

In the summer of 1928 Kirsten went to Denmark to bring back the two youngest girls, Anette and Marie-Louise. They all returned to China together via the long sea route reaching Shanghai in November. Anette describes their arrival in China in her book *Mist on the Window Panes*:

Figure 134: In the summer of 1928 the entire family was reunited in Denmark.

We had woken up in the morning to find the sea around us green no longer, but a muddy brown, and so we knew we were not far from Shanghai. As the morning advanced, we saw more and more junks and steamers but there was still no sight of land – until suddenly – we sighted quite close, the low, muddy flats, only a little more solid than the brown sea itself. The ship's engines started to turn slower now as we sailed up the Yangtze, crossing the Bar and on up the Whangpoo River, and the stream of traffic grew ever thicker. The brown land was still flat and low on each side of us, but paths of green appeared here and there, and we glimpsed the thatched roofs of a village, a water buffalo working a water mill and people wandering to and fro. And the nearer we got to Shanghai, the thicker the stream of traffic on the river grew. Dirty tramps and shiny ocean-going liners passed us, and tugs, tankers, wooden junks, ferries filled to bursting point and gleaming, grey gunboats and destroyers of many nations. In the swirling, eddying, whirlpool current of dirty water, sampans juggled their way with men and women straining at yulos and oars, shouting and swearing as they dodged the heavier traffic. The noise grew deafening too, and there was a honking of horns, a shrieking of shrill whistles and the clang of gongs. Suddenly we had arrived – and there was The Bund with its impressive skyline of modern office buildings, looming up in front of us.

Once they had gone ashore Kirsten and the girls immediately felt at home:

> We felt at home again when in the customs shed we were surrounded by the press of Chinese faces, the special smell of Chinese bodies – grease and garlic and sweat – and the gesticulating and noisy squabbling, or what sounded very like squabbling though it was often quite friendly discussion.
>
> Outside in the street stood the chauffeur with his hand to his cap his face grinning welcome, and as usual ours was the first in the row of waiting cars. – It really was remarkable the way he always managed to have our car just where we wanted it, no matter how many other cars were waiting to pick up their 'Masters'.
>
> We scrambled in and were driven off – but not swiftly – down the Nanking Road. The stream of traffic somewhat impeded our progress and the noise was as usual terrific. For a moment I thought that some festival was being celebrated because besides the many posters and boards of vivid colouring and design, flags of all sorts hung down from shops and houses. But I had just forgotten that it was always like this and quite an ordinary day. The flags, even the ones hanging down all seven storeys from the tops of the Chinese department stores 'Wing-on' and 'Sincere', advertised only ordinary sales. From open windows gramophones blared Chinese music and outside a shop that had recently changed owners, sat a whole orchestra loudly announcing this fact by playing the same melody over and over again: the stringed instruments accompanied by high nasal singing and the beat of a gong. Soon we came to quiet streets and the chauffeur increased the speed but never left off using his horn as he dodged the slower traffic – watercarts and wheelbarrows, rickshaws and strolling pedestrians.

In 1929 Rose-Marie rejoined the family in Shanghai and the entire family spent the summer holiday at Wei-Hai-Wei. In September there was a message from Denmark that Vilhelm's father, old Louis Meyer, had died at the age of 86. He had spent his last summer in Villa Padre in Vedbæk, which he had always loved, on the lovely Øresund coast looking across the sound to Sweden.

FIFTEEN

A Royal Visit, 1930

Crown Prince Frederik's Visit to Shanghai

There is nothing like a royal visit from Denmark to boost the team spirit of a Danish community abroad. The Danish Shanghailanders were therefore delighted at the news that Crown Prince Frederik, accompanied by his brother Prince Knud and their cousin Prince Axel, would be coming to the Far East early in 1930 on board the E.A.C. vessel, the *Fionia*. Princess Margaretha, married to Prince Axel, accompanied them as did Waldemar Bache, chamberlain, who later wrote the book *Dagbogsblade fra Kronprinsens Rejse til Østen* [The Crown Prince's Voyage to the Orient], published 1931. The ship was scheduled to arrive in Shanghai in March.

Figure 135: On the occasion of the royal visit in 1930, the Danish Society gave a dinner at the Hotel Majestic. Kirsten was in charge of decorating the large hall with beautiful floral arrangements on the tables and Danish flags and Chinese lamps.

Thirty years had passed since Prince Valdemar, Prince Axel's father, had visited China in 1900 on board the Valkyrien, as mentioned earlier. In the meantime, although Prince Axel had visited China for the E.A.C., no member of the Danish royal family had officially visited Shanghai since the voyage of the *Valkyrien*.

Extensive preparations were made. In addition to Consul-General Lars Tillitse (who had succeeded Svend Langkjær in 1929), Captain Bahnson and Vilhelm Meyer, the chairman and deputy chairman, respectively, of the Danish Society in China, were put in charge of the arrangements along with their wives. On 9 March the *Fionia* steamed up the Whangpoo River and moored at The Bund. The royal guests were received with pomp and ceremony, representatives of the Chinese government and many Danes having turned out to greet them. On the wharf a Chinese band played the Danish national anthem, 'Kong Christian', and Princess Margaretha was presented with flowers by 10-year-old Marie-Louise Meyer.

The royal guests then paid a visit to the E.A.C. offices on The Bund followed by a visit to the Danish Church at Pahsienjao, where the visitors laid a wreath on the grave of Laurits Andersen's, the founder of the endowment. That evening the Danish Society in China gave a big party for 150 guests at the Hotel Majestic. During dinner a telegram was sent via the Great Northern telegraph station to King Christian X and Queen Alexandrine in Copenhagen with greetings, 'in gratitude for the royal visit to Shanghai', and 25 minutes later the greetings were returned by the Danish King and Queen. All the guests applauded. Copenhagen wasn't really so far away after all!

Figure 136: Great Northern hosted a party on 10 March 1930 for the Danish royal visitors at the French Club. One of the guests, the heir presumptive, Prince Knud, is shown in the centre. A little to his right are Crown Prince Frederik and Captain Bahnson followed by the Danish envoy, Minister Kauffmann (shown in profile) and behind him (right) Vilhelm Meyer. The large ballroom is still in use today at the Garden Hotel.

Bache wrote the following about the party given by the Danish Society:

> The entire function was organized by Mrs Meyer, seated beside the crown prince, and she certainly deserved the thunder of applause that broke out when the crown prince proposed a toast to her. Afterwards there was dancing until the small hours. The party did great credit to the Danes that had arranged it.

The next morning the Danish guests were taken sightseeing in the city. The crown prince hosted a large luncheon on board the *Fionia* for a number of Danes in Shanghai, including Thea, 19, and Rose-Marie, 16.

In the afternoon Crown Prince Frederik and his entourage had tea at Li Ching-mai's large villa with its marble fountains and statues in the garden. Lord Li, as he was called by the Europeans, was the nephew and adopted son of the renowned Chinese statesman, Li Hung-chang, whose mausoleum was shown to the Danish guests. They were also shown the Li family's magnificent collection of jade jewellery. Bache was deeply impressed by the jewels – pearls, diamonds and rubies – and offered the following comments in his description of the voyage:

> It was not difficult to understand what a catch Lord Li would be for a gang of robbers. We were told that he was always very careful to keep away from the Chinese section of the city as he wasn't sure what might happen and he never left his house without an armed retinue.

Figure 137: The Great Northern Telegraph Company set up headquarters on Avenue Edward VII. The edifice was built by Andersen, Meyer & Co. in 1922.

A visit was then paid to the Mercantile Marine Officers Club. In his speech in honour of the royal guests, the chairman, Chief Pilot S.P. Jørgensen, emphasized the importance of the Danish merchant fleet and its activities on the high seas.

That evening the three Danish organizers had divided up the tasks among them. Captain Bahnson and his English-born wife were to be the hosts at Great Northern's ball at the French club, le Cercle Sportif Français. Before that Tillitse and Meyer were to give dinners for the Danish visitors. Later on that evening they all met at the French club. It was an impressive party with 700 guests. Not only were all the Danes in Shanghai invited but also many Chinese, including Lord

Li and his family and a large number of foreign consular officials. The guests danced to the music of Whitney Smith and his band, which alternated from time to time with the British Regimental Band, the Green Howards.

Figure 138: In the entrance hall of Great Northern's building on Avenue Edward VII stood a bust of Edouard Suenson, the man who had brought the telegraph cables ashore in Shanghai in 1870. Today the bust is in the company's headquarters in Copenhagen, but the inscription in English underneath is still visible in the entrance hall to the building in what is now Yan'an Lu: 'Edouard Suenson, the Dane who introduced the telegraph into China'.

At the stroke of 12 all the guests, led by Captain Bahnson, shouted 'hurrah' for the crown prince, who had just turned 29, and the military band played the Danish national anthem. Many of the Danish guests were impressed by the fact that the band played the national anthem so well. But there was a special reason. British Queen Alexandra, the sister of Christian X's father, was honorary colonel in the Green Howards, and the tune was one of the numbers in the band's repertoire. There was dancing and merrymaking to the wee hours.

The next day was Crown Prince Frederik's birthday celebration. First there was a visit to the Great Northern Telegraph Society's main building, where Captain Bahnson showed the guests around, explaining all the cables and telegraphic installations. Then the male participants walked over to The Bund, where Bahnson hosted a stag luncheon at the Shanghai Club. A number of prominent Chinese businessmen and employees of Great Northern were among the guests. First there were drinks in the famous bar and then a festive birthday lunch.

Figure 139: On Crown Prince Frederik's birthday, 11 March 1930, the Danish guests visited Great Northern's building in Shanghai. The Crown Prince, Prince Knud and Prince Axel are shown (centre) and Captain Bahnson (left). The young man on the right is the future director of Great Northern, Bent Suenson, the grandson of Edvard Suenson, who laid down the first marine cables in China in 1870.

In the afternoon the royal Danish guests paid town visits, including a visit to the Meyer family, described by Bache in his travel book in the following terms:

> It was a villa in which a number of interesting *objets d'art* and rarities were collected. Precious carpets covered the floors and the walls were hung with magnificent brocades and paintings. The rarest object of all was to be found in the study. This was a panelled screen inlaid with antique porcelain – a work of art that both Chinese and European museums have tried in vain to acquire. Mrs Meyer, who is known and loved by everyone in Shanghai, both Europeans and Chinese, showed us all the art treasures of her home and generously distributed them. The crown prince was thus given a beautiful piece of tapestry.

Late that afternoon the *Fionia* left Shanghai with the crown prince and his entourage, sailing up the Yangtze River bound for Nanjing, the seat of the Nationalist government. The Danish Minister to Peking Henrik Kauffmann and his wife, as well as Vilhelm and Kirsten, were also on board. Foreign Minister Wang had invited them to Nanjing as guests of the Chinese government on the occasion of the crown prince's visit.

Skippered by Chief Pilot Jørgensen, the *Fionia* was accompanied by a Chinese gunboat to protect the Danish guests from piracy, which was not an unusual occurrence on the large Chinese rivers. Thanks to Vilhelm, four of Shanghai's best Russian musicians were on board to provide music for the birthday dinner. Later the guests took over the entertainment with Vilhelm singing and another guest, the E.A.C. Harbin representative, Consul Henrik V. Jacobsen, performing a few numbers on the Russian cellist's instrument. The evening finished off with magnificent fireworks on board arranged by Prince Axel.

At Generalissimo Chiang Kai-shek's

According to the original plan, the royal Danish guests were supposed to have arrived in Nanjing on 12 March. Chiang Kai-shek, however, had postponed the visit by one day, as he didn't want any official arrangements to take place on the fifth anniversary of Sun Yat-sen's death.

On the morning of 13 March the Danish guests were greeted in the Nanjing harbour by a guard of honour and a band. Foreign Minister Wang, the mayor of the city, and a number of prominent state officials were on hand to receive them.

The first event on the programme was a visit to the ancient Ming graves, right outside Nanjing. For the Nationalist government these graves had great symbolic significance as the Ming dynasty represented Chinese rule before 1644. In the period 1644–1911 China had been governed from Peking by the foreign Manchu Qing dynasty. Now that the Chinese government was re-established in Nanjing, Hung Wu, the oldest of the Ming emperors, who had been buried there in 1398, was the symbol of the good old days. Along the tree-lined avenue leading up to the graves stood a number of large stone animals – lions, camels, elephants and horses – intended to keep the evil spirits at bay.

After visiting the graves the Danish visitors continued in the bright sunlight to President Sun Yat-sen's new mausoleum. Sun Yat-sen's sarcophagus had been removed from Peking to Nanjing in 1929 and the visit of prominent foreign dignitaries to Sun Yat-sen's monument was excellent publicity for the Nationalist government. Crown Prince Frederik laid a wreath on the grave of the former head of state.

The mausoleum was an impressive piece of architecture extending over 800,000 square feet. A total of 400 granite steps led up to the mausoleum itself, in which lay Sun Yat-sen's sarcophagus. The white walls and blue ceiling symbolized the K.M.T.'s colours, a white sun on a blue background. It had taken over four years to build. Andersen, Meyer & Co. had been in charge of all the electrical installations.

The Danish guests were shown the huge inscriptions on the gates. One of them said: *Tian Xia Wei Gong*, i.e. the world belongs to everyone. This was a sentiment that all Chinese in post-imperial China could approve, whether they followed the Nationalist leader, Chiang Kai-shek, or the Communist leader, Mao Zedong. Sun Yat-sen was and remained the spiritual father of the Chinese Revolution.

Figure 140: In Nanjing the Danish guests paid a visit to the Sun Yat-sen mausoleum.

The next event on the programme was a luncheon banquet given by President Chiang Kai-shek, who was described by Bache in his travel book as 'the most powerful and most controversial man in China':

> He never stays more than one day at a time in the same place as attempts are still made on his life and his opponents have put a huge price on his head.
>
> The president had borrowed an impressive house from one of his friends that day to receive the crown prince. We entered a flagstone courtyard enclosed by columns, the woodwork painted sky-blue. The roofs were real Chinese yellow, curving upwards with grey tiles. Military guards were placed on both sides of the courtyard and an excellent band played the Danish national anthem, rattling away at a pace, it is true, to which we are not accustomed. But it was done with the best of intentions and what they were playing was certainly recognizable.
>
> A number of steps led up to a large hall where the famous president was standing to receive us. He was quite tall, looked splendid, and was dressed in a khaki uniform and high boots. He was not a very Chinese type and one particularly noticed his eyes, which were not exactly mild.
>
> We were ushered into the audience room and presentations were made – in Chinese. This was performed by the foreign minister. The president sat down, as did the crown prince and the other princes. The princess remained behind in another room along with the president's wife and a number of Chinese ladies. The conversation was held in Chinese as the president did not speak English or at any rate pretended that he didn't.

Afterwards all the guests had lunch hosted by Chiang Kai-shek and Soong Meiling.

In the afternoon there was tea on board the *Fionia* with table music provided by the Russian musicians. Bache noted that unfortunately President Chiang Kai-shek did not attend. 'It was said that he doesn't like to show himself without an escort – and that would have been impossible on board the ship. His wife

Figure 141: The guests were photographed after the official luncheon in Nanjing given by the president of China. The presidential couple, Chiang Kai-shek and Soong Meiling, are in the front row together with Crown Prince Frederik. The Danish minister to China, Henrik Kauffmann, is on the far right.

was there, however, a very beautiful lady, who spoke excellent English.' In the evening Foreign Minister Wang was the host at a banquet given in the International Club building in Nanjing. There were around 80 guests at the banquet, including several ministers of the Nationalist government as well as foreign diplomatic and consular representatives.

The next day *Fionia* left Nanjing. The Shanghai guests went ashore shortly afterwards, returning home by motorboat. Kauffmann remained on board as the ship continued north along the coast. After the successful conclusion of the royal visit Kauffmann wrote to P. Munch, the Danish foreign minister, assessing the visit in terms of Danish interests:

> The visit to the Nationalist government's President Chiang Kai-shek in Nanjing attracted considerable attention all over China partly because it was the first time that China's new capital was officially visited by foreign princes, and the visit has undoubtedly helped promote a friendly attitude towards us and to make the name of Denmark known among the Chinese.
>
> The Nationalist government warmly welcomed the visit if for no other reason than that it added to the prestige of the Nanking regime, but apart from that were probably genuinely pleased with the visit and generally did their best to make the stay in Nanking and China as pleasant as possible for the royal guests, despite the difficulties posed by local conditions and civil war. The trip to Nanking took place on board the *Fionia*, providing the visit with a much more beautiful and impressive framework than would otherwise have been possible.

The chaotic, political situation in China and the current aggressive Chinese attitude towards foreign interests in general make it impossible to count on the visit producing any significant, tangible results for our special Danish interests. But as part of the efforts we Danes are making to establish the best possible personal relationship with the Chinese – and which in my opinion we ought to step up in the future – I believe the visit to Nanking has not been without importance. The visits mentioned were also enthusiastically welcomed by all resident Danes.

The Civil War Intensifies

As Bache had put it, the Generalissimo's eyes were not exactly mild. The royal Danish visit fitted in with Chiang Kai-shek's promotion of foreign relations, but the military strategist's thoughts were elsewhere. His main problem was how to defeat his enemies in the C.C.P. The Communist guerrilla forces in the Jinggang mountains were growing day by day and the popularity of the young C.C.P. leader, Mao Zedong, seemed to be increasing, as was to be expected. Chiang was obsessed with the question of how to defeat Mao Zedong, Zhou Enlai and the Red Army general, Zhu De. A great reward was promised to anyone who captured Mao Zedong and the other C.C.P. leaders. Many members of Mao's family in Hunan province had been taken prisoner by K.M.T. soldiers, but Mao had always managed to escape.

In June 1930, under the leadership of Mao Zedong and Zhu De, Red Army units attacked Changsha, the capital of Hunan province. They were successful in taking the city. This victory, however, was followed by a heavy counter-attack by K.M.T. General Ho Chien's forces, backed by American, British, Italian and Japanese warships, which had sailed up the river to their assistance. Changsha was bombarded out of recognition and after a week, the Communists again had to withdraw from the city.

General Ho had held Mao's wife, Yang Kaihu, prisoner. As a special punishment for Mao, Ho had her tortured in an attempt to get her to reveal the names of the Communist workers in Changsha. When this failed, General Ho gave orders for her to be decapitated outside the city walls of Changsha. Mao's sister, Mao Zehong, was shot and many other family members and friends were killed. In Peking Mao's party comrade, the librarian Li Dazhou, was executed by slow strangulation.

In Nanjing Generalissimo Chiang Kai-shek considered the situation. The Communists had established several Soviet republics in China, which would have to be eradicated before it was too late. A total extermination campaign would have to be launched against the Red Army bases, primarily Mao's base in Jiangxi. During the early autumn of 1930 Chiang was busy planning this new strategy.

Chiang was aware that he needed Western support in his fight against the Communists. His wife, Soong Meiling, along with her American-educated sisters, had built up strong sympathy in the United States for China's new government. The popular image in the United States of the Soong family and the Nationalist government was further enhanced in October when Chiang Kai-shek had himself baptized in Shanghai, swearing an oath to live his life in accordance with Christian principles.

In December 1930 Chiang began his first extermination campaign. He himself led the force of 100,000 men against Mao's forces in the Jiangxi mountains. But the Nationalists were unable to beat Mao and his comrades at arms. With guerrilla warfare and the support of the local peasants, Mao was a match for Chiang's forces, and the Nationalist forces consequently had to give up their first attempt at crushing the Communists.

Wei-Hai-Wei

The Meyer family spent the summer of 1930 at Wei-Hai-Wei. The four girls were now aged 19, 17, 14 and 10. In her book *Mist on the Window Panes*, Anette describes what it was like to go for walks in the area:

> We passed streams where women chatted as they slapped and beat their washing on stones, and almost naked children with spindly legs and distended tummies stood still to stare at us with round eyes, and dirty fingers stuck into fly-ridden mouths. We would clamber up the hills where silk-cocoons spun on mulberry bushes and race across the fields of peanuts. We pulled some peanuts up and munched them raw in spite of their not very pleasant taste but assured each other that we liked them merely to tease Mademoiselle [Renée], who said we must not eat them ...
>
> In the villages wonks barked at us and made a fearful noise as we approached, but they were cowardy-custards and ran away with their tails between their legs if one shoo'ed at them. The villagers returned our smiles and the little girls who sat hunched up on doorsteps working with filthy fingers the most exquisite embroidery, would willingly pause in their work and shyly spread out for us to see and admire, the glowing silks in brilliant colours that contrasted so strangely with their own sun-faded blue cotton garments.

In 1922 the British, who had had sovereignty over the little coastal enclave in Shandong province since 1898, had entered into negotiations concerning the return of the area to the Chinese. While Hong Kong and the New Territories, over which the British had also been granted sovereignty until 1997, had developed into a significant international commercial centre and port, Wei-Hai-Wei had not become the expected important naval base. Although the British Navy did make use of the bay as a Far Eastern base, the small area on the coast had developed into what was primarily a holiday resort for Shanghailanders. The British had thus no problem accepting the actual contents of the treaty. The problem for them was rather whom to negotiate the treaty with. Whereas in 1898 there had been an imperial regime in Peking controlling all of China, the domestic situation in China in the 1920s, as we have seen, was characterized by internal power struggles.

However, after the Nationalist government had been installed in Nanjing in 1928, China had a government with whom the British could negotiate. In April 1930 the British envoy, Sir Miles Lampson and the Chinese Foreign Minister C.T. Wang signed a treaty according to which Wei-Hai-Wei was to be returned to China on 1 October 1930. According to the treaty, the British were to enjoy free use of the naval facilities in Wei-Hai-Wei for the next 10 years with an extension option. The rights of the foreign owners of summerhouses were also respected.

Figure 142: Summer in Wei-Hai-Wei, 1930. Kirsten, her four daughters and some of their friends.

As a consequence of its special status, the Wei-Hai-Wei enclave had managed to stay out of civil war. As the area had been duty and tax free, the town that was now returned to the Chinese after 32 years under the British flag was an enterprising and prosperous little port.

Vilhelm was optimistic that summer in Wei-Hai-Wei. Even though the Generalissimo was not exactly popular with the foreign business community in Shanghai, one had to admit that after many years of civil war, China was once again a single state. It is true that the disturbances of recent years had drawn Shanghai into the Chinese power struggles. But surely that was over now and the Shanghailanders were confident that they would be able to continue their own lifestyle in their mini-republic.

SIXTEEN

The Pinnacle of Success, 1930–1931

Daily Life on Avenue Road

Upon their return from Wei-Hai-Wei early in the autumn of 1930, Anette and Marie-Louise began to attend the Danish School, which now had more than 20 students distributed over four classes. English was the language most commonly used by Shanghailanders and the Meyer girls, particularly the two youngest, spoke English together more and more frequently. It was thus important for them to learn Danish properly and Kirsten insisted that the four girls speak Danish with their parents.

At the end of the year the house was again the scene of a number of Christmas and New Year celebrations. Although no one suspected it at the time, this was to be the last Christmas Kirsten and Vilhelm would celebrate with all four daughters. After a pleasant Christmas Eve spent with numerous Danish guests, the family attended a Christmas luncheon the following day given by Lewis and Hope Andrews, American friends of the family. That evening there was again a dinner at the Meyers' home, this time for the family's British friends. Thea's and Rose-Marie's faithful beaux were also invited, two officers from the British regiment, the Green Howards. They drove up to the house bringing with them a special Christmas gift for the hostess, who always had to feed so many people – a pig, held on the back seat by two men.

During the Christmas season there were many paper hunts. Originally these were for men only, but over the years young women riders also wanted to join in the fun – and there Rose-Marie was among the first prize-winners. This was not a sport that Vilhelm enjoyed, but many of the other Shanghai Danes took part with great enthusiasm.

Vilhelm's nephew, Caj Gericke, went out to Shanghai again in January 1930. He had been so taken with his short stay a few years before that he had managed to secure himself a job with Andersen, Meyer & Co. Gericke was to work in the electric installations department. Many buildings were under construction in the city and A. M. & Co. were involved everywhere. Gericke had travelled across Siberia by train and was met at the station by K.V. Aagesen, who found him lodgings in the new Y.M.C.A. building at Bubbling Well Road. This was a fine place to stay for newly arrived bachelors. Rose-Marie invited him to a rug-by match shortly after his arrival and before long young Gericke was an inte-gral part of the Shanghai social scene. As the Chinese New Year approached, Gericke made the following comments:

> Mellon told me that according to the Chinese religion no one can enter into the
> New Year with debts and consequently they sell out a lot of things cheap in the

days before. Those who can't live up to their obligations drown themselves in the Whangpoo River and it's said that around New Year it's filled with corpses. I'm glad we don't have the same religion in Denmark because then Denmark and Sweden would be connected!

Caj Gericke often went to dinner at his uncle's house, and enjoyed taking part in the musical evenings. Thea had become an excellent ukulele player and had a beautiful singing voice. Vilhelm had received a magnificent record player from the United States, much admired by the friends of the family, who came over to listen to the latest records.

Many years later Marie-Louise jotted down some reminiscences from this period. She was 11 years old at the time:

It was a splendid gramophone! General Electric's latest model and it didn't have to be cranked up. It was a really huge piece of furniture on four legs, made out of mahogany, with cupboards that could be opened underneath, in which there were loudspeakers and room for records, and a lid on top on which the gramophone was placed. It stood in the library and played an important role in our daily lives. This was where I heard H.C. Lumbye's *Drømmebilleder* for the first time and I still remember every note. We wore it out for it was one of our favourite records to dance to. We pushed the chairs aside, put on all kinds of scarves and shawls and let ourselves be carried away by the music while we threw ourselves into the dance either individually or in what we considered to be a graceful *'pas-de-deux'*. Mostly it was Anette and me, but Thea and Rose-Marie sometimes joined in the dancing. This, however, was to other records. They taught us to dance the charleston and practised the latest foxtrot, waltz or tango steps. Thea was the man and led Rose-Marie around most elegantly. Later it was our turn. They were considered the best dancers in Shanghai. I don't know if anyone realized how much they practised and worked at it.

Whenever I had the chance I sneaked down and played a record. Once I went too far. None of the grown-ups was home so I went down into the library as usual to play. The window in a corner of the room facing the street was open. The music was quite loud and then I thought it might be fun with a bit of an audience. I got out Thea's ukulele, turned up the music even louder, placed myself on the window sill and pretended that I was the one playing the ukulele. And sure enough, it didn't take very long before a large crowd of Chinese gathered around, pointing and laughing up at me. And I at them. But then Mama came driving home and oh how mad she was! What did I mean by showing off and drawing attention to myself like that! As a punishment the library was off limits to me for a while.

Anette and Marie-Louise took dancing lessons. In their class was a girl called Peggy Hookham, whose father was an engineer at British American Tobacco Company. Anette was a bit annoyed that Peggy danced better than she did. However, jealousy turned to admiration for the graceful English girl, who danced ballet so beautifully. Her admiration was justified – little Peggy later became Margot Fonteyn, the prima ballerina!

The Danish Consulate General, for many years located at Avenue Dubail in the French Concession, now moved its offices to a building on The Bund, no. 26. Ove Lunn had succeeded Lars Tillitse as Consul-General in 1930 and the previous year Alexis Mørch had succeeded Carl Brun as vice-consul. Although

Nanjing had now taken over Peking's role as China's seat of government, the foreign legations were still situated in Peking. The Danish Minister Henrik Kauff-mann had managed to find a suitable building within the Legation Quarter in Peking, across from the celebrated Peking Club. However Shanghai's close proximity to Nanjing and the city's emergence as China's most important commercial centre meant that the consular officials in Shanghai were of great importance in this period. Shanghai had become an international metropolis.

The Anniversary Book

It was on 31 March 1931 that Andersen, Meyer & Co. had registered as a commer-cial firm in Shanghai. Twenty-five years later the firm was a large international contracting business and Vilhelm was in regular communication with the Nan-jing government, especially with the minister of industry, H.H. Kung, Chiang Kai-shek's brother-in-law.

The anniversary would be celebrated in style. An extensive anniversary publi-cation was prepared in English describing in text and pictures the corporation's history, organization and activities, including mention of some of the most im-portant foreign suppliers. As a gesture to the host country, the entire text was also translated into Chinese.

The book is introduced by a letter of congratulation to Vilhelm Meyer from the minister of industry, H.H. Kung. The anniversary book shows the wide range of activities characteristic of Andersen, Meyer & Co. Ltd. In 1931 the firm had a total of 1,200 employees, around 100 of whom were foreigners.

The company's directors had their seat in the head office on Yuen Ming Yuen Road. In addition to the president and general manager, they consisted of Vice-Presidents Clifford H. French, treasurer, and W. Wright, sales manager. The third vice-president, the Dane Paul N. Forum, was the manager of the com-pany's New York office on Madison Avenue. All three had been with the com-pany for many years.

In the firm's office buildings on Yuen Ming Yuen Road more than 500 Chinese were employed in addition to a number of foreigners. It was from here that the company's activities all over China were administered. The company had established a total of nine branches, covering much of China. The branches were located in Harbin, Mukden (Shenyang), Qingdao, Jinan, Peking, Tianjin, Hankou, Hong Kong and Canton. The head office in Shang-hai was responsible for activities in the four surrounding provinces of Jiangsu, Zhejiang, Anhui and Fujian thus covering such important cities as Nanjing, Suzhou, Hangzhou, Ningbo and Fuzhou.

The buildings on Yuen Ming Yuen Road also contained the company's showrooms facing the street, where potential buyers could study all the different products ranging from small electrical appliances to complex machinery and motors. The sales section was divided into nine departments, as outlined below.

The Textile Machinery Department had been established in 1915 when Vilhelm had become the agent for Saco-Lowell Shops in Boston. Complete

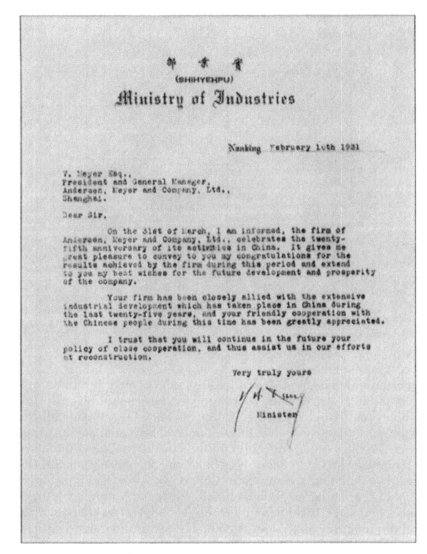

Figure 143: Vilhelm received a congratulatory letter from the minister of industry, H.H. Kung, on the occasion of A. M. & Co.'s 25th anniversary.

cotton mills had been delivered to many locations in China in the intervening years, particularly Shanghai and Tianjin. Hosiery knitting machinery and cotton and silk loom equipment were also supplied.

The firm's Power Plant Machinery Department was in charge of supplying power plants. Ever since the first G.E. light plant had been built in Mukden in 1908, with a capacity of 350 kw, A. M. & Co. had supplied power plants, the total capacity of which exceeded 130,000 kw. This department was also in charge of supplying pumping equipment for waterworks and public swimming pools.

Figure 144: Andersen, Meyer & Co. moved into new headquarters at Yuen Ming Yuen Road in 1908. There were showrooms on the ground floor.

The Electric Department was in charge of sales of electric motors and other electrical products, particularly those supplied by General Electric, including components for Shanghai's street lighting. A. M. & Co. supplied all electrical installations to a large number of buildings in Shanghai such as the Great Northern Building on Avenue Edward VII, the newspaper building, North China Daily News & Herald Co. on The Bund, the Shanghai Municipal Council's administration building, the American Club on Foochow Road, the large European Y.M.C.A. building on Bubbling Well Road, and a number of banks and insurance companies. In addition there was the Sun Yat-sen Mausoleum in Nanjing and the large new Sun Yat-sen Memorial Auditorium under construction in Canton. The department was also in charge of sales of refrigerators and airconditioning units. Finally, the department had a special section in charge of sales of x-ray units to a large number of Chinese hospitals.

The General Machinery Department was a continuation of Vilhelm Meyer's engineering department, established way back in 1908. One of the main jobs of the department was the sale of machinery and materials for China's growing railway operations. The import of American locomotives from Baldwin Locomotive Works was started in 1915. This American company, which had begun selling locomotives to China in 1897, had sold a total of 435 locomotives, 202 of these through Andersen, Meyer & Co., followed up by the import of passenger and freight trains as well as railing from U.S. Steel Products Company. Machinery imports also included entire factory mills for the production of flour.

Figure 145: The Sun Yat-sen Memorial Auditorium in Canton, designed by the Chinese architect Lu Yenzhi, was constructed by A. M. & Co. Some 650 tons of steel structures were used in the building, which was centred around an octagonal dome with curving Chinese roofs. Construction was initiated in 1929 and completed in November 1931. It was an impressive structure, for due to the special steel girder building technology, there wasn't a single column in the 150-foot high dome room. The auditorium was primarily financed by funds collected from overseas Chinese, who wished to raise a huge monument to Sun Yat-sen, the revolutionary hero of Guangdong province. The building has been kept up over the years and is still in use as a theatre and concert hall. The 60-year-old auditorium – with its large statue of Sun Yat-sen outside – is today one of Canton's major tourist attractions (see Fig. 177).

The Building Construction Department, which was one of the most important departments, was managed by the Danish engineer, John E. Rainals. As a result of the new concrete and steel construction techniques the company was able to erect all kinds of buildings ranging from factories, power plants, office buildings, port facilities, bridges, waterworks, oil tanks, business centres, department stores to apartment complexes, hotels, schools, banks, theatres, hospitals, sports facilities and libraries. The Sun Yat-sen Memorial Auditorium was a special project in Canton. A. M. & Co. had been given the task of building an auditorium in the Chinese style with seating for 5,000 spectators using Western construction techniques (see Fig. 177).

The Building Supplies Department, established in 1917, could supply anything in building materials from cement, tiles and floorings to roofing materials, lifts and paint.

The Plumbing and Heating Department was also established in 1917. This department imported plumbing equipment such as radiators and water-pipes, diversifying into oil burners and boilers. This was a huge market in China. A panorama photograph in the anniversary book of all the buildings along The Bund shows that A. M. & Co. was in charge of installing central heating and radiation systems in almost all of them.

Figure 146: The A. M. & Co. management and staff in 1931. In the centre the president, seated, flanked by his two deputy managers, C. French to the left and W. Wright to the right.

The Agricultural Machinery Department handled imports under the management of the Danish engineer, K.V. Aagesen. The department could supply trucks, tractors and other agricultural equipment primarily from the large American firms International Harvester Export Co. Inc. and McCormick-Deering.

The Drug and Chemical Department was set up in 1916 as something of an experiment. Would it be possible for the Western pharmaceutical industry to gain a footing in the Chinese market, which had completely different traditions in the area of medicine? However, with the founding of a number of new hospitals in China, the door was open to foreign medicine, particularly from American firms such as Parke Davis & Co. and Johnson & Johnson. Even cod liver oil from Bergen, Norway, was on the list of the department's wide range of articles.

In addition to the nine sales departments, there were a number of administrative units. The Accounting Department was in charge of all foreign transactions. A total of 17 different currencies entered into the accounts and had to be converted into the local Shanghai dollar. The Finance Department was managed by the Japanese K. Hara, while the Cable Department was run by the Chinese K.B. Tsang, who, having been with the firm since 1 May 1906 (a total of 25 years less one month), was the most senior member of the entire staff.

Finally there were two manufacturing departments located in the Yangshupu district. Since its beginnings in 1921 the firm's machine shop had undertaken the manufacture of a wide range of steel products and now had a staff of 150 workers. There was also the window-sash shop, which since 1929 had manufactured the A. M.C.O. steel windows that were greatly in demand.

Figure 147: A. M. & Co. built many cotton factories including this one supplied by Saco-Lowell Shops of the Boston area.

The Anniversary Book also gave information on the firm's nine branch offices in China:

In 1931 the Tianjin and Peking offices were managed by R.E. Gilleland. After the seat of government had moved from Peking to Nanjing in 1928, the Peking office had declined in importance. The Tianjin office had a staff of 50.

Elias Gutter, a Dane, was head of the Harbin office in northern Manchuria, established in 1926. He had a staff of 12.

Another Manchurian branch, opened in Mukden in 1919, employed a total of 30 people.

The Hankou office covered all the inner provinces around the Yangtze River and had a staff of 30.

In Shandong province the firm had opened an office in Jinan in 1916, also covering some of the neighbouring provinces. Since 1898, Shandong had first been dominated by Germany, then taken over by Japan, and since 1922 was again Chinese.

In 1929 A. M. & Co. opened an office in the port of Qingdao, which subsequently became the leading office in Shandong province. In 1931 both offices taken together had 18 employees.

The Hong Kong and Canton offices, directed from Hong Kong, had been established in 1917 and 1920. In Hong Kong the office was located on the important shopping street Des Voeux Road. The two branches taken together had a staff of 35. In 1931 the Canton office, located on small Shamian Island, was in charge of the daily management of A. M. & Co.'s large projects in southern China: building a bridge across the Zhujiang River to connect

Figure 148: A. M. & Co. also imported steam pump machinery from the United States. The machinery in the picture was delivered to the Shanghai Water Works.

Canton with China's southernmost provinces, and building the huge Sun Yat-sen Memorial Auditorium.

Finally, the Anniversary Book also contained a reference to some of the numerous foreign firms that were Andersen, Meyer & Co.'s main suppliers. The book described a total of 38 suppliers, 33 of which were American. Among the most prominent were International General Electric Co., Saco-Lowell Shops and Baldwin Locomotives Works, all of which were represented on the board of A. M. & Co. In addition there were International Harvester Export Company, Inc., American Radiator Company, Crompton and Knowles Loom Works, Davis & Furber Machine Company, Riley Stoker Corporation, Worthington Pump and Machinery Corporation and the Scherzer Rolling Lift Bridge Company.

The remaining suppliers consisted of three British companies (Agricultural and General Engineers Ltd, Fielding & Platt Ltd, and Uskside Engineering Company Ltd) and the Belgian firm La Céramique Nationale, which manufactured ceramic tiles, and finally the German textile firm, Peter Wolters.

The 25th Anniversary Celebration

Right before the anniversary celebrations started in earnest, Anette was confirmed. This took place on 29 March in the Danish Church, where she had been prepared for confirmation by the new clergyman, Pastor Søe. That evening there was a confirmation party at home, primarily for the family's Danish friends, including the Bahnsons and Bent Suenson of Great Northern, the Rainals and Cai Gericke of A. M. & Co, the Lunns and the Mørchs from the Consulate General, and Pastor Søe and his wife.

The next day marked the start of the anniversary festivities. That evening the house on Avenue Road formed the background of a large anniversary cele-

Figure 149: All the guests gathered in the sitting room on the occasion of the anniversary celebration at home on Avenue Road. Vilhelm is in the centre with Anette on his lap and Kirsten on the left.

bration. Vilhelm had remodelled the veranda into an extra chamber, thus making it possible for 150 guests to attend the ball at the house.

The guests, dressed in dinner jackets and long evening gowns, arrived at 9 p.m. The added wing appeared to advantage with beautiful old Chinese brocades hanging on the new walls. A band provided music from the start and the guests flocked to the dance floor. A little later Vilhelm gave his welcoming speech. He thanked all the Andersen, Meyer & Co. employees present. Two members of the staff who had been particularly instrumental in getting the Anniversary Book issued were presented with gifts. Then Vilhelm read aloud some of the cables he had received, including one from International General Electric Company and one from A. M. & Co.'s board in New York. All A. M. & Co. employees greeted the last telegram with delight, for when Vilhelm read it aloud they learned that thanks to the anniversary they would all be given an extra half-month's pay!

There was dancing again followed by supper. The gratified president and general manager obliged his merry guests with a few songs. The party didn't break up until 3 am. Everyone had a marvellous time. 'It was an absolutely terrific party and I had a great time', wrote Caj Gericke.

The next day, 31 March, was the actual day of the anniversary. There was a reception at the head office, where the large showrooms on the ground floor were emptied to make room for the guests. There was a table for the gifts and a bar. Many people came to congratulate Vilhelm, who stood there receiving them together with Kirsten and their four daughters.

Among the many gifts was a special gift to Vilhelm from Kirsten. This was a silver cup of the type usually won as a prize at sporting events. It was not particularly beautiful, but distinctive, with large curved handles. A. M. & Co.'s well-known triangular trademark, designed by Kirsten in 1916, with the dates 31 March 1906 and 31 March 1931 were engraved on one side. On the other side were Kirsten's and Vilhelm's initials K.V.M. Written in Kirsten's large, characteristic handwriting the following words were engraved:

> From the one who believed in you
> from the very beginning
> and was never disappointed

That evening there was a banquet for the staff. This took place at the large restaurant Wing-On where places were set for 450 guests. Caj Gericke described the dinner in the following terms:

> When we arrived we were received with a large smile and handshake by King Fah while Ah Zee ran around giving orders as to who should sit where. He impressed me by yelling and screaming even more than usual, since the row he usually makes is generally second to none. We sat at round tables with 10 people at each and in accordance with Vilhelm's orders we were mixed so that Europeans didn't sit at the same table. I had Mr Tsu on one side and King Fah on my other side since I needed someone to show me how the food should be eaten. It was interesting to see how strictly it was insisted upon that neither blue- nor white-collar workers should sit at the same table as coolies.
>
> While we were waiting for everyone to arrive we had a few almonds and when everyone had come we dug in. What a spread! There were 20 different dishes!

The president and general manager, sitting in the place of honour flanked by his wife, A. Wright and Ah Zee, gave a speech thanking the employees for all the years that had passed since the firm had first seen the light of day 25 years before. After Vilhelm and Kirsten Meyer had retired, the party continued, becoming particularly lively, according to Caj Gericke:

> Afterwards we had whisky and cigarettes and then all the Chinese played the Chinese 'finger game' roaring with enthusiasm. The 'finger game' is played by two people standing with their right arm bent and making a fist and then they simultaneously stretch out their arms and if one shows 2 and the other 3 fingers, the person who said 5 wins, but if nobody hits on the right number they continue. It goes on at a furious pace and they enjoy themselves tremendously.

The anniversary received extensive press coverage. On the day of the anniversary the following mention of Vilhelm was made in the *North China Daily News*:

> To the newcomer to Shanghai it is rather difficult to picture the head of Andersen, Meyer & Co. as having ever been anything other than the president of a great business corporation, as his dominating personality, grasp of financial subjects, and conspicuous business ability mark him out as having had essentially from the beginning the attributes which now place him at the head of one of the most energetic business firms and the director of several of the most important local concerns in Shanghai. Nevertheless one has to recall that Mr Vilhelm Meyer arrived in 1902 to take up a subordinate position in the East Asiatic Co.

The history of A. M. & Co. is described in the article, as are Vilhelm Meyer's commercial ventures in China. The article continues:

> From what has been written above, there can be no possible lack of appreciation of the rare business of the central figure of the firm which has grown up to such great proportions and importance in China. The fact, however, is that if Mr Meyer had not taken up a business career, he could just as easily have made a success of things on the grand opera stage, and then he has a sense of humour, which is almost Scottish in its pawkiness. For instance the standing joke about Andersen, Meyer is that while the general manager is a Dane, the sales manager is a Scotsman, while the treasurer is French. Mr French, the treasurer, is American of the Americans, and accordingly very popular in all circles in Shanghai.

The article mentions all the numerous cables and gifts received by the firm on the occasion of the anniversary:

> The interesting thing about many of them is that they are from groups of the company's Chinese staff, including workmen from the Chinese Machine Shop and over 100 warehouses, these indicating the goodwill which has always existed between the Chinese and foreign staffs. The Chinese staff numbers 1,200, many of whom have been with the firm for periods of between 10 and 20 years.

Vilhelm Meyer is asked in the article whether the Chinese are capable of handling positions as managers and office workers. Vilhelm responds that this depends on the degree of co-operation between Chinese and foreigners. He continues:

> Provided that when young Chinese are taken into a firm, proper assistance and guidance are given them so that they may develop into useful members of a firm, they are entirely capable of doing so.
> Young engineers from technical schools have developed into extremely useful men in the firm and as time progresses and the younger generation become technically educated, it should be possible to use them more and more in co-operating with foreign firms. For all electrical work, book-keeping etc. they rise right up to the top as they have done in Andersen, Meyer & Co.

Vilhelm also explains why it was crucial for the firm to have foreign engineers from the suppliers' countries:

> With reference to the foreign staff Mr Meyer pointed out that the greatest number had been with the company for many years, and were all specialists in different lines of engineering. Where a specific manufacturer's products are handled, an engineer belonging to the country manufacturing these products acquainted with the engineering practice of the country, is employed. While Andersen, Meyer & Co. handle large American manufactures, British and Continental products also constitute a considerable part of business.

The article also refers to the many congratulations which the firm had received from Chinese and foreign business connections on the occasion of the anniversary. One of 'the most important telegrams received', from Owen D. Young, chairman of the board of General Electric Co. in New York, is quoted in the article:

> I have just learned that Andersen, Meyer & Co. are celebrating the 25th anniversary of their foundation on March 31. Your firm has rendered such outstand-

ing services to the Chinese people and those outside China who have served the Chinese through you that I cannot permit such a significant date to pass without extending my heartiest congratulations on what you have done, and recording my faith and hope that in the next quarter century you will do much more.

The next anniversary function, held at home on 5 April, was primarily for friends of the family – 200 in all. Once again the guests danced into the wee small hours – after which Caj Gericke and several other young gentlemen went on to the Casanova Night Club, not returning home until around 5 am. 'And then we had to get up at 7. It was awful!'

The anniversary was also covered in Denmark. The Danish newspaper *Berlingske Tidende* described the history of the firm on the basis of the Anniversary Book. The article concludes in the following manner:

> The eminently informative commemorative volume shows the extent of Andersen, Meyer & Co.'s wide-ranging activities. The firm is known all over China, has built a number of public works, erected factories in all kinds of fields and runs an extensive construction business. Its close financial ties to America have not obliterated its Danish stamp. It employs a large number of young Danes. Vilhelm Meyer, the president, is still head of the entire enterprise. He was greatly feted on the occasion of the anniversary.

The Danish Chamber of Commerce in Shanghai

Even though Andersen, Meyer & Co. was an American corporation, Vilhelm – as president of the Danish Society in China – was heavily in favour of establishing a Danish Chamber of Commerce in Shanghai. A number of countries had set up chambers of commerce and Vilhelm felt that Danish businesses, too, would benefit from a forum geared to protecting their interests. The Danish Consulate General, however, did not feel any particular need for this and was additionally concerned about the risk of a competitive organization.

Vilhelm discussed the question with his old friend, Carl Johan Knipschildt, who after several years with E.A.C. had started his own company. The two men agreed that it was a good idea for private Danish firms to join together in a chamber of commerce, while the Consulate General would continue as the official representative of Denmark with regard to the Shanghai authorities.

In order to build a bridge between the two institutions, Vilhelm recommended that the Danish Consul-General always chair the Chamber of Commerce's general assemblies and that a close co-operation between the Chamber of Commerce and the Consulate General be established. When Vilhelm was elected president of the Danish Society in China in January 1931, he immediately took steps to set up a committee to look into the question.

After the anniversary celebrations Vilhelm and Kirsten left for Denmark on 14 April. On the eve of their departure Vilhelm was glad that the plans to create the chamber of commerce were now so far advanced that it would be founded within a few days. This proved correct. At the first meeting on 22 April 1931 at the E.A.C. office, 12 Danish businessmen representing a corresponding number of Danish firms gathered together. Vice-Consul Alexis Mørch chaired the meeting

Figure 150: For many years the E.A.C. Shanghai headquarters were located at the Union Building on the corner of The Bund and Canton Road. The Danish Chamber of Commerce in Shanghai was founded at a meeting here in April 1931.

in the absence of the Consul-General and the Danish Chamber of Commerce in Shanghai was founded. The following were present at the first general meeting:

J.J. Bahnson, Great Northern Telegraph Company
S. Frederiksen, E.A.C.
M.L. Justesen, Anglo–Danish Shipping Company
I. Behrens, Shanghai Milk Supply Company
T. Møller, F.L. Smidth
Edvard Trock, Larsen & Trock
S.J.F. Jensen, Jensen's Chemical Laboratories
Carl Johan Knipschildt, C.J. Knipschildt
Arne Eskelund, A.H. Eskelund & Co.
Aage Corrit, A. Corrit
Erik Crone, E. Crone
Constant A. Krogh, C.A. Krogh

At the meeting the participants passed the bylaws that had been drawn up, which stated that the special aim of the chamber of commerce was 'to promote and protect Danish commercial, industrial and shipping interests in Shanghai and to communicate in this regard with the authorities and others'.

The first board consisted of Knipschildt, Bahnson, Frederiksen, Corrit and Trock, Knipschildt being the chairman.

SEVENTEEN

A Worldwide Enterprise, 1931

Danish Holiday

Naturally, Vilhelm had enjoyed occasional holidays during the course of his many years in China, but he felt that this was the first time he and Kirsten had been able to get away for an extended period of time. After the success of the anniversary they needed to go to Denmark for a while to rest on their laurels. Thea and Rose-Marie were to remain behind in Shanghai because of school, staying with Hope and Lewis Andrews.

Although Anette and Marie-Louise were very happy in the small Danish School in Shanghai, Vilhelm and Kirsten felt that it would be best for the two girls to go to boarding school in Europe. They wanted to send the girls to a school in Denmark, but Anette had begged fervently to be allowed to go to England, the home to which so many of her friends were returning. Anette managed to persuade her parents and the two sisters were entered at the girls' boarding school, Langford Grove, in the south of England.

Anette and Marie-Louise said goodbye to their classmates in the Danish School and left for Europe with their parents in April. Their travelling companions were Ove Lunn, the new Danish Consul-General in Shanghai, his wife Ruth Lunn, and their son Otto. They sailed on the *Dairen Maru* to Qingdao and on to Dalian in Manchuria. From there the route went by train to Harbin, where they visited Henrik V. Jacobsen, general manager of E.A.C., followed by the long train journey across Siberia.

From Moscow the train passed through Poland to Berlin, where several Danish family members had come to meet them. They all spent a few days together sightseeing in Berlin. The Meyer family then continued on to London where they were met at Victoria Station by Mary and Ronald MacLeod, now living in England. Kirsten then accompanied her two youngest daughters to Langford Grove.

In early May Vilhelm went on a business trip to New York by ship, returning to London the following month. Kirsten, who had been staying with the MacLeods in London, had visited the girls regularly and upon his return Vilhelm went down to the new school, too.

Vilhelm and Kirsten travelled on to Denmark and were joined by Anette and Marie-Louise in Copenhagen at the end of July. Now the real holiday began, visiting family and friends. In August the Meyer family moved into the Hotel Trouville in the coastal resort of Hornbæk. It is still remembered that Vilhelm told the hotel manager not to bother about bedclothes as they had brought their own silken sheets with them from China.

Of all his five brothers the one Vilhelm felt closest to was Ernst, who had also received a business education and had taken over his father's wholesale business, Beckett & Meyer. In 1922 Ernst Meyer had become president of the Danish Chamber of Commerce, a post he held until 1933. Of the five Meyer sisters Vilhelm and Kirsten were particularly attached to Emilie (Mille) and her husband, the manufacturer William Heering who lived in the merchant house, *Heeringsgård,* in Copenhagen.

A family dinner was held at the elegant Copenhagen restaurant Nimb. Vilhelm's 10 siblings and Kirsten's two sisters with their spouses and children attended. There were 55 guests in all and there were speeches and songs in honour of the 'Chinese contingent'. Vilhelm's and Kirsten's health were toasted, and in songs and speeches it was predicted that many long years in China lay ahead of them.

This is worth a moment's reflection: the old Chinamen generally returned to Europe; and this included not only the large ships that sailed to the Far East, but also the European businessmen and their families who spent many years in China. For Vilhelm and Kirsten Shanghai was now their home, but they wanted to return to Europe in their old age. Vilhelm had only just turned 53 and Kirsten was 47, so it was not yet time. They, too, believed that many happy years in Shanghai still lay ahead of them.

Interview with the President of A. M. & Co.

While the family was on holiday in Hornbæk, Vilhelm was approached by a journalist from the Danish newspaper *Politiken.* The journalist was interested in writing about the 25-year-old Shanghai firm and its president and general manager. The interview took place in the garden room of the hotel while outside the rain poured down. The article appeared on 14 August under the pompous headline 'The Danish Firm That Industrialized the Heavenly Kingdom'. The article introduced Vilhelm in the following terms:

> While every schoolchild in this country has heard of E.A.C. and the activities of its director H.N. Andersen, only very few are aware of the significance of the name of Andersen, Meyer & Co. or have heard the name of its president and general manager, Vilhelm Meyer. And yet the latter firm is just as important in the Far East, both in terms of size and impact, and just like E.A.C. it was built by a Dane.

The article then traced the development of the firm since its beginnings in 1905, with a start-up capital of 100 dollars, right up until 1931, when the firm had a capital of roughly 20 million Danish kroner and a staff of more than 1,200. The article continues:

> The reason why our countryman, one of the most renowned Danes in the East, is so seldom referred to at home is simply that he has never sought publicity for himself or his company. Many people hadn't really heard of the firm until this winter when it celebrated its 25th anniversary and the world press gave coverage to its amazing growth over the past quarter of a century – and now that the founder of the whole thing, the president and general manager himself, is home

on his first real holiday in 25 years, we have succeeded in breaking down what amounts to the great wall of silence with which he likes to surround himself.

Vilhelm Meyer has not forgotten his Danish despite his 25 years in the Far East. Only when speaking on the phone or when directly discussing business matters does he have a tendency to lapse into those short, concise English sentences so characteristic of business language. If you ran into him on the streets of Shanghai – well, a Dane would be able to tell that here was a fellow countryman, his appearance has only become superficially Americanized during all those years abroad.

When questioned about the secret of his overwhelming commercial success, Vilhelm referred to the two trunks of samples he always had with him in the days when he used to travel around Denmark as the agent of the firm of Moses & Son, G. Melchior. He felt that the secret of running a large business was building it up from the bottom and retaining a firm grasp of every detail. He had never forgotten his two trunks and the fact that he was able to keep track of them at all times. Although the firm's activities in China had gradually become considerably more wide-ranging, Vilhelm nevertheless felt that he understood them thoroughly.

After describing how the firm had developed into a very large contracting enterprise, Vilhelm discussed China's development over the past decades, the extent of which one could hardly even imagine in Denmark. At the turn of the century China imported machinery for approx. $ 1.5 million. In the intervening 30 years that amount had increased to $ 50 million.

> I have been working out there in a completely revolutionary era when the old was replaced by the new and Western technology entered into an alliance with the Eastern desire for expansion. Our firm has seen the fall of the imperial dynasty and the rise of revolutionary governments. But it has always been our principle never to get mixed up in politics, which is why throughout all developments we have been able quietly to get on with our business and continually gain new ground. We have sold anything that might help the country move forward, but never war equipment of any kind, only purely practical articles that China has an ever increasing need for.

Vilhelm explained how he had developed the concept of complete industrial plants all ready for operation:

> Andersen, Meyer & Co. is no longer based on imports, but on work and manufacture within China itself. You might say we 'sell the key to an industry'. Let's say, for instance, someone wants to put up a new cotton mill or power station or shipyard or any other kind of completely up-to-date industrial plant. We make our bid – and if we get the order we build it complete within our own organization. Our construction experts build the factory, our machine shop installs the power plant and special-purpose machinery, our electrical department manages its share of the business, and so on and so forth. When the plant is completed all the owner has to do is put the key in the lock and open his doors for business. We've also drawn up his production plan and working schedules for him. The factory is actually operative.

The interview also touched on developments in Japan, of great concern to Vilhelm. In order to prevent unemployment, the Japanese kept their own factories running at any cost. They had embarked upon a drastic dumping policy, totally destructive of world trade. There were numerous examples of the Japanese putting in bids in China with prices 30–40 per cent under the world market level. Vilhelm further emphasized that the Japanese were no longer merely imitating Western industry – they were now carrying out research programmes that would put them at the leading edge of the industrialization process.

When asked whether it was still possible in the East for a young man with a quick mind and the desire to work hard to build up something big the way Vilhelm Meyer had done, Vilhelm replied, almost surprised, that of course it was possible – not only in the Far East, but all over the world. The right man on the right spot would always be able to make good if he himself wanted to.

Back in Shanghai

With Anette and Marie-Louise settled in their school in England, Vilhelm and Kirsten returned to Thea and Rose-Marie in Shanghai. The house on Avenue Road had been the family's anchor for many years, but since Vilhelm had moved in 30 years ago a number of changes had taken place in the surrounding neighbourhood. It was no longer so fashionable and many of the Western businessmen and their families had moved further west. Vilhelm and Kirsten had also discussed moving from time to time. They wanted to move to Hongqiao in the western outskirts of Shanghai, where there were already some lovely houses. They had no wish to give up their old home, however, just to build a smaller house in rural surroundings to be used on weekends.

The well-known businessman Sir Victor Sassoon had a lot for sale in Hongqiao where he himself had built a hunting lodge in Tudor style with a tall roof and timbered frame. Vilhelm and Kirsten had a weakness for Sir Victor Sassoon. He was a scion of an old Jewish family whose activities in London, Bombay, Hong Kong and Shanghai were on a par with the renowned firm of Jardine, Matheson & Co. In 1931 he had decided to leave Bombay and settle in Shanghai as he felt that his large fortune would have more favourable conditions there than in India. His firm had built the city's most modern hotel on The Bund. With its marble floors and all the most modern conveniences, including central heating supplied by Andersen, Meyer & Co., the Cathay Hotel rapidly became *the* new luxury hotel in town.

Sassoon had also built several modern apartment complexes and office buildings and bought a number of sites, both within the city and further out. It was said of him that he owned half of Shanghai. He was given a seat on a number of boards, including the board of the Yangtze Trust Company, and the International Investment Trust Company together with Vilhelm.

Vilhelm and Kirsten agreed to buy a site in Hongqiao and the papers were signed in December 1931.

The Bund

The Meyer family thrived in Shanghai's international atmosphere. No other city in the world was so cosmopolitan: a meeting place of many nationalities in a synthesis of Western and Chinese culture. Vilhelm was particularly fascinated by The Bund – that unique section along the river, unparalleled in the world. Andersen, Meyer & Co. had installed the plumbing and heating systems in almost every big building along The Bund.

Vilhelm loved strolling down The Bund along the river, observing the individual buildings. Standing next to the large monument from the World War, located on the borderline between the French Concession and the International Settlement, he could follow the old system of house numbers, going all the way back to the early years of the British Concession. No. 3 was the old Shanghai Club, on this location since 1864, whose present quarters had been built in 1910. He went there from time to time to meet with business colleagues over a drink in the long bar or have a good dinner.

The next building, no. 4, was the seat of E.A.C. and several other companies. Despite a bad start with E.A.C. almost 30 years ago, Vilhelm was now on the best of terms with the large Danish firm, which had really gained a foothold in the growing Asian market.

Further on was no. 7, where Great Northern Telegraph Company had established its head office in 1882. The beautiful building that now stood on the site had been built by the Danish Telegraph Company in 1907 and taken over by the Commercial Bank of China in 1921.

No. 9 was the location of China Merchant Steam Navigation Company. Then came the impressive structure completed by the Hong Kong Shanghai Banking Corporation in 1923. The new building with the large dome in the middle had become a well-known feature of Shanghai's renowned waterfront.

The following building, no. 13, was Shanghai's Customs House, built in 1927. There was now a large clock on top, replacing the chimes used on former customs house buildings. Vilhelm smiled at the thought that those chimes, the tones of Big Ben in London, had always given the Shanghailanders the feeling of having brought something of their own culture with them to China.

Vilhelm was particularly fond of the beautiful building, no. 15, formerly the headquarters of the Russo–Chinese Bank, later named the Russo–Asiatic Bank. The building had been built in 1901 and Vilhelm had worked there for a few years after leaving E.A.C. in 1902. Those were instructive years. The building had now been taken over by the Central Bank of China.

Next door, no. 16, was the Bank of Taiwan. It had been built in 1926 by the Japanese, who for many years had enjoyed sovereignty over Taiwan.

The next building, no. 17, with its two small domes, was owned by The Bund's most important news organ, the *North China Daily News*. The renowned Russian artist, Sapajou, who had painted Vilhelm's portrait several times (see his cartoons of Vilhelm, Figs 111 and 130) worked here for many years.

Further on stood the Palace Hotel at no. 19. The hotel had been erected in 1906 and was one of the favourite meeting places of the Danish business com-

Figure 151: The Bund, Shanghai's famed waterfront. The building with the roof shaped like a pyramid is Sir Victor Sassoon's Cathay Hotel. The imposing building on the left is the headquarters of the Hong Kong & Shanghai Banking Corporation.

munity. It now had a serious competitor in the new Cathay Hotel, located on the other side of Nanking Road, Shanghai's renowned, colourful main shopping street. Vilhelm remembered the beautiful, low houses, which used to house E.D. Sassoon's offices. But the new Sassoon House was an impressive construction with its green roof, shaped like a pyramid, and its consistently art deco style.

The next building, no. 22, had always fascinated Vilhelm. He could remember when the house had been built back in 1907 as a renaissance castle with towers and spires. The German Club Concordia had been located there, but the building had been taken over by the Bank of China after the War.

Further on was no. 26, the headquarters of the Yangtze Insurance Association, built in 1929 and distinguished by its French mansard roof. The Danish Consulate General had just moved in and Denmark had thereby acquired an official address on The Bund.

Since 1851 the large British commercial house, Jardine, Matheson & Co. had been located at The Bund no. 27. Before Denmark sent her first official envoy to Shanghai in 1896, a number of Jardine, Matheson & Co's partners had acted as honorary consuls for Denmark. The present, impressive building, the EWO building (Yi He Yang Hang) had been inaugurated in 1922.

At the end of The Bund, across from the old Public Garden, stood the British Consulate General, located there since 1852. The beautiful, old building surrounded by a lush garden had been built in 1872.

And then Vilhelm had reached Garden Bridge, built in 1907, leading over to Hongkou. On the other side he could see the large buildings, including the German and Japanese Consulates General. This was where he had worked at the Danish Consulate in 1905–09 and where he had been married in 1909.

Figure 152: View over the Huangpu River from the Cathay Hotel, today the Peace Hotel.

A Good Year

The 25th anniversary had helped highlight Vilhelm's abilities and energy. As a businessman he was one of the best – a good negotiator who kept his word, and who had the complete confidence of both the foreign suppliers and the Chinese importers. His jovial and often informal style made him very popular. With his fat cigar, witty repartee and ringing laughter he could loosen up the most difficult negotiations.

He was respected and liked as an employer, too. Both the foreign engineers and the Chinese employees looked up to their large Danish company president, who steered A. M. & Co. through good times and bad with a firm hand and a natural authority. He attached great importance to the competence of the staff and insisted that they be able to work independently on the numerous construction projects carried out in many areas of China. If the foreign engineers weren't good enough, they had to seek employment elsewhere. And although he gladly employed Danish staff in the firm, they received no special treatment. Those that were weighed and found wanting had to find themselves another job.

Vilhelm was excellent at making money for both the firm and himself. He made extensive investments of his own money in securities in Shanghai, Copenhagen and New York. Many Chinese in Shanghai had a predilection for gambling and games of chance, which rubbed off on Vilhelm. Whether it was on the Shanghai Stock Exchange or at the racetrack, Vilhelm would often play for high stakes despite the greatness of the risk. During the course of his life he experienced both heavy losses and big winnings.

However, he was also the sort of man who let others benefit from his prosperity. Any Dane in Shanghai in financial straits knew that Vilhelm Meyer was never approached in vain. He had gradually become the leading figure of the Danish community. He also contributed a great deal of money to the Danish Charity Society over the years. Vilhelm could be very generous when it came to the beautiful antiques in his home, too. If a guest was particularly taken with a lovely Chinese vase or a perfect little figurine, Vilhelm would often give it to the somewhat astonished guest.

He followed political developments in China closely, not because he was particularly interested in politics, but because he wanted to understand the changing conditions that his firm would have to work under. His refusal to serve as go-between when it came to weapons and other military equipment was generally known. He set his own ethical limits on his commercial activities.

Vilhelm was popular on the home front, too. His four daughters adored him, both when he praised them and when he occasionally teased them with a roguish smile. Anette describes the relationship between her parents in her book *Mist on the Window Panes*:

> As for Papa – he was very proud of her and never tried to hide his admiration. He was not as Mama, reserved with strangers, but got on well with people of all sorts, liking them how and as they were, and few things seemed able to shock him or bring him out of balance. This was not because he was soft – far from it – but because he had an essential sureness, a capacity to stand on his own feet, and he could also be alarmingly stern and concentrated when there was work to be done or the occasion demanded it. Papa loved too a pretty face, and it was his nature to be a flirt. He was usually quite open about it and it didn't worry Mama because she knew that for him she stood as a being apart, bearing no real comparison to anyone else. Once I heard her say to the then just grown-up Thea – 'You know, I think people sometimes pity me and say – "her husband must lead her quite a dance at times, do you think she knows?" And of course I know, but I'm not to be pitied in the very least. Papa just can't help flirting with pretty women and often I feel quite sorry for the little fools who feel embarrassed in my presence and think they've "stolen" him from me! Of course I sometimes get annoyed too, but never much more than that, because you see, I know I'm the only one who really matters to him', but then the laughter left her voice as she continued: 'Jealousy is a terrible thing and a very sad thing, because it shows uncertainty and a lack of faith. Thank goodness I have never had cause to be really jealous, though at times it may have seemed as if I had. I hope for you, that you at my age will be able to say the same, and be as happy in your marriage as I have been in mine.'

Throughout her entire life Kirsten was enchanted by and in love with Vilhelm and the love was mutual. The fact that Vilhelm was a real charmer in the company of ladies came as a surprise to no one, but when Kirsten would say lightly, 'Don't be a fool, Vilhelm', she elegantly demonstrated her ability to tame her zestful husband.

Kirsten's efforts in the home were part of the secret that lay behind Vilhelm's success. She saw to the furnishings, chose colours and together with Vilhelm selected the Chinese rugs, pictures and other beautiful things that were the hallmark of the house. The house was hospitable and guests thronged there, for Kirsten knew how to create a home atmosphere that was a mixture of warm, Danish family life and social elegance. She was on excellent terms with the servants and had a general's grasp of the logistics of planning the numerous social functions held in the house.

Kirsten experienced both the trammels of Victorianism and the looseness of the roaring twenties, but was always able to find the right balance. With her beautiful eyes, calm presence and gentle voice she was ever the lovely, dignified lady of the house. Over the years Kirsten, always dressed in exquisite taste, had become a woman of the world.

The children loved their mother, who always had time to talk to them. Gathering all four of them on the sofa in her room she would read them stories. It was wonderful. Anette characterizes her mother in the following terms:

> I don't think that she was particularly intelligent or even clever, but she was wise and wide awake, well read and with an instinctive knowledge about things and people and though she lived so long in the East she never lost her sense of values. She was not pretty in the ordinary sense, and perhaps she was not really beautiful – her nose tilted slightly too much upwards for real beauty – but she was very lovely. Her dark hair that turned white so early, was swept up high on her head and in this fashion suited the fine lines of her face. She never changed the set of it and kept it long when most others cut theirs short. She had beautiful hands and a sheer, pale complexion, but what one first noticed about her were her eyes – they were so intensely clear and blue. Only when she flared up in sudden anger did they seem to turn grey and flash like steel and then even the bravest would find it hard to meet their blaze. But she seldom got really angry and there was a calmness about her and a certain innocence or integrity that somehow made most people want her to see them in the best light, and those who worried themselves sick or made complications for others, usually forgot to be malignant or neurotic in her presence.

The year 1931 was a good one for Vilhelm and Kirsten. The 25th anniversary of A. M. & Co. had proved that the firm was now one of the biggest and most important in Shanghai. And while the Depression of 1929 had an impact on the economies of the industrialized Western nations and on world trade, it did not affect Shanghai, which had experienced a spurt of economic growth in the period 1927–31. China's currency was based on silver; consequently a drastic fall in the price of silver on the international market meant a correspondingly drastic devaluation in China. This led to rising Chinese exports and increased credit opportunities abroad. While the rest of the world was experiencing poverty and depression, China, and in particular Shanghai, was enjoying a period of prosperity and economic growth. Recent years had shown that to a great extent it was possible to continue to keep Shanghai out of the Chinese power struggles while the city also enjoyed the benefits of China's privileged position on the world market.

Everything pointed to Vilhelm and Kirsten being able to spend many more productive years in Shanghai before returning to Denmark. However, this was not to be: 1931 was the last year to bear witness to the indomitable optimism and unfailing energy which characterized Vilhelm and Kirsten's life within the Shanghai community.

EIGHTEEN

Clouds on the Horizon, 1932–1933

The Japanese Attack Shanghai

In the autumn of 1931 Japanese troops occupied all of Manchuria in Northern China. The action was completed within a few months and a bitter hatred of the Japanese spread all over China. The Chinese initiated a boycott of Japanese goods and shops.

The increased hatred of the Japanese could also be felt in Shanghai. Early in 1932 an episode took place that involved members of a militant Japanese Buddhist sect, who wanted Japan to seize power over all of Asia. On 18 January a crowd of Chinese attacked five Buddhist monks, one of whom was killed. The Japanese residents of Shanghai, now numbering nearly 30,000, i.e. three times as many as the British, were clearly the largest foreign population group. They retaliated by setting fire to a Chinese factory. Two Chinese perished in the fire. The Japanese Shanghailanders, who primarily lived in the Hongkou area ('Little Tokyo'), north of Garden Bridge, requested military aid and protection from Japan against the implacable Chinese.

Three days later the Japanese Consul-General presented General Wu, the mayor of the Chinese section of town, with an ultimatum. Those responsible for killing the Japanese Buddhist monks must be punished, the boycott of Japanese goods must cease and anti-Japanese organizations must be disbanded. General Wu was not in a position to fulfil the last two conditions.

The Kuomintang's 19th Army was in Shanghai at the time. General Cai Ting-kai commanded approximately 31,000 men recruited in Canton. Chiang Kai-shek in the seat of government in Nanjing did not want the K.M.T. forces to be deployed against the Japanese. Seen from Nanjing, the real enemy was and would always be Mao's Communists in Jiangxi province 500 miles further south. Chiang had already despatched three 'extermination expeditions' south to Jiangxi in order to crush the growing Red Army. But the expeditions had failed and Chiang was now planning his fourth southern campaign.

On 26 January in Shanghai, the local Chinese authorities proclaimed a state of emergency for the entire Shanghai area surrounding the International Settlement and French Concession. The situation for foreign residents was confused. Over the years the newly arrived Japanese had gained acceptance by the Europeans and Americans. The Japanese had quite early been given two seats on the Shanghai Municipal Council and had been allowed to become members of the Shanghai Club, a privilege denied the Chinese. The question that now arose was whether the other Shanghailanders should support the Japanese, whose fate as foreigners they shared to a certain extent, or should they support the Chinese forces, who wanted all foreigners thrown out of the country? There was also the good old expedient, previously found so successful, of trying to keep out of it entirely. The situation became critical and on 26 January the Shanghai Municipal Council also declared a state of emergency. The soldiers of the Shanghai Volunteer Corps were positioned along the borderline between the International Settlement and the rest of Shanghai in order to keep the area out of a possible military conflict. The Danish S.V.C. volunteers also took up their positions. S.V.C.'s Japanese volunteers were sent to Hongkou bordering on the Zhabei district, where Chinese 19th Army units had positioned themselves.

That evening Admiral Shiozawa, commander-in-chief of the Japanese flagship *Azumo,* anchored in the Whangpoo River, sent 400 marines from the Japanese garrison in Hongkou to Zhabei 'to protect the Japanese and maintain law and order'. Their objective was the train station in Zhabei and if everything had gone according to plan, the entire operation would have been over within a couple of hours. This was not what happened, however. Contrary to expectations, General Cai's forces fought the invading Japanese. The next day Admiral Shiozawa ordered the entire Zhabei area bombarded. But the Chinese held their ground.

Despite the fact that an additional 20,000 Japanese soldiers were sent in over the following weeks and despite heavy artillery shelling and bombing by Japanese planes, the Chinese forces maintained their positions in Zhabei. Zhabei was levelled beyond recognition during the heavy shelling. While fire and black clouds of smoke rose over Zhabei, more than 600,000 Chinese refugees tried to flee into Hongkou and over Garden Bridge into the centre of International Shanghai. They took with them all they could carry on bamboo poles, in rickshaws or small carts.

Shanghai in the Line of Fire

At school in Langford Grove in England, 15 year old Anette anxiously followed on the radio and in the newspapers reports of the heavy shelling of Zhabei, only a few miles away from the house on Avenue Road. On the day after the first shelling she wrote in her diary: 'Awful things in papers about S'hai. Awful war. Japanese bombing killed 300 Chinese. Chapei in ruins.' The next day, 20 January, she writes that the situation in Shanghai has grown much worse and that Shanghai's foreign colony is in great danger. British troops are on their way from Hong Kong. The following day she writes: 'Troops sent from America. Total number 12,000. Even more danger. Ships ready to take them away. SO frightened.' No mention of Shanghai was made in the diary for a few weeks. But in mid-February Anette had a comforting letter from her mother, who reassuringly wrote that she and Thea and Rose-Marie had gone inland three days before the bombardment started and that they were all fine. The sisters had been sent to Hong Kong where they were now staying with friends.

Figure 153: In January 1932 Japanese troops attacked Chinese units in Zhabei, a northern suburb of Shanghai. Japanese soldiers are here shown in action. Although the International Settlement managed to keep out of military operations, the Japanese attack was to prove the beginning of the end for the special status that Shanghai had enjoyed since 1843.

After 34 days of resistance to a superior Japanese force, the 19th Army was forced to retreat in early March. The peace negotiations were initiated at the British Consulate General, with the British envoy to Peking serving as mediator. From his office Vilhelm could follow the hectic activity at the nearby British Consulate General as diplomats and military personnel continuously drove in and out.

On 5 May the warring factions signed a treaty whereby the Chinese were forced to accept the establishment of a neutral zone around Shanghai. The 19th Army was withdrawn from the city and transferred to Fujian province. Peace was restored. But the Shanghailanders were in a state of shock. This was the first time that the International Settlement had been directly involved in extensive military operations. The Japanese need for *Lebensraum* had been clearly demonstrated in the transformation of the three Manchurian provinces into a Japanese protectorate, Manchukuo. The former Manchu emperor, Puyi, who as a boy had abdicated as China's last emperor of the Qing dynasty, was now reinstated as the head of Manchukuo on Japanese terms.

Although the Shanghailanders did not yet fully realize it, the Japanese attack was the starting signal for the countdown. The days of International Shanghai were numbered. In effect, what put an end to Shanghai's continued existence as China's international metropolis were the imperial dreams of Japan. The Western business community in Shanghai did realize, however, that they and their families were now in danger of finding themselves in the direct line of fire between the two mighty neighbouring Asian countries, China and Japan. Would it be possible for Shanghai to avoid being sucked into this conflict?

The Danish Society in China

Not even the Japanese attack on Zhabei could alter the Danish Shanghailand-
ers' decision to go through with the annual general assembly of the Danish
Society as planned. It took place on 29 January at the Palace Hotel on The Bund.
As the Japanese forces were initiating their bombardment of the Zhabei area,
the Danes met to discuss questions of common interest. The chairman, Vilhelm
Meyer, presented the annual report. The membership was now 116. One of the
special events of the year mentioned by Vilhelm was the founding of the
Danish Chamber of Commerce in Shanghai.

Figure 154: Paper hunts (see Chapter 11, sub-section on 'The Danish Community') were one
of the Shanghailanders' favourite sports. Captain J.J. Bahnson, Henrik Brockenhuus-Schack
and Bent Suenson, all of Great Northern, are shown here. Tearing along, jumping ditches
and streams, the wet riders would gallop their Mongolian ponies to the finish line where a
great crowd collected to cheer them.

The topic that primarily occupied Vilhelm's thoughts was the question of
Danish participation in the Shanghai's International Settlement's political decision-making process. True, the composition of the Shanghai Municipal Council was not determined by nationality, but it was nevertheless apparent that foreigners eligible to vote normally elected their own countrymen. The British consequently continued to hold most S.M.C. posts followed by the Americans and
the Japanese. Vilhelm felt that if all Scandinavians entitled to vote could agree
on a common candidate, there would then be a good chance of getting a representative on the Municipal Council. He emphasized that it was a demanding and
responsible position, which must be assumed with no thought of financial
remuneration.

Vilhelm explained at the meeting why he himself was not a candidate. In the first place Clifford French, his vice-president at Andersen, Meyer & Co. and also the president of the Shanghai American Chamber of Commerce, had been elected to the Shanghai Municipal Council the previous year. Second, Vilhelm felt that a Scandinavian representative should be recruited from a company that was entirely Scandinavian. At the general assembly it was agreed that Captain Bahnson would be a candidate for the annual Municipal Council election in April and that everybody should work to ensure that the Scandinavian voters in Shanghai pledge their votes to the Danish candidate. Bahnson's election bid was successful and he was elected to the Municipal Council in April 1932.

Figure 155: In 1932 Vilhelm and Kirsten built their weekend house 'Sletten' in Hongqiao.

'Sletten' at Hongqiao

Chiang-Kai-shek's campaign against the Communists, the Japanese occupation of Manchuria and the recent Japanese shelling of Shanghai provided something for Shanghailanders to think about in 1932. However, most of them retained their confidence and faith in the future. They rebuilt the bombed houses and again set in motion the machinery of trade, manufacturing and shipping.

Vilhelm and Kirsen, reunited with Thea and Rose-Marie after the girls' stay in Hong Kong, wished to preserve their life in Shanghai, too. They were now busy planning the construction of the new house in Hongqiao. Vilhelm had bought a number of neighbouring lots so that he owned a total of 110 mu (18 acres). A small bungalow was already on the site. This was to be the core of the family's new Danish-inspired house. It was to be called *Sletten* after the area in Denmark where Kirsten had spent her summer vacations as a child, north of Copenhagen.

The name (which is Danish for 'the plain') was also very suitable for Hong-qiao, not a particularly exciting place on the face of it. The area was quite flat with no real vegetation, although there was a small stream. The bungalow was the last building on the road towards the Hongqiao airstrip. Further on there were flat, bare fields interlaced with brooks and rivulets. This was where many of the Shanghai paper hunts took place.

Figure 156: The Danish flag outside Vilhelm and Kirsten's weekend house 'Sletten' could be seen far and wide across the flat terrain at Hongqiao.

Vilhelm and Kirsten made plans for their new grounds. A small lake would be dug and a garden laid out. They sold their houseboat, which for many years had served as a weekend home. The family's boat-keeper, Laodah, was happy to move to Hongqiao with his family and look after the new house. Then the extensive construction started with all the digging and shovelling. Contractors, architects, gardeners and their assistants and many others took part in the project. Kirsten went to Europe with Thea and Rose-Marie in April. Vilhelm remained behind, alone but very busy getting the house and garden in Hongqiao finished.

Thea's Wedding

Once in England, Kirsten took Thea and Rose-Marie to visit Anette and Marie-Louise at Langford Grove. Thea was now 21 years old and wanted to take singing lessons in London. Denmark's envoy to Britain, Count Preben Ahlefeldt-Laurvig and his Russian wife, Mary, long-time friends of the family and resident in London since 1921, had invited Thea to stay with them. This was where she met Kai, the 29-year-old son of the house. He was second lieutenant in the Royal Danish Guards and had taken over Nordenbrogaard, the family farm on Langeland.

In Denmark, Kirsten rented a beautiful house on the Øresund coast for the summer holiday. It belonged to the Dinesen family who lived nearby at Rungsted Lund. Karen Blixen, née Dinesen, who was the same age as Kirsten, had just returned home after many years on her African farm in Kenya. (Under the nom de plume of Isak Dinesen, Karen Blixen would later gain world renown for her book *Out of Africa*.) Kirsten and her four daughters enjoyed the delights of the Danish summer in Rungsted, bathing, playing tennis and visiting with family and friends. In August Kirsten felt under the weather and tired. She entered a private clinic in Copenhagen, but was told that there was nothing wrong with her.

Thea was invited to visit Kai Ahlefeldt-Laurvig on Langeland. She took Marie-Louise along, who proved a very zealous chaperone. Kai did manage to propose, however, and Thea to accept! This took place on 22 August and everyone was delighted. Thea's three sisters were fond of their future brother-in-law, even though it made them sad to think that the quartet of the Meyer sisters could no longer be preserved intact.

Figure 157: Vilhelm and Kirsten's eldest daughter, Thea, was married to Count Kai Ahlefeldt-Laurvig in November 1932 at the Garrison Church in Copenhagen. Thea's three sisters were bridesmaids.

When Count Ahlefeldt in London was informed of the engagement, he immediately sent a congratulatory cable to his old friend in Shanghai. It merely read: 'Congratulations. We'll have beautiful grandchildren.' Not surprisingly, Vilhelm was somewhat taken aback at the message, since news from Kirsten and Thea of the engagement had not yet reached him!

At the beginning it was not clear where and when the wedding would take place. The parents of the bride lived in Shanghai, the parents of the groom lived in London, while most family members and friends lived in Denmark. The wedding date was consequently set for 2 November in Copenhagen.

In October Vilhelm travelled to Copenhagen where the family rented an apartment in the centre of town not far from the church where the wedding was to take place. Vilhelm and Kirsten celebrated their own 23rd wedding anniversary on 27 October. The two youngest girls went to Copenhagen from England to attend the wedding. These were busy days for the entire family with crowds of guests coming and going and hectic wedding preparations.

The only thing that marred their happiness was old Grandmama Ottilie Bramsen, who at 80 felt she was too old to attend. This saddened Kirsten, who still remembered that her mother had not attended her own wedding in Shanghai either.

It was a festive wedding. Among the guests were Crown Prince Frederik, Prince Axel and Princess Margaretha, all of whom had been part of the royal visit to Shanghai a year and a half earlier. The bride's large family, on both the Meyer and the Bramsen sides, were well-represented by the Copenhagen business community while the guests on the groom's side counted family and friends from the large provincial landed estates. There were also Danish friends from China such as Sophus and Minna Black, Henrik and Charlotte Kauffmann, Bent Suenson and Denmark's newly appointed Minister to Peking, Oscar Oxholm and his wife Inge. All in all, 200 guests were invited to the wedding.

The Copenhagen newspapers covered the large wedding with the relish of the popular press. The groom, dressed in the red dress uniform of the Royal Guards, arrived with his parents. When all the guests had found their places in the church everyone waited for the bride and her father:

> A silence falls on the church, but it's a strangely vibrating, excited, unsolemn silence. Then the sound of light, almost jingling horses' hooves is heard outside. The bride's carriage pulls up. Everyone rises and Count Kai Benedikt steps forward to receive his bride. The curtains are pushed aside and the bride stands there for a minute in the opening, on her father's arm. She is all in white, her wedding bouquet is of white carnations and white orchids with dark purple points. Her veil trails several metres behind her on the floor. Behind her and her father walk her three younger sisters, Rose-Marie, Anette and Marie-Louise, dressed in identical light green dresses, carrying bouquets of lilies-of-the-valley. The face of the bride is one large smile, her eyes fixed on the groom who kisses her hand when she reaches him in front of the choir opening. The tones of a psalm are heard from the choir. Then the young couple step up to the altar where they are wedded by Dean Valentiner.
>
> An old wedding psalm concludes the ceremony and the bride and groom followed by the large wedding procession drive off to dinner at the Hôtel D'Angleterre.

Kai and Thea went to Switzerland and Italy on their honeymoon. In Venice they were joined by Vilhelm, Kirsten and Rose-Marie, who were on their way back to Shanghai. More than six months had passed since Kirsten had returned to Europe with her two eldest daughters. They had not planned for Thea to remain in Denmark, but were happy for her. Kirsten's own prolonged engagement had been a trial. Thea's had only lasted a few months.

The happy newly-weds waved goodbye on the wharf as the large ship steamed out of the harbour, its course set for the Far East.

Anette and Marie-Louise had returned to school at Langford Grove. Anette had become a proficient flautist, Marie-Louise played the piano and they both performed at the school's Christmas concert. They spent the Christmas holiday in London with the Ahlefeldt family and Thea and Kai.

Eskelund, the Dentist

Vilhelm, Kirsten and Rose-Marie returned to Shanghai in December 1932. One of their Danish friends in town was Arne Eskelund, one of the founders of the Danish Chamber of Commerce. Eskelund had arrived in Shanghai in 1917 and was an able businessman. His brother, Niels, who had been a dentist in Bangkok for many years, was now in China. Arne had urged him to try to establish himself as a dentist in Shanghai. Niels' son, who later married a Chinese woman, wrote a book about his father in which his father describes his life in the East, *Min Far Trækker Tænder ud* [My father pulls teeth].

The following is the description of Niels Eskelund's arrival in Shanghai by ship up the Whangpoo River in 1932. Thirty years had now passed since Vilhelm Meyer had gone to Shanghai for the first time and, for better or worse, the city had developed into a great international, industrial centre and port:

> I stood in the bow gazing expectantly at the green banks of the river. In the background were stately yellow pagodas and partially hidden behind clumps of bamboo trees were golden temples with graceful upward curving roofs. Flat, broad faces laughed at us from the rocking junks gliding past on the muddy river.
>
> We reached a bend. Suddenly the green fields and small huts disappeared and in their place were ugly grey stone buildings. Clouds of heavy smoke poured out of countless factory chimneys. The river was suddenly transformed into a harbour. Moored alongside the quays were ships with the flags of all the countries of the world fluttering from their masts. There were warships too: British, American and Italian gunboats dwarfed by a grey battle-cruiser. I recognized a Danish ship that I had often seen in Bangkok. It had looked impressively large on the Mekong River, but here it looked like a tugboat.

Arne Eskelund was waiting for him on the quay with his car and chauffeur. Their first stop was the Astor House in Hongkou, the oldest and still one of the best hotels in town:

> The chauffeur made his way through a confusion of rickshaws, bicycles, wheelbarrows and trams as if by magic. Little Japanese girls in colourful kimonos minced by on high wooden sandals, sweating Indian policemen cursed and swore as they vainly attempted to regulate the traffic, cars honked, trams clanged while the Chinese, unmoved and imperturbable, strolled through the chaos as though they were in their own homes.

From the hotel they proceeded to Arne Eskelund's house located in the fashionable villa area at the end of Bubbling Well Road.

First we went tearing along The Bund, Shanghai's business street along the river. Ragged Chinese dock workers sauntered by on the pavement. They didn't seem to belong there at all among the massive Western buildings. The pavements were a sea of pale Chinese faces, slender bodies in long blue tunics, small feet in soft cloth shoes. Strange written characters embellished the colourful posters and deafening Chinese music boomed from the shops' loudspeakers. The crowds soon thinned and we were driving along a wide street – Bubbling Well Road. This was where the race-track, movie theatres and foreign clubs were.

Niels Eskelund later became better acquainted with Shanghai:

Sometimes I had trouble believing I was in China. Hardly any of the foreigners I met had Chinese friends. The only Chinese I had contact with were waiters, rickshaw coolies and business connections. The Shanghai Club was the most exclusive in town. Not even Chiang Kai-shek would have gained admittance unless he had dressed up as a waiter and sneaked in through the back door.

Every day I saw new and fascinating things. Shanghai was truly an international city. In the French Concession there was 'little Moscow' with its onion-shaped church spires, *zakuska* restaurants and thousands of beautiful Russian women with seductive eyes. The population there were refugees from the Russian Revolution and the sworn enemies of the Bolshevik government.

Eskelund also visited the old Chinese section, which constituted original Shanghai:

Here I virtually never saw any other foreigner – Nantao was Chinese territory and the whites felt uncomfortable surrounded by thousands of mysterious yellow faces. For my part there was no more mystery in yellow than in white faces – I felt just as connected to the Chinese as to my own solid countrymen.

The poverty I saw was dreadful but didn't seem to make a particular impression on those who suffered it. For some reason poverty is much more degrading in Europe and America than in the East. There is nothing more depressing than a poor proletarian home in the West. The European poor are always so bitter and troublesome, which the Chinese coolies are not, because they do not consider being poor to be shameful. The Chinese don't worry about all the things they don't have, which may be the reason why they even take poverty in good spirits. They know how to get pleasure from the small things in life. Even the poorest coolie in China can always afford a friendly smile.

New Danish Envoy

In 1932 Minister Kauffmann left the Danish Legation in Peking to assume the position of Danish minister to Norway. He was succeeded by Minister Oscar O`Neill Oxholm, who had embarked for China with his wife and two daughters early in 1933. The family arrived in Shanghai in terrible shape owing to bad weather and extreme changes of temperature on the stretch between Hong Kong and Shanghai. On his arrival in Shanghai in pouring rain, Denmark's new envoy had to be carried ashore on a stretcher with a temperature of almost 40°. In her memoirs of China, Inge Oxholm wrote that she had heard that one didn't get sick in China, 'You just die'! This was hardly an encouraging arrival on Chinese soil.

Figure 158: Oscar O'Neill Oxholm (1889–1949) was Denmark's minister to China from 1932–39. He is shown here at his desk at the Danish Legation in Peking. In 1935 Oxholm moved with the Legation to Shanghai (The Bund no. 26.) Fifteen years later, in 1950, the Danish Legation moved back to Peking, capital of the People's Republic of China.

The Oxholm family spent several weeks in Shanghai, staying at the new Cathay Hotel. When Oxholm had recovered he presented his credentials to the Chinese government in Nanjing. During his stay in Shanghai he also had the opportunity to study political and economic conditions in China. Since Peking was now virtually in the periphery of the vast Chinese area, Shanghai with all its Western consuls, businessmen and press was clearly the best place to follow political developments in China. Many of the foreign diplomats in Peking spent long periods of time in Shanghai.

While the Oxholm family were in Shanghai they became acquainted with many Danes in town including the Meyer family. Inge Oxholm writes the following in her memoirs:

> The Danish community was large, with many prominent personalities, some of whom had very pronounced opinions, but we met most of them and formed many friendships.
>
> Vilhelm Meyer, the general manager, and his lovely wife held a special position in Shanghai and owing to their great hospitality and warmth their home was a gathering place for Danes, Chinese and diplomats as well as leaders of the large foreign commercial houses, led by the British. Everyone was a friend of the house and we met many people there who became very important to us both as friends and purely professionally.

Kirsten's Illness Worsens

Danish church affairs were closely connected to Danish school affairs, the size of the Danish community in Shanghai being crucial to their joint efforts. The figure peaked in the late 1920s with nearly 500 Danes, but began to decrease in the early 1930s. This was primarily due to the Japanese threat. In 1933 Pastor Søe had to admit that the number of Danish churchgoers and the number of Danish school children had now fallen so drastically that there was no longer a sufficient basis to maintain the Danish Church and Danish School in Shanghai. Many Danes were genuinely saddened when Pastor Søe left Shanghai in April 1933, as they realized that his post would not be filled again.

As mentioned above, Bahnson of Great Northern had been elected to the Shanghai Municipal Council in April 1932. At the Danish Society's general assembly in January 1933 the chairman, Vilhelm Meyer, announced that Bahnson would no longer be the Scandinavian candidate since he was returning to Denmark for a prolonged stay. It was a condition for candidacy to the Shanghai Municipal Council that the candidate's place of residence be within the International Settlement and that he pay taxes there. Unfortunately, surveys had shown that no other eligible candidate among the city's Scandinavians was willing to run in April. Vilhelm thus had to note with regret that the 'Danish seat' on the Municipal Council would henceforth have to be relinquished.

Figure 159: In February 1933 the Danish Society arranged a large carnival in Shanghai. Kirsten is shown in the centre. Vilhelm, chairman of the Danish Society, is shown above in a dark costume, just right of the door.

Vilhelm was re-elected a chairman of the Danish Society in China and got his new Danish employee, Elias Gutter, elected as the new board secretary. A few weeks later the Danish Society held its first big function of the year. It was a Danish party and the guests had to be dressed in Danish folk or peasant costumes. The participants could bring guests, but only if they were Scandinavian, too. The party was a success, but it was apparent to everyone that Kirsten Meyer, the wife of the chairman, was not well. She seemed tired and had dark circles around her eyes. Kirsten was ill. She was admitted to hospital in Shanghai where she was diagnosed as having breast cancer. It did not improve her condition when she received a telegram from Denmark informing her of the death of her 80-year-old mother, Ottilie Bramsen.

Vilhelm realized that Kirsten needed treatment. He deemed it advisable for her to go to Stockholm, where cancer research was highly advanced. In the spring of 1933 they left Shanghai onboard the *Bremen*. In Southampton they picked up Anette and Marie-Louise. They continued to Bremerhaven and Hamburg and from there by train to Copenhagen. The family lodged at the Hôtel D'Angleterre. The mood had changed considerably since Thea's wedding a few months earlier.

Figure 160: Anette attended the Carnival arranged by the Danish Society. Here she is with Mogens Pagh of E.A.C., the future president of the company.

Vilhelm and Kirsten continued to Stockholm where Kirsten was admitted to hospital. She insisted that she could manage perfectly well in Stockholm, where she could easily be visited from Copenhagen, and that Vilhelm should therefore return to Shanghai. Sad and lonely, Vilhelm crossed the cold snows of Siberia by train on his way back to Shanghai.

Kirsten was operated on and then treated with radium. In August she spent a summer holiday in Gausdalen, Norway, where she was joined by her three youngest daughters and later by Vilhelm. After another stay in Stockholm,

Kirsten and Vilhelm returned to Copenhagen in September. Kirsten took Anette and Marie-Louise down to Nordenbrogaard on Langeland to visit Thea, who was pregnant. Vilhelm and Rose-Marie again returned to Shanghai.

On 19 September Thea gave birth to a daughter. It was a wonderful experience for Kirsten, so rarely able to take part in important family events in Denmark, to be present at the birth of her first grandchild, who was to be called Kirsten. The christening took place on a cold day in October and Kirsten held her grandchild at the baptismal font. She was pale and quiet, but faced the future with a certain confidence. The operation had gone well and she was looking forward to being with Vilhelm again in Shanghai and decorating the house and garden in Hongqiao. The 49-year-old 'Grandmama' had a good rest at Nordenbrogaard. On 27 October, her wedding anniversary, she looked back to that day 24 years before when she had married Vilhelm. Would they be able to celebrate their silver wedding anniversary in Shanghai with the whole family as they so longed to do?

In November Kirsten returned to China. She had Anette with her while Marie-Louise returned to boarding school in England. The train drove through Germany where the Nazi advance was visible everywhere in the form of flags and swastikas. They sailed from Venice via the Suez Canal to Shanghai, arriving in December.

Vilhelm and Kirsten went out to their house in Hongqiao as often as they could. On the occasion of their large housewarming party, one of their Danish friends gave them a tall, white flagpole complete with a large Danish flag. This was raised in the garden and was visible at a great distance across the flat landscape. Rose-Marie and Anette were eager participants in the traditional paper hunts. The riders often finished their hunt by riding out to the Danish flag that fluttered over the Meyer family's house at 'Sletten'. Tea would be then be served to the sore and tired riders.

The family spent a traditional Christmas Eve in Hongqiao with Danish friends, a Christmas tree and Christmas carols. The next day there was a paper hunt, tea and a large dinner for a number of other friends.Then there was New Year's Eve, celebrated with a dinner and dance at the house on Avenue Road. The guests were in full evening dress and very merry. Kirsten, however, was not well and did not participate. True to tradition, the young people went on to the old British Country Club later in the evening, where they danced long into the night.

Chiang Kai-shek's Campaign against the Communists

Outside Shanghai the situation was tense. Chiang Kai-shek had continued his campaign against the Communist bases, initiating his fourth campaign in April 1933 with 500,000 Nationalist soldiers. Zhou Enlai had been in charge of defending the Chinese Soviet republic in Jiangxi province. The Communists, by a supreme effort, had again succeeded after six months of heavy fighting in beating back the Nationalists. In the course of 1933 the Communist forces had grown to more than 300,000 men.

With the entrance of Hitler on the political scene in Europe, Chiang Kai-shek gained a new ally who shared his inveterate hatred of Communism. Hitler sent a team of 64 German officers to China. Wearing swastika armbands they trained Nationalist troops in modern warfare techniques.

The German officers' strategy, approved by Chiang Kai-shek, was to surround the Communists in Jiangxi. The plan was to build long defence lines of concrete bunkers, thereby enabling the Nationalist government army to cut off the Communists completely from the outside world. The lines could slowly but steadily be moved closer and closer to the Red Army bases. When the noose was finally tightened, escape would be impossible.

At New Year 1933–34 Chiang Kai-shek in Nanjing was planning his fifth military campaign, which he was confident would lead to the final defeat of Communism.

NINETEEN

The Final Years, 1934–1935

Kirsten Leaves Shanghai

In the spring of 1934 the family spent a great deal of time in Hongqiao. Vilhelm would drive to town every day and Kirsten was busy making arrangements to plant the numerous flowers, bushes and trees that had arrived from Denmark. The beautiful Poulsen roses thrived in the new surroundings. The house was now complete. There were ducks and geese in the yard, and Chinese carp were released in the lake.

In her book *Mist on the Window Panes* Anette describes the family's house and garden on the outskirts of Shanghai:

> Mama spent hours in the garden, talking to the gardener and planning improvements. Both she and Papa had spent a great deal of time when in Denmark last, at the famous Poulsen Nurseries and not only roses in great number but also trees taller than a man and bushes of many sorts had been selected and sent off to Shanghai by sea. They arrived at about the same time as we did and – like the fishes – they thrived in their new surroundings. Soil and climate suited them and not long after they had been planted they looked as if they had never grown anywhere else but here in the garden at Hungjao.
>
> This garden was neither completely Chinese nor completely as might be seen in Denmark. A formal rose garden was laid out in front of the house, but instead of a sundial in the middle, there stood four Chinese ladies of marble, holding up a birdbath. Flagged paths twisted through bamboo groves and past other graceful statues of marble that gleamed white against the groups of dark Danish fir trees that stood as background. Two great Ming horses of stone overlooked the lawn where in summer the tennis courts were laid out, Mandarin ducks swam on the lake, their shiny, metallic feathers reflected in the still water, or they settled themselves noisily among the clusters of iris that grew along the edge. A couple of punts were moored to the miniature landing stage and four fat geese with heads held high, waddled single-file over the bridge to their island home – an intricate house of stone that Laodah had built to surprise us – it had windows and a door and a tiny tiled roof of many colours.

Kirsten's illness had made it necessary for Vilhelm and Kirsten to spend a great deal of time away from Shanghai in 1933 so that Vilhelm no longer felt he could satisfactorily carry out the duties of the chairman of the Danish Society in China. At the general assembly of March 1934 he therefore retired completely from the board of the society.

In spite of the operation she had undergone in Stockholm, Kirsten still didn't feel well. She sometimes had very painful headaches and was often bedridden. The headaches grew worse and in April her doctor advised her to go to

Peking for an examination. Kirsten, Anette and Amahsan took the train to Peking where Oscar and Inge Oxholm met them and drove them to the illustrious, old Peking Hotel. The doctors in Peking weren't able to help either and Kirsten returned to Shanghai, discouraged and anxious. The doctors were in no doubt that Kirsten still had cancer and should probably make another trip to Stockholm.

One day in early May when the family was in Hongqiao, Kirsten called Rose-Marie and Anette to her. She told them that she had to go to Europe with Vilhelm and that the two girls would spend their summer holiday at Wei-Hai-Wei as planned, but without their parents this time. As she spoke, calm and collected, tears rolled down her cheeks. The girls had never seen their mother cry before and realized the gravity of the situation. But Kirsten also told them that although she wouldn't be able to celebrate her 50th birthday in China at the end of May, the whole family would be reunited in Shanghai at the large silver wedding celebrations in October.

A few days later Vilhelm and Kirsten sailed past The Bund bound for Europe. Rose-Marie and Anette waved goodbye on the quay. They knew their mother had had cancer, but surely that was over now and if the situation were really serious, wouldn't their parents have taken them along to Denmark? They expected to see them again in a few months.

Kirsten cried quietly as the ship left The Bund. It was almost 25 years since she had sailed up the Huangpu River with her father to marry Vilhelm. She was – at 49 – still beautiful and stately, but the combination of the harsh climate of the East and the ravages of her illness had marked her and she no longer looked young.

Kirsten's 50th birthday on 31 May 1934, was no festive occasion. Vilhelm and Kirsten were in Stockholm, where Kirsten underwent further examinations. In June they both returned to Denmark. Kirsten, after a visit to Nordenbrogaard, was admitted to hospital near Elsinore where she felt she was in good hands. One of the attending physicians was young Niels Krarup, engaged to Kirsten's niece, Kirsten Heering. She was the daughter of Vilhelm's sister, Emilie, and had been named after her Shanghai aunt.

Vilhelm was aware of the gravity of the situation, but could not imagine a life without Kirsten by his side. Living with Kirsten was the way things should be. She was the most important element of his life. If, or rather when she died, he had no desire to remain in Shanghai. Nothing indicated that his four daughters would remain in the Far East. Rose-Marie was a possible exception as she was seeing a good deal of Hugh Barton, a young businessman. He was the son of the former British Consul-General in Shanghai, Sir Sidney Barton, and had a promising future in Jardine, Matheson & Co. But Vilhelm was also aware that Shanghai's special status would soon be history.

The portents of the political and military upheavals that lay ahead were clear enough. The international economic depression, which had set its mark on the rest of the world a few years before, had finally reached China. From the record year of 1931–32, China's exports had fallen by almost 50 per cent and imports by 35 per cent. Trade was stagnating and Shanghai's economic climate was clearly deteriorating.

On the political scene, the battle between the Nationalists and the Communists was in full swing. In February 1934 Chiang Kai-shek had mounted his fifth campaign involving over a million Nationalist soldiers. The Kuomintang forces and their advisors, the German officers, had commenced operations to isolate the Communists in Jiangxi province. The soldiers had orders to shoot anything that moved within the cut-off area, including the local peasants.

The future of China was not only decided by domestic, political conditions. Hitler was preparing for war in Europe and Japan's territorial ambitions in the East had led to the first Japanese annexations and attacks on China.

During his stay in Copenhagen Vilhelm mulled over his family's future. Kirsten was ill, his own health was not so good anymore, and the political situation was worsening. This all made it clear to him that he would probably have to sell his business assets in China before it was too late. His most important asset was the block of shares in Andersen, Meyer & Co. Ltd, for which the best buyer would be International General Electric in New York. Not only did the company control a large share unit already, but it also had the economic clout to continue A. M. & Co. in China despite imminent international upheavals. The G.E. management had previously expressed an interest in taking over Vilhelm's holdings.

Kirsten and Vilhelm agreed that Vilhelm should return to China. Thea and Kai would visit Shanghai in October. Thea would remain and return to Denmark with Rose-Marie and Anette in the spring and Vilhelm would follow them to Denmark in June. So on 8 August Vilhelm set sail from Cherbourg on *H.M.S Majestic* bound for New York where he intended to discuss the future of Andersen, Meyer & Co. with General Electric. From there he would continue on to Vancouver and Shanghai. However, he had just arrived in New York on 14 August when he received telegrams from Thea, Mille and Kirsten's physician informing him that Kirsten had had a serious relapse. He returned immediately on the same ship to Cherbourg and from there to Elsinore, where it was apparent that the end was near.

From Elsinore he wrote a letter to his two daughters in Wei-Hai-Wei, Rose-Marie and Anette, now 21 and 17 years old. The letter was dated 28 August 1934 and was written in English:

My own Darlings,

It has been terrible to send you the telegrams I have sent you this week – but I felt you would wish to know the truth rather than suddenly be faced with the great sorrow which is staring us in the face.

As I wrote you before when I left for China, Mama seemed to have recovered – the doctors were satisfied that it was a matter of rest only – the doctor here was satisfied that the eye trouble was rheumatism and would clear up – a few days after however she suddenly got a relapse and when Doctor Berwin visited her on the 12th of August he was definitely certain that it was cancer which had attacked her eye and spread attacking her liver and lung. He told Mille that there was no hope, but only a matter of time – days, weeks or months, he couldn't tell – but definitely no hope. I arrived in New York on the 14th, got a telegram from Thea who immediately got up here and I arrived back at Montebello on the 23rd.

My darlings, I didn't know a person could change in two weeks as Mama had. She was glad to see me and knew me – she spoke in a whisper only but was quite clear in her mind – had no idea how ill she was and did not suffer – the doctors saw to that. I haven't left her since, but day by day she has grown weaker. Today she doesn't even know me or Thea – These are terrible days darlings and in a way I am glad you are spared them and will remember your mother as you saw her last. I don't believe she can live many days more. Thea and Kaj have been marvellous but it has nearly broken Thea down – Marie-Louise saw Mama two days ago and will hardly see her again. She is staying with Aunt Mille.

Darlings, my thoughts are with you all the time – it must be terrible for you to go and wait for the message which of course you have understood is bound to come soon – and I hope I have done right in preparing you for it, than to wait till all is over. You know how I love you and although I realize that neither I nor anything can compensate you for the loss of Mama – I will try to make your future as happy as we all know she would like it to be.

Love to you darlings from Papa

Kirsten Dies in Denmark

Kirsten passed away peacefully on 30 August 1934, at Montebello Hospital. Vilhelm and Thea were at her side. The sad news was cabled to Rose-Marie and Anette in Wei-Hai-Wei and to Marie-Louise at Langford Grove.

Sophus Black, the family's old friend from Peking, who had just returned to Denmark after 30 years in China, wrote an obituary in the Danish newspaper *Berlingske Aftenavis,* which beautifully sums up Kirsten and Vilhelm's happy life in the East:

> Nowhere will the news of Mrs Kirsten Meyer's death be received with greater and more genuine grief than in the Far East – by many, many Chinese, by the Danes spread to the far corners of China, and by the international and Danish communities in Shanghai.
>
> Throughout the 25 years Mrs Kirsten lived there, the East was her home and from the very first she was the centre of a large circle of friends of all nations, who gathered in the hospitable home on Avenue Road in Shanghai, well-known to any Dane who has ever visited China. Her tall, elegant and erect figure was universally admired and her gentle, calm, graceful air captivated everyone. Her great generosity and goodness made her universally loved and respected. Add to this a strong artistic sense joined to a highly developed and refined taste, and it is no wonder that her gifts were made use of on whatever occasion such talents might be required. She was a true helpmate to her husband and her rare qualities were an excellent support in his vast, far-flung business, which represents the biggest American firms in the world. In America the best families in the banking and business world were to be counted among her best friends. It was typical of her that in the place of honour in her salon hung a large portrait of her husband's first Chinese comprador.

Figure 161: Kirsten died of cancer on 30 August 1934, at the age of 50.

Black also mentioned the old Manchu palace in Peking, which formed the setting for the Chinese antiques, 'chosen with love and appreciation of the distinctive art of an ancient culture before it had become fashionable among foreigners to recognize it'.

Kirsten Meyer had once told Black that she had had so much happiness in her life that there surely must be trouble ahead.

> But she accepted trouble and illness in the same gentle, quiet way with never a word of complaint. And she, who seemed to have many, many bright years before her, is now dead. We, her friends from the East, express our thanks for all the rich memories she has given us.

In Shanghai Captain Bahnson informed the *Shanghai Times*, which printed a full obituary on 1 September 1934:

Mrs Vilhelm Meyer

Shanghai residents will hear with deep regret of the death of Mrs Vilhelm Meyer, wife of the head of Andersen, Meyer & Co., Shanghai, which occurred at Elsinore, Denmark on August 30. Mrs Meyer had been in bad health, and with her husband, sailed for home in the spring of this year. It was naturally hoped that the trip, and a period in her own country, would restore her to health, but unfortunately such was not the case, and she passed away as stated.

Sincere sympathy will be extended to her husband and her four daughters; and of the latter, Thea, the eldest was married last year to Count Ahlefeldt-Laurvig, son of the Danish Minister to St James, London, and a member of one of the oldest and most distinguished families in Denmark. Rosemarie and Anette are at present in Wei-Hai-Wei, and Marie-Louise, the youngest, is in England at school.

The deceased was, before her marriage, a Miss Kirsten Bramsen, daughter of Mr Aage Bramsen, the head of a big insurance company in Copenhagen. She came to Shanghai accompanied by her father 25 years ago, and she and Mr Meyer were to have celebrated their silver wedding shortly.

Gifted with a strong artistic sense, Mrs Meyer possessed some talent as a painter in oils and water colours, and this artistry showed itself to a remarkable extent in the tasteful arrangement of her own home. She was always a great and gracious hostess, and her fine social sense contributed in no small way to the success which her husband enjoyed here. Of a handsome appearance with exquisite taste in dress, Mrs Meyer was always an outstanding personality at any social gathering which she graced.

Her first interest was always her family and her home, but she had wide sympathies and never turned a deaf ear to any charitable demand.

It will be remembered that she did a great deal for the British troops from the time they were first stationed in Shanghai, and members of all nationalities have frequently received general assistance from this lady.

Her social circle here was a wide one, and she numbered members of almost all nations among her personal friends. The Danish community always relied upon her to give the artistic and decorative touch to their functions and by her own countrymen and women and many others Mrs Meyer will be greatly missed.

At home in Denmark the funeral service took place at Bisbebjerg Crematorium. Many of the people who had celebrated Thea's wedding less than two years before, when Kirsten had still been in good health, came to the crematorium to bid her farewell. A string quartet played Tchaikovsky. The service concluded as the congregation sang Kirsten's favourite psalm. There were also many wreaths and flowers from far-off friends in the United States and China. The urn was buried in Vestre Cemetery in Copenhagen.

Vilhelm Returns to Shanghai

It was a numb, emotionally paralyzed Vilhelm who left the cemetery. Life had become unreal and empty and he felt depressed and weak. He was no longer in any doubt that Shanghai would soon be a finished chapter for him and his daughters. He was anxious to start winding up his affairs in the East and from Copenhagen he proceeded directly to New York.

He negotiated with Clark Minor, who had been vice-president of International General Electric from 1924–25 when he succeeded Anson W. Burchard as president of I.G.E. Throughout the intervening years Vilhelm and Minor had built up a solid relationship of goodwill and trust. The two friends agreed that G.E. should buy up Vilhelm's holdings in A. M. & Co. As the price would have to depend on the total value of the business, it was deemed advisable for Minor to travel to Shanghai in order to assess the financial situation.

Vilhelm took the train to Vancouver with Clark Minor and his wife Allice, and from there sailed on the *Empress of Canada* to China. Li Ming, Vilhelm's old friend from Shanghai, was also on board during the long voyage across the Pacific. Kirsten had only been dead for a little over a month and Vilhelm was not himself. He couldn't sleep and often wondered restlessly around the deck at night without an overcoat. He caught pneumonia and had to stay in bed.

The ship's doctor realized that this was not merely a case of pneumonia, but that Vilhelm also had pernicious anaemia, a malignant form of anaemia. The doctor informed Clark Minor in confidence that Vilhelm Meyer did not have long to live. On 3 October Vilhelm, knowing he was dying, insisted on making his will. He gave directions on the shipping company's writing paper that after his death his body was to be cremated and the ashes brought back to Denmark to be buried next to Kirsten's. His four daughters were to divide the assets he left between them. His two employees, Elias Gutter and Valdemar Steensby, were to serve as executors of the estate in Shanghai. In connection with the realization of the estate's assets, they were to employ the following advisors: Ludvig Trier, broker, in Copenhagen, Li Ming, bank director, and Michel Speelman, director, in Shanghai. In addition, he particularly requested Clark Minor in the United States to look after the interests of the four heirs in connection with the sale of the A. M. & Co. stock. The will was signed on board ship by Vilhelm, with Clark Minor and Li Ming as witnesses.

As things stood, Clark Minor thought it would be best for Vilhelm's two daughters, Rose-Marie and Anette, who were staying with the Oxholm family in Peking at the time, to join their father on the last stage of the voyage from Yokohama to Shanghai. Minor cabled Oxholm from the ship. Rose-Marie and Anette, accompanied by A. M. & Co.'s Tianjin branch manager, hurried to Yokohama where they were reunited with their father on board the *Empress of Canada*. They accompanied him on the last stage of the voyage to Shanghai. They could see that their father was very ill, but did not yet realize how serious it was. He was overjoyed to see them. Lying in his cabin he presented them with some of the jewellery Kirsten had asked him to give them a few weeks before.

In Shanghai he was immediately taken by ambulance to Country Hospital. On his silver wedding anniversary he lay in his hospital room, remembering 27 October 1909, that beautiful, sunny day 25 years ago. He had shared 25 wonderful years with Kirsten. This was so different from the large silver wedding party they had both so much been looking forward to. After a few weeks' stay in hospital, Vilhelm insisted on going home to Avenue Road. Almost six months had passed since he had left his house in Shanghai.

Clark Minor remained in Shanghai for six weeks studying Andersen, Meyer & Co.'s financial assets. He drew up a contract which he and Vilhelm signed on 23 November. General Electric would take over the stocks, all of which were in New York, and the cash price for them would be deposited in Vilhelm's bank account in New York. The conclusion of the negotiations was celebrated with a dinner for Clark and Allice Minor at home on Avenue Road.

This had not been an easy task for Clark Minor. He had known Vilhelm for a number of years and they had established an excellent spirit of co-operation and a solid friendship. Minor had no children himself and felt very close to the

Figure 162: Clark H. Minor (1878–1967) succeeded Anson Burchard as president of International General Electric Company in 1925. In December 1934 Minor bought Vilhelm's stocks in A. M. & Co. for I.G.E. When Vilhelm Meyer died in 1935, Minor succeeded him as president of A. M. & Co. until 1945 and also succeeded William de Krafft as chairman of the board of the company from 1937 to 1950.

four Meyer girls. Nor was it easy to protect the buyer's interests while looking out for the welfare of the seller's heirs. Minor felt, however, that he had drawn up a fair contract.

In early December Clark and Allice Minor took leave of Vilhelm and returned to the United States. It felt strange to Vilhelm no longer having any financial interest in the firm he had started in Shanghai almost 30 years before. But he knew that as a businessman it was always vital to know the right time to buy and sell, and his position was clear. His business arrangements meant that his four daughters were no longer bound to Shanghai in the event of his imminent death.

The Long March

Chiang Kai-shek's ruthless war against the Communists in Jiangxi continued into the autumn of 1934. Decimated, the Red Army was faced with total annihilation if no attempt was made to break through the Nationalists' stranglehold and join up with other Red Army bases in China. On 16 October the Communists seized the initiative, breaking through the white Nationalists' lines. This was the start of the heroic and gruelling expedition across China later known as the Long March. Around 100,000 men fought their way out of Jiangxi province, making their way up to Shaanxi province in northwestern China. It would take a whole year before they reached their goal and 80,000 soldiers would die along the way either in combat or of exhaustion. Those who reached Yan'an after a year's march across China had covered 6,000 kilometres on foot.

On 7 January 1935 the Red forces took the city of Zunyi in Guizhou province. The casualties resulting from breaking through the Nationalist blockade had been enormous. Half of the original 100,000 men had been killed as they crossed the Xiang River, the last of the main Nationalist blockade lines. It was time to reconsider political and military strategies.

Over the next few days a stormy meeting took place in Zunyi in the C.C.P. Politburo. Mao Zedong's views carried the day. Mao had felt for a long time that the military leaders were making a big mistake by having the soldiers march through the countryside in one long column. He thought they should apply the mobility and guerrilla tactics he himself had used in the Jiangxi period – marching in several columns and carrying out lightning raids. Mao also opposed the C.C.P. leaders' dogma that the primary C.C.P. recruiting base should be the urban workers rather than the peasants in the rural districts. His ideas were supported at the Zunyi meeting by a number of leading Communists, including Zhu De, Liu Shaoqi, Lin Biao, Deng Xiaoping and Zhou Enlai. At this meeting, which proved to be a turning point in the history of the Chinese Revolution, Mao became the new leader of the Communists.

Figure 163: The two comrades-in-arms, Mao Zedong and Zhou Enlai, led the Communists' fight against Chiang Kai-shek's Nationalists. They are shown here in Yan'an in 1935 after the Long March.

When Edgar Snow, the American writer, later visited Yan'an – as the first Western journalist – it struck him that peasants and workers were not the only ones to take part in the Long March. He met several well-educated Chinese, too, who had left well-paid, secure positions to join the Communist movement. Some of them had worked for large foreign firms, such as Jardine, Matheson & Co. and Andersen, Meyer & Co – and had excellent recommendations to show for it.

In his book *Red Star over China*, Snow tells the story of Chu Tso-chih (Zhu Zuo-zhi), one of the well-educated Chinese, an engineer, who as a young man had written a textbook for engineering students and had been employed by the Shanghai Power Company. After several years with Andersen Meyer & Co., Zhu had set up his own lucrative engineering consulting firm. Edgar Snow continues:

> Until recently he had a practice of $10,000 a year in South China, where he was a consulting engineer and efficiency man, and had given it up and left his family to come up to these wild dark hills of Shensi and offer his services to the Reds for nothing. Incredible! The background of this phenomenon traced to a beloved grandfather, a famous philanthropist of Ningpo, whose deathbed injunction to young Chu had been to 'devote his life to raising the cultural standard of the masses'. And Chu had decided the quickest method was the Communist one.
>
> Chu had come into the whole business somewhat melodramatically, in the spirit of the martyr and zealot. It was a solemn thing for him; he thought it meant an early death, and he expected everyone else to feel that way. I believe he was a little shocked when he found so much that he considered horseplay going on, and everybody apparently happy. When I asked him how he liked it, he replied gravely that he had but one serious criticism. 'These people spent entirely too much time singing!' he complained. 'This is no time to be singing!'

Vilhelm Dies in Shanghai

Anette, having contracted appendicitis, spent most of December in hospital. Vilhelm's condition grew worse again so he too was hospitalized. On 21 December Vilhelm formalized his will, which was duly attested by Vice-Consul Mogens Melchior, then serving as acting Consul-General while Ove Lunn was on leave in Denmark.

Vilhelm and Anette were both discharged on 22 December and true to tradition they held a Danish Christmas Eve at home with Rose-Marie and Anette as the hostesses. Vilhelm, however, was not well enough to join the party and had to remain upstairs in bed. Over the following days he rallied a little. Close friends with whom he could joke and laugh visited him, but everyone knew his days were numbered.

He told Rose-Marie and Anette that he was in communication with Kirsten, who often called to him, and that he would die soon. He remained in his room where his two daughters could sit by his bedside talking with him. Although only 56 years old, he had become an old man within a short time. Anette later described her sick father:

> His thick hair was now quite white and was a little longer than usual. He looked like a lion in captivity but there was strength in him yet. His broad shoulders

Figure 164: Mogens G.I. Melchior (b. 1903) was acting Consul-General when Vilhelm returned to Shanghai in October 1934. Melchior, as the highest Danish authority, witnessed Vilhelm's will as public notary and took charge of the funeral arrangements after Vilhelm's death. Melchior was also the executor of Vilhelm's estate and made arrangements for Rose-Marie's and Anette's continued stay in Shanghai.

were not bowed though the coat wrinkled loosely, no longer filled out, and his hands, small for such a big man, lay quietly inactive in his lap. He had a big, heavy head, but his features were delicate, and his grey eyes that sloped a little downwards, were staring into space at something we could not see. Again I felt as I had when a child – small and insignificant beside him. Suddenly he turned to us and smiled: 'Twenty-five years. And every year better than the last. Till now. How lucky I have been.'

In Peking Minister Oxholm knew that Vilhelm did not have long to live. On 2 January he wrote to Melchior in Shanghai letting him know of Mrs Oxholm's imminent arrival in Shanghai so as to be of use to Rose-Marie and Anette. Oxholm mentioned in the letter that Vilhelm's close friend, Carl Johan Knipschildt, had told him in confidence that 'it's been a long time since Meyer's affairs have been in such good order'. He wrote about Meyer's illness:

It seems incomprehensible to me that nothing can be done to save the life of this strong man, but according to the doctors there is no hope. I received a New Year's telegram from Meyer, the wording of which seemed to indicate that he had sent it personally. I couldn't help hoping there might be a slight chance of his pulling through and that we might be able to keep him for a time in Shanghai. His death will be felt here as a great loss to us Danes in so many ways.

On 8 January Vilhelm slept all day. There was no contact with him and in the afternoon, a little past 5 p.m., he quietly passed away. The news of Vilhelm Meyer's death rapidly spread throughout Shanghai. Two rabbis were among the first to arrive at Avenue Road prepared to take charge of the funeral ceremonies. Rose-Marie and Anette, both of whom were christened and confirmed, were uncertain what to do. Although their father was of Jewish descent, he had never been a believer. Indeed, their mother was actually buried at Vestre Cemetery in Denmark where their father also wished to be buried. They hurriedly telephoned an old Jewish friend of the family, the lawyer, Ellis Hayim, and explained the situation. Hayim explained to the two rabbis that there would be no Jewish funeral and two days later the funeral services were held at International Funeral Directors. Many of the family's Danish, English, American and Chinese friends attended the beautiful ceremony. Several of the mourners had respected the request not to send flowers, but instead made a donation to the Danish Charity Society or the Ladies' Benevolent Society.

First Vilhelm's Russian friend, V. Shushlin, sang Beethoven's 'In Questa Tomba Oscura' accompanied by Maestro Mario Paci on the piano. This was followed by a Danish psalm, sung by the Danish participants. Michel Speelman spoke about Vilhelm's great business contribution to China. Captain Bahnson of Great Northern spoke about Vilhelm's numerous activities in China, stressing his work for the Danish community. Another Danish psalm was sung, and finally Shushlin sang 'Wolfram's Song to the Evening Star' from Wagner's *Tannhäuser*, a song Vilhelm himself had loved to sing. In the song Wolfram begs the evening star to send a greeting to Tannhäuser's beloved Elizabeth, who has just died.

At the same time, 1,000 miles away, in Zunyi, Guizhou province, the Communists were embarking on their epoch-making meeting of the Politburo. As mentioned above, 41-year-old Mao Zedong was put in charge of the Communist Party and the Long March to the north. This was to prove the beginning of a radically new chapter in China's long history, but no one outside Zunyi realized this at the time.

'The Greatest Dane in the East'

There were full obituaries in the Chinese and Danish newspapers. The *North China Daily News* printed a long description of Vilhelm Meyer's life in China from the early years under the empire to the final years as president of one of the largest foreign firms in China. Vilhelm Meyer was characterized in the following terms:

> Big men have a reputation for a good humour and friendliness, and that certainly was the case with Mr Meyer, for a smile accompanied his gigantic form in whatever company he might be, and with him there were no hard and fast rules as to social distinctions. A man of any degree, once met in business or the social whirl, he counted as a friend for all time and he never would pass without a cheery word or a smile of recognition. Even leaving out his widespread business connections and his public work, this big, hearty, friendly, and courteous gentleman will be greatly missed in many parts of the Far East, and particularly in Shanghai.

The Shanghai Municipal Council paid a glowing tribute in the *Municipal Gazette* to Vilhelm Meyer's long-term contribution to several of the Municipal

Figure 165: When Vilhelm died this plate was presented to the G.E. and A. M. & Co. headquarters in New York: IN MEMORY OF V. MEYER, FOUNDER AND PRESIDENT OF ANDERSEN, MEYER & CO. LTD 1906–1935.

Council committees. The Municipal Council flag was flown at half-mast on the administration building.

A few days after the funeral another Shanghai newspaper commented on the numerous tributes to Vilhelm's largeness of heart and personal generosity.

> During the last few days many warm tributes have been paid to the memory of the late Mr Vilhelm Meyer, whose funeral took place on Thursday. Not the least of the tributes have come from the most unexpected quarters, which have revealed the extent of Mr Meyer's personal generosity and largeness of heart.

Stories have been told of the most unexpected offers of help to men and women whose misfortunes had been brought to his notice. Moreover he showed an unfailing capacity for giving assistance to young people who, being newcomers to Shanghai, required guidance and encouragement amid the strangeness of this cosmopolitan city. Mr Meyer had a particular knack of winning confidence and of making it clear that, in spite of his many activities, he was always ready to help lame dogs over stiles or to offer hospitality which so magically disappears in a foreign land.

A resolution was passed at a meeting of the board of Andersen, Meyer & Co. in New York expressing sincere grief at Vilhelm Meyer's all too early demise. His New York connections emphasized his outstanding 'ability to convey to his hearers vivid pictures of his business, his problems, his many interests and the constantly changing conditions in those vast provinces of China in which the business of his transactions was transacted'. Vilhelm's business crisis of 1920 – 22 is described as follows:

> When the Pacific Development Company was at its zenith, an exchange of shares was accepted by Meyer, and Andersen, Meyer & Co. became a part of the ambitious business dream which came to such a rude awakening when the values of commodities fell in 1920. The relationship was severed and with the assistance of his friends, Meyer reorganized the company and started up the hard hill of recovery. The task has taken nearly 15 years of work under world conditions of extreme difficulty, but throughout those years his courage never faltered, and now his work is over.

The resolution was sent to his four daughters in Shanghai with the expression of the board's deepest condolences.

The Danish papers, too, printed full obituaries. Under the headline 'Vilhelm Meyer, the Greatest Dane in the East, is Dead' the newspaper *Politiken* described the '100 dollar firm which became the million dollar enterprise Andersen, Meyer & Co.'. It was now one of the biggest enterprises in Shanghai, the article went on. Life in China had suited Vilhelm Meyer admirably. Opportunities always await those who have the eyes to see them, continued *Politiken*. 'Meyer could see them and was not afraid to seize them even though the gamble entailed a certain risk'. *Politiken* continued:

> He was both able and humane. Having a man like Vilhelm Meyer as their countryman meant a great deal to the Danes in Shanghai. He and his wife were very hospitable and numerous young Danes established valuable connections in their home. He continued to feel that he was a Dane and was only superficially marked by the great foreign sphere in which he worked.
>   It was characteristic of him that over the years the business he created has dealt in just about everything – except war equipment. He believed in China as the market of the future but whenever wars or revolution swept the country he always adopted a wait-and-see policy and he never took sides. Consequently he was more highly esteemed in the turbulent East than most.

Several Danish newspapers also mentioned Vilhelm and Kirsten's legendary social life and Vilhelm's great talent as a singer. The newspaper *Dagens Nyheder* wrote that all touring celebrities were guests of the house as a matter of course.

'Vilhelm Meyer lived in style and there was always the intoxicating air of a party about him.'

Vilhelm's two old friends from Shanghai, Sophus Black and Paul N. Forum, wrote in *Dansk Samvirkes* journal about Vilhelm's business career in the Far East:

> From the very beginning Meyer realized what China's awakening meant for its industrial development and he concentrated his energies on the gradual yet rapid build-up of his organization with this development in mind. Meyer's idea was to provide the necessary technical know-how for the rather unformed ideas put forth by provinces, cities or individual Chinese. He was successful in carrying out his ideas, gradually gathering about himself a staff of able, young engineers and businessmen with training in different fields. Whenever possible Vihelm Meyer always sought to attach young Danes to the enterprise and although, as things developed, it became necessary to hire engineers of other nationalities to carry out tasks in which large American specialist firms such as General Electric Co. had an interest, there are nevertheless still Danes in the firm in senior positions who have been with him from the beginning.

Forum and Black emphasized Vilhelm's personal charm, which helped win him numerous and influential friends wherever he went and which resulted in close connections with a number of leading world enterprises for which A. M. & Co. was the sole agent in China. They also emphasized the excellent cooperation Vilhelm had enjoyed with the Chinese for many years. Vilhelm's two old friends from China sum up in the following terms:

> In conclusion we would like to quote the two last lines of a letter signed by Mr William de Krafft, chairman of the board of Andersen, Meyer & Co., a statement which will serve as an appropriate epitaph, for it clearly shows the high esteem in which he was held:
>
> 'With the death of Vilhelm Meyer we have all lost a close friend, the company has lost its greatest asset and the world has lost an exciting and colourful personality.'

Vilhelm's funerary urn was shipped from Shanghai to Copenhagen, where it was buried in Vestre Cemetery next to Kirsten's. Only four months had passed since Kirsten's funeral.

TWENTY

Epilogue

After the transfer of power in 1949, China's borders were more or less closed to foreigners for many years. Vilhelm's and Kirsten's daughters had thus no idea what had become of the Meyer's home and business premises in China. But in 1991–92, when the country had again embarked on an 'open door' policy in regard to the outside world, it was possible for me to visit the places the family had frequented in China.

As will already have become apparent, this book is built up chronologically, and in principle it ends with Vilhelm's death in January 1935. However, in order to frame the events of the past in a contemporary perspective, in the following pages I trace a number of aspects up to the present day.

Shanghai Becomes Chinese

The Communists' Long March ended in October 1935 in the city of Yan'an in Shaanxi province. Mao Zedong and his Red Army had succeeded in surviving Chiang Kai-shek's five campaigns. In 1937 Japan attacked China, and Japanese troops marched on Peking and Shanghai. The common enemy from without united the two warring factions for a time, causing them to co-operate in taking joint action against Japan.

In the autumn of 1937 Japanese units fought Chinese Nationalist troops for supremacy over Shanghai. Once again, as in 1932, Shanghai's International Settlement and the French Concession kept out of the actual fighting. Once again the victorious Japanese occupied Shanghai. The Japanese also took Peking and Tianjin. Nanjing, for 10 years the seat of the Nationalist government, fell at the end of the year in a bloody massacre. Chiang Kai-shek moved the seat of his government further inland to Chongqing in Sichuan province. Refugees poured into Shanghai. By the end of 1937 the combined population of the two international sections, which at the start of 1937 numbered 1.3 million, had increased to a total of 4 million inhabitants.

The Shanghailanders' privileged position came to an end in December 1941 with the Japanese attack on Pearl Harbor, which drew the United States into World War II. All foreign residents of Shanghai who were citizens of one of the Allied countries were interned by the Japanese. Many of Vilhelm's and Kirsten's American and English friends, including Lewis and Hope Andrews, were forced to spend several years in Japanese prison camps at various places in China. Since Denmark was occupied by Germany, the Danish Shanghailanders were free to remain in Shanghai.

In January 1943 the Allies agreed to comply with China's long-held wish to abolish the old, unequal treaties. Thus the remaining exterritorial rights, which had benefited Shanghai's foreign population for a whole century, came to an end almost overnight. The free city of Shanghai did not exist any more. The Shanghailanders were not consulted by their home countries. Indeed, most of them were in Japanese prisoner-of-war camps.

After Japan's surrender in August 1945, Chiang Kai-shek's Nationalist troops occupied Shanghai. The following year marked the start of the final confrontation between Chiang Kai-shek and Mao Zedong in a civil war that was to last for several years. The Communists were the victors. Slowly but surely the People's Liberation Army won back province after province from the Nationalists. In May 1949 units of the P.L.A. under the command of Marshal Chen Yi succeeded in taking Shanghai without a struggle. Several months later, in October 1949 at Tiananmen Square in Peking, Mao Zedong proclaimed the founding of the People's Republic of China. At Mao's side stood not only his faithful comrades from the Long March, including Zhu De, Zhou Enlai and Liu Shaoqi, but also Sun Yat-sen's widow, Soong Qing Ling, who had openly joined the Communist side, believing that her sister, Soong Meiling, had betrayed the revolutionary cause by marrying the Nationalist leader, Chiang Kai-shek.

During the final phase of the civil war, Chiang Kai-shek was forced to flee to the island of Formosa (Taiwan) with his Nationalist supporters. The government of the Republic of China remained in control of the island, where they were joined by several of the Triad gang leaders. Many members of the Shanghai Chinese business community, including Li Ming and James Lee, chose to settle in Hong Kong.

Postwar Sino–Danish relations

The Danish Consulate General in Shanghai had moved from Avenue Dubail in the French Concession to The Bund no. 26 in 1931. Shanghai had become increasingly interesting to the foreign legations, many of which moved there from Peking, since it was closer to Nanjing (the seat of the Nationalist government from 1927) than to Peking. The Danish Legation moved to Shanghai in 1935, sharing the address on The Bund with the Danish Consulate General.

Denmark was among the first Western countries to recognize Mao Zedong's new Peking government after the transfer of power to the Communists in 1949. On 9 January 1950 the formal recognition took place, and on 11 May 1950 diplomatic relations were established between the Kingdom of Denmark and the People's Republic of China. Minister Alexis Mørch presented his credentials to Chairman Mao Zedong in Peking on 24 June 1950.

The new China had no use for foreign consulates and within a short time the Danish Consulates in Harbin, Tianjin, Qingdao, Hankou, Xiamen and Guangzhou were closed down. The Danish Legation in Shanghai was transferred back to Peking. The Danish Consulate General in Shanghai, whose task it now was to assist the remaining Danes in their conversion of Danish firms into an acceptable Chinese model, continued to be in operation for a number of years. The last Danish civil servant in Shanghai was Uffe Himmelstrup, who left the Consulate General in 1957. The Consulate continued to operate with a Chinese staff until 1963 when it was finally closed down.

In 1956 China and Denmark agreed to strengthen their diplomatic ties by converting their legations into embassies and appointing their envoys as ambassadors. In June 1974 the Danish Embassy in Peking moved to the newly established embassy quarter, Sanlitun, in the northeastern section of Peking. At the entrance to the ambassador's residence sits a large, beaming stone figure of Buddha – Darduse. For many years he has contemplated the countless Chinese and Danes visiting the Danish envoys and ambassadors to Peking. He probably also remembers Johannes V. Jensen, Johannes Poulsen, Sophus Black, Vilhelm Meyer and all the other Danes, who in the early part of the century so delighted in the merry Darduse.

After China re-opened its doors in the early 1980s there was once again a need for foreign consulates. The Danish government resolved to establish a consulate general in Shanghai. Svend Auken, Danish minister for energy and environment, together with Sha Lin, the deputy mayor of Shanghai, reopened the Royal Danish Consulate General in 1994. I was given the post of Danish Consul-General in Shanghai and the following year I was appointed Denmark's ambassador to China.

In April 1999 the Royal Danish Consulate General in Guangzhou was re-opened by the Danish Minister of Health, Carsten Koch and by Vice-Governor, Li Lanfang.

The Buildings

The Old Manchu Palace in Peking

In my quest to find Vilhelm Meyer's former houses, I met in Copenhagen with Sophus and Minna Black's eldest son, Christen Black, who had been born in Peking in 1918. In the end this led me to the old Manchu palace in Peking.

On a visit to Peking in 1991, I spent a few hours wandering around the area east of the Imperial Palace with an old photograph as my only clue. This search proved fruitless, although it did give me the opportunity to admire many beautiful courtyards whose surrounding grey-roofed, low buildings still bore witness to the old Peking. Nevertheless I was on the right track. The conclusive information was provided by Mr Feng, the waiter of the Danish ambassador and his wife, William and Alice Friis-Møller. Mr Feng remembered the name of the little lane, Hutong Da Yuan Bao, in which the house was believed to have been located. The lane, now called Hutong Da Yuan Fu, is located behind the Hotel Peking and there we found the old compound.

In the beginning I wasn't completely sure this was the right place. However, certain carvings on the red doors were one of the things that proved to me I was on the right track. Everything looked quite different from in the old photographs. The main building was not easily recognizable, chiefly because the liv-

Figure 166: I succeeded in locating the Meyer family's old Manchu palace in 1991. The main building, which was the core of Great Northern Telegraph Company's Danish Mess at the start of the century, today forms part of Donghuamen Hospital.

ing area had been extended so that the covered veranda corridors were now incorporated into the building itself.

Today the buildings are part of Peking's Donghuamen Hospital and what was formerly the main building is now a dentist's clinic. The clinic assistant showed us the spots on the columns and the ceiling where paintings from imperial times were still visible, when the house had been inhabited by the Manchu prince and his family. In a small corridor I could see the ceiling joists with their painted birds, animals and landscapes, which my mother had contemplated as a little girl in the 1920s and later described in her memoirs of China. The Black family's house on the little hill was still there, too.

A. M. & Co., the Biggest American Firm in Shanghai

I visited Shanghai for the first time in 1991. Many of the old buildings from the 1920s and 1930s are still standing. This is particularly true of the impressive river bank, The Bund, where the characteristic buildings have not changed much in the intervening years. They have all been renamed, however, or have new functions. The illustrious old Shanghai Club is the Dongfeng Hotel today and the famous bar, once the fashionable meeting place for Shanghai's foreign business community, has been taken over by Kentucky Fried Chicken. Only a small section of the longest bar in the world has been preserved, but the columns and marble floors still bear witness to past glories.

Sir Victor Sassoon's Cathay Hotel on The Bund is now jointly managed under the collective name of the Peace Hotel along with the Hotel Palace, the favourite Danish meeting place during the interwar period. A Chinese jazz

Figure 167: The author in front of the main building, which today houses the dental clinic of the Donghuamen Hospital. It was primarily the carvings on the door that made it possible to establish that this definitely was the original location of the old Manchu palace. (Compare with Figs 65, 76 and 100).

band, the members of which are so advanced in years that most of them surely remember old Shanghai, play every evening in the high-ceilinged restaurant of the former Sassoon Hotel. The rich marble walls and elegant lifts bear witness to the fact that this was one of the most stylish hotels in Shanghai in the 1930s.

I walked from the northern end of The Bund, now called Zhong Shan Dong Lu after Sun Yat-sen, to Yuan Ming Yuan Lu, which runs parallel to it. This was where the A. M. & Co. headquarters were located in the old days. I brought a picture from the Anniversary Book of 1931 with me, showing the firm's main building (see Fig. 77). There was no problem finding the buildings, which, standing on both sides of the street, were all there.

The main building was still adorned with the characteristic striped awnings. The buildings were in very poor repair, however, in comparison with the glory of the past. They now housed the classrooms of a technical school and apartments where the offices used to be. Washing hung from the windows, and on the ground floor – which in former times were the well-lit showrooms displaying the latest innovations in imported machinery from the United States and Europe – there was now a motor cycle repair shop.

Curious to see what had become of Andersen, Meyer & Co., particularly after the Communist victory in 1949, always referred to as the Liberation, I got hold of a new Chinese reference work on the history of Shanghai. There was a

Figure 168: In 1958 the factory at Yangshupu received a visit from General Zhu De, the then deputy secretary general of the C.C.P. Chairman Mao Zedong has also visited the factory.

section on the old company 'Shen Chang Yang Hang', quoted below as translated from the Chinese:

> The firm was founded by the Dane, Meyer, in 1906 (the 32nd year of Emperor Guangxu). It was originally located in Siking Road in Shanghai and dealt in Danish goods.
>
> In 1915 Meyer transformed his firm into an American corporation, Shen Chang, the parent company of which was Shen Chang Commercial Enterprise in New York, which sold American machinery and equipment on the Chinese market.
>
> In 1920 Burchard, who was the director of G.E., one of the eight big American corporations, became the chairman of the board of Shen Chang and Meyer was made general manager.
>
> The Shen Chang factory in Yangshupu was built in 1921. The factory started out by repairing and storing imported goods and manufacturing steel window-frames, but developed its production to also include small and medium sized machinery. The manufactured products were sold under the Shen Chang and G.E. label all over China, South East Asia and Africa.
>
> Shen Chang was taken over by the Japanese during the Japanese Occupation and forced to manufacture war equipment. After the victory over Japan, G.E. sent Schelcke to China to assume the post of general manager of Shen Chang. The Chinese, Gu Lansun, was made deputy manager and production was increased.
>
> Directly prior to the liberation of Shanghai there were a total of 293 machines in the factories belonging to Shen Chang. Shen Chang was the biggest American firm in Shanghai.
>
> After the liberation the firm was taken over by the government and the name changed to 'Shanghai Boiler Works' and 'Shanghai Electric Power Station Supplementary Machine Factory'.
>
> Shanghai Boiler Works is now so advanced that it can manufacture boilers for 300,000 kw power plants. It is also among the most important factories in the nuclear power industry, producing 9 megawatt accelerators and x-ray scanners on a level with foreign standards.

美 商 慎 昌 洋 行
ANDERSEN, MEYER & CO., LTD.
ESTABLISHED 1906

HEAD OFFICE:
21 YUEN MING YUEN ROAD
SHANGHAI, CHINA
TEL. 12590

BRANCHES:
NANKING • TIENTSIN • PEIPING • TSINAN • TSINGTAO • HANKOW
HONGKONG • CANTON • NEW YORK AND LONDON

AGENTS FOR

International General Electric Co., Inc.	American Radiator Co.
Saco-Lowell Shops	Keuffel & Esser Co.
Baldwin Locomotive Works	Parke, Davis & Co.
Worthington Pumps & Machinery Corp.	G.E. Medical Products Co.
International Harvester Export Co.	Mosler Safe Co.
Standard Sanitary Mfg. Co.	Combustion Engineering Co.

Figure 169: After the sale of A. M. & Co. to General Electric in 1934, the firm continued doing business in Shanghai. An advertisement for the firm in the *China Trade Monthly*, 1947, is shown here.

By collating this description with the information I had acquired from the Company Registers in Delaware, where A. M. & Co. had been registered in 1925, I was able to form a picture of the firm's operations in the years following Vilhelm Meyer's death and the G.E. takeover of the Shanghai firm.

Clark Minor, president of I.G.E. and Vilhelm's close friend, was made the new president of A.M & Co. in 1935. A. M. & Co.'s office in New York moved from Madison Avenue to the large G.E. building at 570 Lexington Avenue. In Shanghai Vilhelm Meyer's long-time colleague, R.E. Gilleland, was appointed deputy manager of A. M. & Co. in charge of daily operations. As mentioned above, A. M. & Co.'s machine shop in Yangshupu was used by the Japanese for weapon manufacture during World War II. Shortly after the Japanese capitulation in 1945 Elias Gutter, one of Vilhelm's Danish employees, assumed the management of A. M. & Co. General Electric later sent the American, C.V. Schelcke, to Shanghai as the firm's new manager.

Andersen, Meyer & Co. continued its operations in China in the postwar years. Clark Minor was made chairman of the board and was succeeded in his post as New York president by W.R. Herod, a colleague from G.E. The main suppliers continued to be major American firms, including General Electric, Saco-Lowell Shops and Baldwin Locomotives.

After the founding of the People's Republic of China in 1949, a large number of foreign firms in Shanghai were nationalized, including Andersen, Meyer & Co. Ltd, which came entirely under Chinese control in 1950.

Figure 170: Andersen, Meyer & Co. Ltd became a Chinese firm in 1953. Prime Minister Li Peng is shown here visiting Shanghai Boiler Works in Minghang in 1993 in connection with the celebration of the 40th anniversary. In the picture are also Wu Bangguo, who was secretary-general of the C.C.P. in Shanghai at the time, and is vice-premier in Beijing today, and Huang Ju, mayor of Shanghai in 1993 and secretary-general of the Shanghai C.C.P today. Xu Yudong, head of the Shanghai Boiler Works, is to the left of the Prime Minister.

The New York Board of A. M. & Co. was consequently forced to note that the corporation no longer had any real assets and in the following years the company was exempted from U.S. corporation tax. As it gradually became clear over the years that whatever assets there might be would have to be abandoned, the New York board decided to liquidate. The formal liquidation of Andersen, Meyer & Co., Ltd, took place on 22 September 1961 in Wilmington, Delaware. Some 56 years had passed since the three young Danes, Andersen, Meyer and Petersen, had become partners in 1905.

The firm continued in China as a Chinese company under a new corporate structure. In 1953 the factory in Yangshupu was renamed Shanghai Boiler Works and five years later it took initial steps for a move to Minghang in the eastern part of Shanghai. The factory in Yangshupu continued as the Supplementary Machine Factory.

When I was in Shanghai in 1991 I inquired whether it might be possible to visit Shanghai Boiler Works. We consequently drove along the river to the Yangshupu district. At the factory, thanks to the company Anniversary Book of 1931, I was able to recognize some of the large machine sheds, formerly part of A. M. & Co.'s machine shop.

We were shown around the machine sheds, which didn't seem to have changed much since 1949. I felt a thrill when I suddenly caught a glimpse of A. M. & Co.'s characteristic triangular trademark on the outer wall of one of the large sheds. I felt like an archaeologist discovering an ancient written character which very few others could decipher. General Electric's well-known trademark was visible next to it – G.E. in a circle. Time had worn down the two large trademarks on the wall and they were no longer distinct. My Chinese escorts and the surrounding workers, however, were visibly impressed when I showed them the Anniversary Book and told them that it was my grandfather who had caused these machine sheds to be built in 1921 and that it was my grandmother who in 1916 had drawn the trademark still visible on the wall.

Figure 171: In the Yangshupu District, facing the Huangpu River, stand the old machine sheds and storage rooms built by A. M. & Co. in 1921. Today the sheds form part of the Shanghai Power Equipment Co., Ltd (S.P.E.C.). The outlines of the G.E and A. M. & Co. trademarks, still barely visible on the wall, are a testimony to the former foreign owners.

During my time as Danish Consul-General in Shanghai in 1994–95, I revisited the old factory in Yangshupu, now called the Shanghai Electric Power Station Supplementary Machine Factory. I also visited the Shanghai Boiler Works in Minghang, which employs a staff of more than 5,000 and is responsible for one-third of the production of boilers for power plants in China. Xu Yudong, the director, told me that it was this factory that had supplied a steam generator for China's first nuclear power plant in 1989.

I also revisited Shen Chang Yang Hang's main building in Yuan Ming Yuan Lu. In the entrance hall there was still a large brass frame proclaiming the firm's former name and the names of the two Danes who founded it in 1906, Andersen and Meyer. This building in Yuan Ming Yuan Lu was renovated in 1996–97 and now appears brand new. It is the head office of Shanghai Telecom.

On my first visit to Shanghai in 1991 I visited the building on Avenue Edward VII (now Yan'an Donglu) built by Andersen, Meyer & Co. for the Great Northern Telegraph Company in 1922. Although the building, which now housed a number of small Chinese enterprises, was in poor repair, the directors' office on the top floor with its dark mahogany furniture, wooden panelling and ceiling lighting in the functionalist style had been preserved. There was now a canteen on the ground floor, in the room where Captain Bahnson had proudly held forth on Great Northern's enterprises in China (see Fig. 139) on the occasion of the royal visit in 1930. In the entrance hall the spot where Edouard Suenson's bust had formerly stood was still visible (see Fig. 138).

The present-day headquarters of the Bank of Bangkok in Shanghai, no. 7, now modernized, used to be Great Northern's original headquarters. It is the only building on The Bund of Danish origin.

Other – more historic – buildings in Shanghai were easy to find. Both Sun Yat-sen's and Zhou Enlai's villas in the French Concession have been turned into museums. This is also true of the school building in which Mao Zedong helped found the Chinese Communist Party at a secret meeting in 1921.

The old French club building, Cercle Sportif Français, was still there with its sweeping staircases and magnificent halls. The tall, modern Garden Hotel now looms directly over the low building. Across the street from the French club there now stands another modern hotel, Jin Jiang Hotel, where President Nixon and Premier Zhou Enlai signed the communiqué in 1972 that was to pave the way for the re-establishment of diplomatic relations between the United States and China. The two nations had not been on speaking terms since the Communist victory over Chiang Kai-shek in 1949. Once again the doors were open to Americans.

19 Avenue Road

It seemed doubtful whether I would be able to track down the old home at no. 19 Avenue Road. First of all the four Meyer sisters thought that the house had been torn down many years ago. Second, I knew that the house number had been changed, first from no. 19 to no. 47 and most recently, I believed, to no. 653, while the name of the road had been changed from Avenue Road to Beijng Xilu.

Arriving at Beijing Xilu 653 I was still far from sure I was in the right place. What met my eye was a brand new, not yet completed, six-storey school building, in a schoolyard where construction workers were in the final stages of their work. We talked to some of the teachers who didn't immediately recognize

Figure 172: The Meyer family house on Avenue Road no. 19, today Beijing Xilu no. 653. The house served as a school in 1940–60. The building shown here is on a video recorded just before the house was torn down to make room for a new school.

the old photograph I had of the villa. However, when I brought out a photo of the living room (see Fig. 90), one of the workers remembered removing a pillar very similar to the pillars in the picture. One of the teachers also thought that the large arches visible on the veranda in the old photo were identical with the arches on the school building that had been torn down the year before to make room for the new building. A video recording had been made of the old school building prior to its demolition and we all eagerly trooped up to the teachers' room in one of the side buildings to watch the video.

As soon as the former school building appeared on the screen there was no longer any doubt – this was definitely the Meyer family's old house! In 1940 the building had been turned into a middle school and the veranda had been remodelled as classrooms by filling in the veranda arches to form a new outside wall. The house had served as a school for 50 years until the building was demolished in September 1990. The garden in which the four Meyer girls used to play as children now served as a schoolyard.

My new Chinese friends shared my delight in having found the house where my mother had spent her childhood so many years ago and where my grandfather had died. It was obvious that the traditional Chinese respect for ancestors gave rise to a genuine interest in my project. The local inhabitants, workers and teachers eagerly studied my old photos of the 1920s and 1930s. I have since visited the school on several occasions and donated several complete

Figure 173: The Bund 1991. The Peace Hotel (centre) was built by Sir Victor Sassoon in 1931 and was then known as the Cathay Hotel.

sets of Hans Christian Andersen's fairytales, highly popular in China, to the school library.

'Sletten' in Hongqiao

Finding 'Sletten' in Hongqiao was somewhat more difficult since its precise location was far more uncertain. Even though I had excellent photos of the house with me, none of the local Chinese we talked to recognized it.

In the course of our investigation we visited one of the remaining, old Hongqiao villas, Sir Victor Sassoon's Villa Eve. This villa, with its Tudor timber frame and high-ceilinged hunting room was still standing, surrounded by a lovely park with a small lake and beautiful flowers. Today the house is part of the Hotel Cypress Garden. I was aware that in 1937 the house had been bought by Vilhelm Meyer's long-time Chinese friend, James Lee (Li Lu-hsioung, see Fig. 59). When I mentioned this to the manager of the house, he smilingly fetched a large portrait of Lee. He remembered Mr Lee, who had later moved to Hong Kong where he had died several years ago.

In the 1970s the house had been the residence of Mao Zedong's wife, the former Shanghai film actress, Jiang Qing, and the other three members of the so-called Gang of Four. They were later convicted of continuing the radical policies of Mao's disastrous Cultural Revolution, which in the period 1966–76 had thrown China completely off course.

During my term as Danish Consul-General in Shanghai in 1994–95, I continued my search for the Meyer family house in Hongqiao. I finally succeeded:

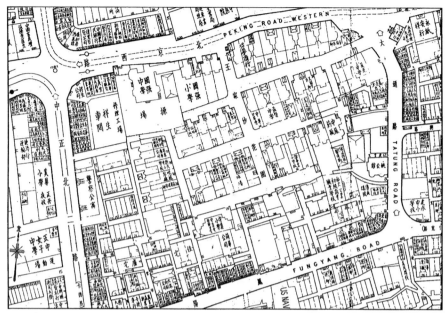

Figure 174: The Meyers' house on Avenue Road was located on a large lot. As shown on this map from the late 1940s, the house was turned into a school with the address Peking Road no. 653. In 1991 a modern six-storey school building was constructed on the spot where the old villa had formerly stood.

the house was situated right next to the airport, where it now serves as a secluded government guesthouse. The house has been altered considerably in the intervening years, but one of the old workers in the area told us that the manager of Shen Chang Yang Hang had once lived there.

Vilhelm's close Chinese friends James Lee and Li Ming had both moved to Hong Kong with their families after 1949. I met several of their descendants in Hong Kong in 1996. James Lee had had a daughter there, Lisa Lee Siu, who is in the public relations business today. The family's title to the house in Hongqiao has been recognized.

Li Ming's grandson Li Ning now works for Henderson Land Development Company Ltd, owned by his father-in-law, Lee Shau Kee. The very large Hong Kong firm is in charge of a number of construction projects all over China, including the Henderson Centre in Beijing as well as Shanghai Sky City.

Wei-Hai-Wei

I arrived at the port of Wei-Hai-Wei in Shandong province late at night during my visit to China in 1991. The city is called Weihai today, but the newest hotel in town uses the old name and is called Hotel Wei-Hai-Wei. Looking out of the hotel window at the bay in the red light of dawn I immediately recognized the large island of Liugong, which appeared in so many of the old beach photos. Wei-Hai-

Wei, however, was no longer a small Chinese village, clustered behind a city wall, consisting of a few thousand inhabitants and the small British Port Edward. The city wall had been torn down long ago and very little remains of the 32 years spent under British rule. Today the city is an important commercial centre with 250,000 inhabitants. Due to its efforts on behalf of the environment, Weihai was proclaimed the cleanest city in China in 1991.

Figure 175: The family's summer house, 'Red Roof', was located on this stretch of beach at old Wei-Hai-Wei. Today there is a promenade where the citizens of Weihai stroll along the water, enjoying the beautiful view.

On my early morning stroll from the hotel down to the water I saw that the entire long, wide stretch of beach, along what the British had formerly called Narcissus Bay, had been replaced by a cement promenade where many of the local inhabitants were performing their traditional morning exercises before going to work. This was where 'Red Roof' had stood on the beach, along with four other summerhouses. Virtually nothing was left of that period. However, a few old sampans on the small stretch of beach whispered of that far-off time over 60 years ago, when small European children from Shanghai, all dressed in white, scampered up and down the beach with their nannies, while British war-ships lay at anchor in the bay, a constant reminder of the British Empire's global presence.

Later that day I drove up along the coast. The beautiful, unspoiled beaches, once the Meyer family's treasured picnic spot, were unchanged. The names were the same in Chinese and English – Half Moon Bay, Dog's Nose Bay and Cat's Eyes Bay – and the cliff in the water still resembled a cat with two eyes. With its pleasant climate and beautiful, clean beaches modern Weihai is planning to

develop the entire area into an attractive holiday resort for Chinese and foreign tourists.

Canton

Early in 1992 I accompanied the Danish minister for industry and energy and
a large trade delegation to China. Our visit included Canton, where we stayed
at the tall, modern White Swan Hotel on the small island of Shamian. This was
the island which for many years had comprised the concession area – the only
area in Canton in former times where foreign commercial firms had the right
to establish themselves and carry on their businesses after 1856.

Figure 176: In the 1920s and 1930s A. M. & Co.'s Southern China branch office was located
in this building on Shamian Island in Canton. Today it has been turned into an apartment
building.

Late in the evening of the first day in Canton after the official programme
was over, I stood high up on my balcony gazing out over Canton and little
Shamian Island. It is only 900 yards long and 400 yards wide and is separated
from the rest of Canton by a narrow canal. The buildings on Shamian Island
clearly bear the stamp of the Western style of architecture in the early part of
the century, as do the buildings on The Bund in Shanghai.

I was aware that the location of Andersen, Meyer & Co.'s Canton office had
been Shamian Island, but I didn't know the address. A picture in the *Anniversary Book* of 1931 showed the stately building bought by the firm, in which it
had remained for many years. If the building was still standing it must be down
there somewhere. Although it was almost midnight, I could see that several
streets were still lit up and a few pavement cafés were still open. So I decided to
take a late evening stroll. There was even a slim chance of my stumbling upon

the A. M. & Co. building in one of the streets. With a firm grip on the *Anniversary Book*, I left the hotel and started out down the first street. Imagine my astonishment when, as I walked past the second house in the street, there it was!

Figure 177: In 1992 a Danish trade delegation visited China. Upon learning that it was Vilhelm Meyer, the Dane, who had been in charge of building the large Sun Yat-sen Auditorium, the hosts (the mayor of Guangzhou and the governor of Guangdong province) added a visit to the auditorium to the programme. The delegation is shown here with Danish Minister for Industry and Energy Anne Birgitte Lundholt. To her left is Denmark's ambassador to China, William Friis-Møller, and to her right is her permanent secretary, the author of this book.

I sat down at a small pavement café and compared the picture in the book with the building on the other side of the street. The exterior of the house had not changed, but there were now many small apartments where the offices used to be. The local Chinese participated with great interest in my comparative studies and shared my delight in my discovery. This was the spot where A. M. & Co. had planned the vast engineering projects carried out in Canton and surrounding Guangdong province, including the Sun Yat-sen Memorial Auditorium built in 1929–31, today one of Canton's main tourist attractions.

On subsequent visits to Canton I also located the area where for many years the foreign factories had stood. The large open square in front of the factories is today Canton's Cultural Park. We also found Danes Island, where the Danish Chinamen used to anchor 200 years ago. Many years later this island was also the location of the famous Huangpu (Whampoa) Military Academy. We found the hill, which used to be called Foreign Devils' Peak. Here we discovered in the grass a number of tombstones from the old cemetery, including stones with names of several Danish sailors and merchants. There was also a monument to Alexander Hill Everett of Boston, 'first Resident Minister of the United States of America to China', who died in Canton in 1847, aged 58. Today these 15–20

tombstones have been put on stone foundations at the foot of the hill, now
called Bamboo Hill.

New York

Most of the time Vilhelm Meyer had spent in New York had been in southern
Manhattan, downtown in the financial district where Wall Street meets Broad
Street. The building at 116 Broad Street facing the East River, the site of Vilhelm's first office space all the way back in 1908 in the firm of Melchior, Armstrong & Dessau, is no longer there. New skyscrapers have shot up. However,
the Pacific Development Corporation building at 80 Wall Street, into which A.
M. & Co. moved in 1920, is still standing. It was in this building that the vast
Pacific project was conceived. At the time the brand new 12-storey P.D.C.
building was among the tallest buildings in Manhattan. Today it seems small.

India House, the villa-like club building, seemed even smaller. This is the
home of Willard Straight's old society of American exporters to the Far East. As
soon as we were in the reception area my wife and I knew that we were on the
right track. For who was sitting there, life size, in black mahogany with a broad
smile and a huge, naked belly? None other than our good, old friend Darduse!

The receptionist was highly reluctant to allow us to enter the respectable,
old club, which is for members only. Nor did it help when I explained that my
grandfather had been a member of the club. She was not convinced. However,
when I inquired whether that wasn't a portrait of Willard Straight, the founder
of the club, hanging above the open fireplace, she realized that I knew something about India House. We were then allowed to enter the building and admire the numerous, beautiful Chinese antiques and old maritime paintings of
American Chinamen.

Antiques

At their deaths Vilhelm and Kirsten left behind them in Shanghai a collection
of beautiful antiques. Some of them are now in the homes of their children and
grandchildren. A large number are in the ethnographic collection of the National Museum of Copenhagen where, along with similar bequests and acquisitions
from other Danes from China, they form part of an extensive and fascinating
Chinese collection.

The first large Chinese donation was made already in 1872 by Peter A.
Kierulff, a Danish merchant in Peking, who lived in China from 1859 to 1884.
Another major donor was Sophus Black, who was said to have known 800 of
the 850 curio dealers in Peking and exactly how to deal with each one of them.
Then there was Thorkild Bülow-Ravens, the Danish engineer in Shanghai em-
ployed by the Chinese Customs Service, whose collection the Danish National
Museum later managed to acquire, and beautiful contributions by Henrik V.
Jacobsen, later general manager of E.A.C.

The Norwegian General Munthe was another great collector. He started sending antiques from Tianjin back home to his native city of Bergen as early as 1906.

Figure 178: In 1935 Vilhelm and Kirsten's four daughters donated a total of 150 Chinese antiques from their parents' collection to the Danish National Museum in Copenhagen. One of those antiques is shown here, a Ming figurine of Kuan Ti, the god of war.

Over the years these numerous objects of art were brought together in the Vestlandske Kunstindustri Museum in Bergen, where they have formed a separate section of the museum ever since Munthe's death in 1935.

After Vilhelm's death in 1935, the four Meyer daughters decided to donate 150 pieces from the total collection to the Danish National Museum. The donations, which went on exhibit in 1936, included clay figurines from Tang dynasty tombs (619–906) and a glazed figurine of a horseman from the Ming dynasty (1368–1644). The most valuable item in the collection was a 2-foot tall white porcelain figurine from the Ming period representing Kuan Ti, the god of war. There were also a number of figurines and temple vessels made of bronze as well as a large number of porcelain vases and bowls.

The Meyer Family

It was not granted Vilhelm and Kirsten to grow old together and enjoy their retirement in Denmark as they had so much looked forward to doing. They only saw one grandchild. But it would have made them happy to know that their progeny would be numerous.

Figure 179: The four Meyer sisters with their families in the summer of 1946 at Norden-brogaard on Langeland, one of Denmark's many islands. Upper row: the three brothers-in-law, Bo Bramsen, Kai Ahlefeldt-Laurvig and Carl Ricard. (The fourth brother-in-law, Hugh Barton, was in England.) Then come the four sisters and their children: from the left: Marie-Louise with Christopher and Bolette (the second son, Joachim, was born a year later); Thea with Kirsten and Preben flanking their father; followed by Ulrik and Merete. Rose-Marie's daughter, Susannah, is in front of her and Anette is at the far right with her sons, Lennart and Peter Vilhelm. The four sisters were to have a total of 10 children and 26 grandchildren in all.

As mentioned above, Thea, the eldest daughter (1910–98), married Kai Ahle-feldt-Laurvig (1903–85), who later became Count of Tranekær Castle in Lange-land. They had four children and 13 grandchildren. In the next generation, 11 great-grandchildren have been born.

Rose-Marie (b. 1913) married the Englishman Hugh Barton (1911–87) in Shanghai. He was employed as tea-taster at Jardine, Matheson & Co. in Shanghai. They stayed in Shanghai from 1949–51, prevented from leaving by China's nation-alization of Jardine, Matheson & Co.'s assets in China. Hugh Barton was then made director of Jardine, Matheson & Co. in Hong Kong, a post he held until 1963. They had a daughter and two grandsons and later lived in London for many years.

Anette (1916–76) returned to Denmark in 1935. She studied literature at the University of Copenhagen where she later took a Master's degree. In 1942 she married the future attorney-at-law Carl Ricard (1902–93) in Copenhagen. Their descendants number two sons, four granddaughters and one great-grandson.

Figure 180: The youngest of Vilhelm and Kirsten's 26 great-grandchildren was born in 1992. He was christened on 14 June 1992, and named Vilhelm after his great-grandfather who had been born on the same date, 114 years ago. In 1994 little Vilhelm went to Shanghai with his parents and the following year to Beijing. Here 3-year-old Vilhelm is shown with his parents in front of the Royal Danish Embassy on his way to his first day in his new nursery school in the Western Academy of Beijing.

After the deaths of her parents, the youngest daughter – my mother, Marie-Louise (1920–89) – returned to Langeland at the age of 14, where she lived at Nor-denbrogård with her sister and brother-in-law, attending the local school. After attending boarding school in Switzerland, she studied at the Music Conservatory in Copenhagen where she took her final exams in piano music in 1941. The same year she married Bo Bramsen (b. 1912), publisher and author. As will appear in the genealogical table in the Appendix, Bo Bramsen was the cousin of Marie-Louise's mother, Kirsten Meyer. Bo and Marie-Louise Bramsen had three children and seven grandchildren.

Up to the present Vilhelm and Kirsten have thus had a total of 10 grandchildren, 26 great-grandchildren and 12 great-great-grandchildren. They would be happy to know that their descendants still benefit from the close family ties created many years ago in the home on Avenue Road in Shanghai.

Figure 181: In April 1998 most of the grandchildren of Vilhelm and Kirsten Meyer and of William and Mille Heering visited China with a large group of friends. Here are the grandchildren with their spouses, in front of the Temple of Heaven in Beijing.

In April 1998 I invited a group of cousins – grandchildren of Vilhelm and Kirsten Meyer – with their spouses and friends, a total of 42, to see modern China and to visit some of the places where the Meyer family had spent so many happy years. In Beijing we visited the old Manchu Palace, the former Danish Mess. In Shanghai we went to see the middle school on the grounds where the Meyer house on Avenue Road used to be, and we visited the former A. M. & Co. headquarters on Yuan Ming Yuan Lu, close to The Bund. We also went out to see the old A. M. & Co. machine shops in the Yangshupu district near the river. In 1995 the company had been turned into a Sino–American joint venture, Shanghai Power Equipment Company Ltd (S.P.E.C.), with Westinghouse Electric Corporation as the new American partner.

At the Shanghai History Museum we held a special ceremony where a brass frame with the company name 'ANDERSEN, MEYER & CO', recently removed from the old A. M. & Co. headquarters in Yuan Ming Yuan Road, was handed over to the Museum together with a set of old photographs. Our visit was televised on Shanghai television and CNN and was also reported in a number of local newspapers. One of these was read in Australia by Wang Renliang, whose paternal grandfather had been a cook for the Meyer family in the 1930s. He wrote to me and I had the opportunity to meet his uncle, Wang Ruixiang, in Shanghai in March 1999.

Wang Ruixiang was born in 1919 and had stayed in 19 Avenue Road as a young teenager. He remembered his early years with the Meyer family with great pleasure. Every Christmas Eve the Meyers invited the cook's three sons and the housekeeper's son to join the Christmas party. The boys danced around the Christmas tree in the Danish tradition with Mr and Mrs Meyer and their daughters and joined them in singing Christmas carols. The boys would also receive Christmas gifts from Mrs Meyer and the girls.

Figure 182: In 1998, when a group of Kirsten and Vilhelm Meyer's grandchildren and their friends visited China, they took part in a ceremony at the History Museum of Shanghai, where some relics and photos of A. M. & Co. were handed over to the museum.

During those years the boys' fathers would take them out to the Meyers' weekend house in Hongqiao whenever their help was needed. The Meyers had many friends, both Chinese and foreigners, and the house was always full of people. Mr Wang told me that Mr and Mrs Meyer were always kind to their household staff. When Mr Meyer died in 1935 the members of the household all had to move elsewhere and find new jobs. They had all felt like members of a big family which had ceased to exist.

This was the first time that I had met a Chinese who had actually known my grandparents and my mother from the old days in Shanghai. I met with Mr Wang, his son Wang Huizhong and grandson Wang Tianling in their small flat in Shanghai. The Wang family opened their doors to me and made me feel very welcome in their home. Somehow I felt that we had come full circle.

Figure 183: Three generations: descendants of Mr Wang, who worked as a cook with the Meyer family in the early 1930s – his son Wang Ruixiang, grandson Wang Huizhong and great-grandson Wang Tianling. Shanghai, 1999.

Appendix

The Meyer and Bramsen Families

Vilhelm Meyer and Kirsten Bramsen came from rather different family backgrounds. Vilhelm's family, of German–Danish–Jewish origin, counted both merchants and rabbis, while Kirsten's Danish–German–Norwegian background was characterized by business and insurance people and one clergyman. Both families had immigrated to Copenhagen in the mid-eighteenth century and their descendants had become part of the established Copenhagen bourgeoisie.

The Meyer Family

Vilhelm Meyer's grandfather's grandfather's grandfather's father (going back seven generations in total) was named Meyer Abraham and was a merchant in the city of Hausen near Frankfurt am Main. He was killed during the pogroms of 1689 and one of his sons, Jacob Meyer (c. 1680–1766) moved north to Altona near Hamburg. His son, Amsel Jacob Meyer (1728–98) moved to Copenhagen as a young man, where he took out a municipal licence to trade in 1750. One of Amsel's six children was Salomon Amsel Meyer (1759–95), who established himself in 1784 with the licence of trader.

Salomon's son, Jacob Salomon Meyer (1783–1845), took out the trade licence of wholesaler in Copenhagen and married Jette Meyer, whose mother was descended from an old family of rabbis. Jette's maternal grandfather, Hirschel Levin (1721–1800), had served as a rabbi in London, Halberstadt and Mannheim and was the chief rabbi of Berlin from 1772 to 1800.

One of Jacob and Jette's 11 children was Alfred Jacob Meyer (1896–80), who became a wholesale dealer in Copenhagen like his father. He had a draper's shop where he lived with his family. He was later active in the banking business. He married Sophie Melchior, the daughter of the well-known Copenhagen merchant, Gerson Melchior (1771–1845).

Gerson, along with his father, Moses Marcus Melchior (1736–1817), had established the commercial firm of Moses & Son, G. Melchior, in 1796. Gerson and his wife Birgitte, née Israel, had 13 children. The business was later carried on by two of their sons, Moritz Melchior (1816–84) and Moses Melchior (1825–1912).

Alfred and Sophie Meyer had nine children including Louis Meyer (1843–1929), who began his business education at the age of 15 in the family firm, Moses & Son, G. Melchior, with his two uncles Moritz and Moses Melchior. In 1866, when he was 23, his uncles lent him money to start up the firm of Beckett & Meyer with the 23-year-old Englishman, Hugh Beckett.

In 1867 Louis Meyer married Thea Friedlander (1845–1908), the daughter of the stationer, Sally Friedlander (1808–69) (see Fig. 3).

The firm of Beckett & Meyer first took up sugar imports and later coffee, fertilizers, molasses, syrup, cigars and tobaccos. In 1870 Beckett & Meyer acquired premises at Gl. Strand no. 40 in Copenhagen. In 1876 Louis Meyer bought the adjoining building where he and Thea made their home. At this point the family already had seven children. Thea bore five more children in the following years including – in 1878 – a son, Vilhelm (see Fig. 6).

The Bramsen Family

Kirsten Bramsen's ancestors originally came from Schleswig in what is now Danish Southern Jutland. Kirsten's grandfather's grandfather's grandmother's father, Nis Madsen Bramsen (c. 1625–85), was the owner-farmer of Steveltgård in Øsby Parish near Haderslev. His daughter, Maren Bramsen, and her husband, Jep Erichsen, inherited the farm in 1675. They had two sons, Nis Jepsen Bramsen (1677–1736) and Erich Jepsen Bramsen (1678–1735). Both sons, one in Copenhagen, the other in Sdr. Bjert near Kolding, had numerous descendants.

Nis Jepsen Bramsen left Øsby Parish in the early eighteenth century and settled in Højer on the west coast of Denmark. He and Susanne, née Lihme, had a son, Simon Nicolai (1732–1805), who moved to Copenhagen in the 1750s. Simon Nicolai Bramsen took employment in Copenhagen as a textile worker. He had seven children with Anne Marie, née Hencke, including Ludvig Ernst Bramsen (1777–1828), who started out in life as a copy-clerk in the Schleswig-Holstein-Lauenborg Fire Insurance Office, later advancing to bookkeeper, office head and, in 1824, councillor. Ludvig married Marie Christine, née Beutner, whose family came from Germany. They had a total of eight children including a son, Ludvig.

The youngest of a large family of sisters and brothers, Ludvig went to Cuba at the age of 21. He was christened Ludvig like his father, but called himself Luis in Cuba, retaining the name for the rest of his life. Luis Bramsen (1819–86) first worked in a cigar factory, sending some of its cigars to Denmark. These were the first Havana cigars available in Denmark. In 1842 Luis moved to New York where he opened a cigar shop on Broad Street in Manhattan.

In 1843 Luis met a Danish family in New York who had just arrived from Denmark – Niels Frederik and Christine Lassen and their five children. Niels Frederik Lassen (1793–1865), who was the son of Peder Lassen, clerk in the Asiatic Company (see Fig. 12), had been chief prosecutor in railway matters in Copenhagen and judge in Frederikshavn, but had decided to emigrate with his family to St Louis, Missouri. Luis fell in love with the eldest of Lassen's four daughters, Camilla (1820–79). They were married in October 1843 in St Louis and settled in New York City. However, the young newly-weds were given a hard time by Camilla's father, who insisted on interfering in Luis' business. This was finally too much for the young couple and they returned to Denmark in October 1844.

In Copenhagen Luis took out a trading licence as a wholesaler and was very successful selling cigars. In 1848 Luis became interested in the insurance business and acquired the Danish agency for Northern, the British insurance company. Luis and Camilla had a total of nine children between 1845–63. In 1858 they had a large villa built in Frederiksberg. In 1864 Luis founded the insurance company Nye Danske.

Luis and Camilla's eldest daughter, Harriet Bramsen (1846–1913), married the merchant Peter N. Heering (1838–1924), who became the head of his father's firm, Peter F. Heering. As can be seen in Appendix II, Peter and Harriet's son, William Heering (1876–1936), married Vilhelm Meyer's youngest sister, Emily.

Another of Luis and Camilla's children was Ludvig Bramsen (1847–1914), who succeeded his father as director of Nye Danske and who was minister of the interior from 1899 to 1901 (see Fig. 31). William Bramsen (1850–81) also deserves a special mention. He went to China at the age of 20 where he worked for the Great Northern Telegraph Company in Shanghai (see Fig. 14).

Aage Bramsen (1855–1921) grew up in Frederiksberg, the seventh of Luis and Camilla's nine children. After taking his degree in 1874, he spent three years in England, Germany and Switzerland studying marine insurance. In 1877 he took a position with his father's firm Nye Danske.

While on a vacation in Norway on a steamer in the fiords near Bergen, the 27-year-old Aage met Ottilie Grip (1852–1933), who was three years older. They were married the following year (see Fig. 7).

Ottilie's father Rolf Olsen Grip (1812–83) descended from an old Bergen merchant family. Rolf Olsen Grip was the Russian vice-consul as was his father Joachim Grip (c. 1785–1833) before him. Rolf's mother, Cathrine, née Olsen (1789–1822), was of an old Bergen shipmaster's family. Her paternal grandfather Ole Olsen (1720–92) was a merchant skipper and her father Rolf Olsen (1750–1810) was the municipal chief of police.

Ottilie's father died shortly after the wedding and her 69-year-old mother, Charlotte Amalie Grip (1814–1906), then moved to Copenhagen where she remained until her death in 1906 at the age of 92. Charlotte Grip was the daughter of the doctor of the Kristiansand brigade, Johan Adrian Wolff (1787–1867), who had moved to Norway from Germany at the age of 21. According to family tradition his mother Marie née Debeau (c. 1770–1830) was descended from a French Huguenot family.

Ottilie's maternal grandmother Anne Margrethe, née Kyhn (1787–1872), was the daughter of the vicar of Kvikne Parish, J.J. Kyhn (c. 1750–1820) and Charlotte Amalie, née Hassing (c. 1750–1820).

Aage Bramsen became an independent insurance director and took on the agencies in the Nordic countries for a number of foreign insurance companies including Helvetia and Italia. Aage and Ottilie had a total of four children (see Fig. 8) Kirsten, the eldest, was born in 1884.

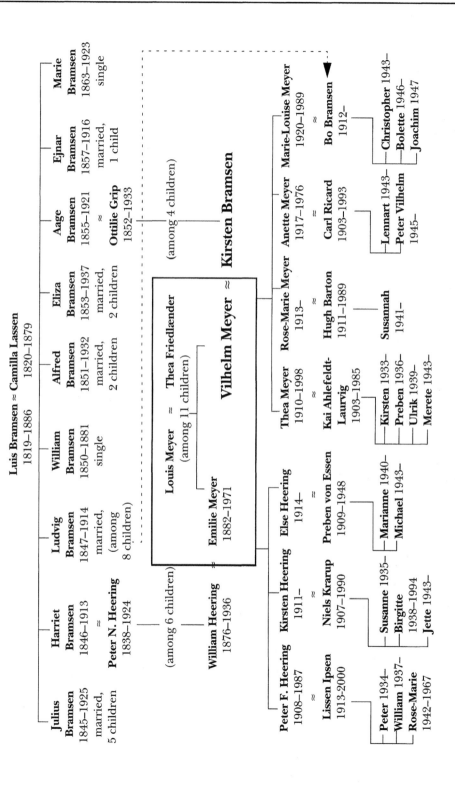

Source Material

Vilhelm and Kirsten did not leave many written records of their life and activities in China. However, diaries, memoirs, letters, reports, biographies, articles and books have made it possible to reconstruct a great many of the Meyer family's comings and goings as well as the structure of the firm Andersen, Meyer & Co. I have also found a number of photographs depicting far better than words the people, places and events mentioned in the book.

Unpublished Sources

The source material includes early diaries written by Kirsten Bramsen, her daughter, Anette Meyer Ricard, and her nephew, Caj Gericke. In addition there are Gerda Nielsen's letters from Shanghai in the period 1920–23. The handwritten memoirs of Emilie Heering, née Meyer, and of Minna Black, née Dich, also deserve special mention. In the Danish Record Office I examined the documents of the Shanghai Consulate, later Consulate General, and in the Danish College of Heralds, I read about the lives of a number of Danes mentioned in the book. Finally I found information on Andersen, Meyer & Co. in the United States in the Company Registers in Dover, Delaware, and Albany, N.Y., respectively.

Published Sources

Abend, Hallet: *Treaty Ports – A Rich Pageant of Life Where East and West Agreed to Meet.* New York, 1944.

All about Shanghai – A Standard Guidebook. Published by the University Press, Shanghai, 1934.

Andersen, H.N.: *Indberetning til Grosserer-Societets Komité angaaende Forholdene i Øst asien* [Report to the Danish Chamber of Commerce concerning the situation in the Far East]. Copenhagen, 1900.

——: *Tilbageblik* [Looking back]. Copenhagen, 1914.

——: *Udvikling* [Development]. Copenhagen, 1929.

——: *Det Østasiatiske Kompagni hjemme i Danmark og ude i Verden* [The East Asiatic Company in Denmark and the world]. Copenhagen, 1937.

Arlington, L.C. and Lewisohn, William: *In Search of Old Peking.* [Peking, 1935] Oxford, 1991.

Atwell, Pamela: *British Mandarins and Chinese Reformers. The British Administration of Weihaiwei (1898–1930) and the Territory's Return to Chinese Rule.* Oxford, 1985.

Bache, W: *Dagbogsblade fra Kronprinsens Rejse til Østen* [Journal extracts from the Crown Prince's voyage to the Orient]. Copenhagen, 1931.

Barber, Noel: *The Fall of Shanghai.* New York, 1979.

Bille, Steen Andersen: *Corvetten Galathea's Reise omkring Jorden i 1845, 46 og 47* [The corvette Galathea's voyage around the world in 1845–47]. [1st edn 1848–51] Copenhagen, 1930.

——: *Min Reise til China 1864* [My voyage to China 1864]. Copenhagen, 1865.

Botved, A.P.: *København–Tokio–København gennem Luften* [Copenhagen–Tokyo– Copenhagen by air]. Copenhagen, 1930.

Bramsen, Bo: *Bogen om Luis og Camilla Bramsens Efterkommere* [The book on the descendants of Luis and Camilla Bramsen]. Copenhagen,1981.

Bramsen, Marie-Louise: 'Trygge dage i Shanghai – Et dansk hjem i Østen' [Peaceful days in Shanghai – A Danish home in the East]. In Margrethe Spies (ed.), *Fra hytte og slot* [From cottage and castle]. Copenhagen, 1977.

Cavling, Henrik: *Østen. Skildringer fra en rejse til Ceylon, Burma, Singapore, Bangkok, Kina og Japan* [The Orient. Essays from a journey to Ceylon, Burma, Singapore, Bangkok, China and Japan]. Copenhagen, 1901–02.

——: *Efter Redaktionens Slutning* [After the deadline]. Copenhagen, 1928.

——: *Journalistliv* [Life as a journalist]. Copenhagen, 1930.

Chang, John K.: *Industrial Development in Pre-Communist China, A Quantitative Analysis.* Chicago, 1969.

Charlton, Peter: *Australians on the Somme. Pozieres – 1916.* London, 1986.

Clemmensen, Tove and Mogens B. Mackeprang: *Kina og Danmark – 1600–1950, Kinafart og Kinamode* [China and Denmark – 1600–1950, China voyages and Chinese fashions]. National Museum, Copenhagen, 1980.

Clifford, Nicholas R.: *Spoilt Children of Empire – Westeners in Shanghai and the Chinese Revolution of the 1920s.* Hanover, New Hampshire, 1991.

Coble, Parks M.: *The Shanghai Capitalists and the National Government 1927–1937.* Harvard University, 1980.

Croly, Herbert: *Willard Straight.* New York, 1924.

Davidson-Houston, J.V.: *Yellow Creek: The Story of Shanghai.* London, 1962.

Eskelund, Karl: *Min kone spiser med pinde* [My wife eats with chopsticks]. Copenhagen, 1946.

——: *Min Far trækker tænder ud* [My father pulls teeth]. Copenhagen, 1949.

Fairbank, John King: *The United States and China.* Harvard University, Mass., 1983.

———: *The Great Chinese Revolution 1800–1985.* New York, 1987.

Fewsmith, Joseph: *Party, State, and Local Elites in Republican China – Merchant Organizations and Politics in Shanghai, 1890–1930.* Honolulu, 1985.

First General Conference of the International General Electric Company Inc. and Associated Companies. Minutes of the conference. New York, 1920.

Gibb, George L.: *The Saco-Lowell Shops.* Cambridge, 1950.

Gittings, John.: *The World and China, 1922–1972.* London, 1974.

Gorowitz, Bernard and George Wise (eds): *The General Electric Story, 1876–1986.* Schenectady, New York, 1989.

Grut, Edmund: *Kina i Støbeskeen* [China in the melting-pot]. Copenhagen, 1947.

Gunst, Sievert: *Bogen om Louis Meyer* [The book on Louis Meyer]. Copenhagen, 1943.

Hahn, Emily: *The Soong Sisters.* London, 1942.

Hallar, Søren: *Øst for Suez. Rejseskildringer* [East of Suez. A travel journal]. Copenhagen, 1923.

Hammond, John Winthrop: *Men and Volts – The Story of General Electric.* New York, 1941.

Hauser, Ernest O.: *Shanghai: City for Sale.* New York, 1940.

Henningsen, Jacob: *Det himmelske rige* [The heavenly kingdom]. Copenhagen, 1887.

———: *Djung Rhua Dji – Kinesiske typer og skitser* [Djung Rhua Dji – Chinese characters and sketches]. Copenhagen, 1894.

Henriksen, Aage: *Dagligt liv i Peking* [Daily life in Peking]. Copenhagen, 1931.

Hinrup, Hans J. and Gregersen, Bo: *Dansk Kinabibliografi 1641–1949.* [Danish bibliography on China 1641–1949]. Aarhus, 1991.

Hookham, Hilda: *A Short History of China.* London, 1969.

Howe, Christopher (ed.): *Shanghai – Revolution and Development in an Asian Metropolis.* Cambridge, 1981.

Hoyt, Edwin P.: *The Rise of the Chinese Republic.* New York, 1989.

Hyde, Francis E.: *Far Eastern Trade 1860–1914.* London, 1973.

Ibsen, Kai: *Den kinesiske tråd – En dansk familiekrønike* [The Chinese thread – A Danish family chronicle]. Copenhagen, 1981.

Jacobsen, Viggo E.: *Eventyret om Store Nordiske* [The adventure of the Great Northern Company]. Copenhagen, 1943.

Jensen, Johannes V.: *Introduktion til vor Tidsalder* [An introduction to our age]. Copenhagen 1915. (3rd edn 1929)

Jessen, Hjalmar (ed.): *Det var dengang man ... Einar V. Jessens oplevelser 1880–1923* [That was back when ... The adventures of Einar V. Jensen, 1880–1923]. Copenhagen, 1987.

Kaarsted, Tage: *Admiralen – Andreas de Richelieu – Forretningsmand og politiker i Danmark* [The admiral – Andreas de Richelieu – businessman and politician in Denmark]. Odense, 1990.

Kamp, A: *De rejste ud – og gjorde Danmark større* [They traveled abroad – and expanded Denmark]. Copenhagen, 1943.

Kamp, A. and A.J. Poulsen: *Danske i Udlandet* [Danes abroad]. [Copenhagen, 1935] 2nd edn 1956.

Kamp, A., Gunnar Hansen and Aage Heinberg: *De Danskes Vej – Danske Pionerer og dansk Virke under alle Himmelstrøg, Bind I–III* [The way of the Danes – Danish pioneers and Danish activities all over the world, Vols I-III]. Copenhagen, 1950–1951.

Kauffmann, Henrik: *Danmarks Traktatforhold til Kina* [Denmark's treaty relations with China]. Peking, 1928.

Keating, Paul W.: *Lamps for a Brighter America – A History of the General Electric Lamp Business.* New York, 1954.

Keswick, Maggie (ed.): *The Thistle and the Jade – A Celebration of 150 Years of Jardine, Matheson & Co.* London, 1982.

Kjølsen, Klaus and Sjøqvist, Viggo: *Den Danske Udenrigstjeneste, 1770–1970* [The Danish Foreign Service, 1770–1970]. Copenhagen, 1970.

Koustrup, Mette and Sten Lange: *Shanghai – Hverdag i Kina. Før og Nu* [Shanghai – daily life in China then and now]. Copenhagen, 1980.

Lange, Ole: *Finansmænd, stråmænd og mandariner – C.F. Tietgen, Privatbanken og Store Nordiske. Etablering 1868–76* [Financiers, puppets and mandarins – C.F. Tietgen, the Private Bank and the Great Northern. The founding years 1868-76]. Copenhagen, 1978.

——: *Partnere og rivaler – C.F. Tietgen, Eastern Extension og Store Nordiske – Ekspansion i Kina 1880–86* [Partners and rivals – C.F. Tietgen, Eastern Extension and Great Northern – expansion in China 1880-86]. Copenhagen, 1980.

——: *Den hvide elefant – H.N. Andersens eventyr og ØK 1852–1914* [The white elephant – the adventures of H.N. Andersen and the E.A.C. 1852–1914]. Copenhagen, 1986.

Langeland, A. St: *Kina, Japan og Korea* [China, Japan and Korea]. Copenhagen, 1971.

Lanning, G. and S. Couling: *Historic Shanghai* [Shanghai, 1920] Taipei, 1973.

Larsen, Kay: *Den Danske Kinafart* [Denmark's trade with China]. Copenhagen, 1932.

Lee, James Hsioung: *A Half Century of Memories.* Hong Kong, 1968.

Lehmann, Johannes: *Gennem Østen* [Oriental journey]. Copenhagen, 1930.

Linck, Olaf: *En Dansker i Østen* [A Dane in the Orient]. Copenhagen, 1927.

Loth, David: *Swope of G.E. – The Story of Gerard Swope and General Electric in American Business.* New York, 1958.

Macmillan, Allister: *Seaports of the Far East.* London, 1923.

Malraux, André: *La Condition Humaine.* Paris, 1933.

Meyer, Louis: *Bedstefaders Rejse til Amerika* [Grandfathers journey to America]. Copenhagen, 1916.

Montalto de Jesus, C.A.: *Historic Shanghai.* Shanghai, 1909.

Murphey, Rhoads: *Shanghai: Key to Modern China 1840–1936.* Harvard University, Mass., 1953.

Nielsen, Aage Krarup: *Dragen vaagner* [The Dragon awakens]. Copenhagen 1927.

O'Neill, Hugh B.: *Companion to Chinese History.* New York, 1987.

Oxholm, Inge: *Fra Måneport til Blånende Fjorde* [From moon gates to blue fjords]. Copenhagen, 1973.

Pan Ling: *In Search of Old Shanghai.* Hong Kong, 1983.

Pan Ling: *Old Shanghai; Gangsters in Paradise.* Hong Kong, 1984.

Pedersen, Erik Helmer: *Pionererne. Politikens Danmarks-historie* [The pioneers. Politiken's history of Denmark]. Copenhagen, 1986.

Petersen, Sophie: *Danmark i det Fjerne* [Denmark in faraway countries]. Copenhagen, 1936.

Pott, F.L. Hawks: *A Short History of Shanghai.* Shanghai, 1928.

Rasmussen, Steen Eiler: *Rejse i Kina* [Journey in China]. Copenhagen, 1958.

Ricard, Anette: *Mist on the Window Panes.* Copenhagen, 1959.

Rosenberg, Holger: *En Vandringsmand sætter Staven* [A wanderer lays down his staff]. Copenhagen, 1937.

Salisbury, Harrison E.: *The Long March.* New York, 1985.

Seagrave, Sterling: *The Soong Dynasty.* London, 1985.

Sergeant, Harriet: *Shanghai.* London, 1991.

Snow, Edgar: *Red Star over China.* New York, 1935.

——: *The Long Revolution.* New York, 1971.

Spence, Jonathan D.: *The Gate of Heavenly Peace – The Chinese and Their Revolution, 1895–1980.* New York, 1981.

——: *The Search for Modern China.* New York, 1990.

Store Nordiske: *Det Store Nordiske Telegraf-Selskab – Hovedtræk af selskabets historie 1869–1969* [The Great Northern Telegraph Company – main points of the company's history 1869-1969]. Copenhagen, 1969.

Svedstrup, A.: *De danskes Vej.* [Danes abroad]. Copenhagen, 1902.

Sveistrup, C.: *Hovedpunkter af Det Østasiatiske Kompagnis Historie 1897–1909.* [Main events in the history of the East Asiatic Company 1897–1909]. Copenhagen, 1910.

Thomasen, T.: *Fra Nationalmuseets Arbejdsmark 1936* [From the sphere of activity of the National Museum, 1936]. Copenhagen, 1936.

Thornton, Richard C.: *China: A Political History, 1917–1980.* Boulder, Col., 1982.

Tong, Hollington K.: *Chiang Kai-shek: Soldier and Statesman.* London, 1938.

Trosborg, Holger (ed.): *Erindringer og Fortællinger fra Store Nordiske* [Memoires and stories from Great Northern]. Copenhagen, 1919.

Turner, Robert D.: *The Pacific Empresses – An Illustrated History of Canadian Pacific Railway's Empress Liners on the Pacific Ocean.* Victoria, B.C., 1981.

Wei, Betty Peh-T'i: *Shanghai – Crucible of Modern China.* Hong Kong, 1987.

Westwood, J. N.: *Russia against Japan, 1904–05. A New Look at the Russo–Japanese War.* London, 1986.

Wright, Arnold and H.A. Cartwright: *Twentieth Century Impressions of Shanghai.* London, 1908.

Wright, Mary Clabaugh (ed.): *China in Revolution: The First Phase 1900–1913.* Yale University, Conn., 1968.

Newspapers, journals and annual books:

Dansk Biografisk Leksikon [Danish biographical encylopedia]

Kraks Blå Bog [Krak's blue book]

North China Daily News

Picture Credits

The illustrations in this book have come from the following sources:

From archives, libraries etc.

Private photographs and prints:
2, 3, 4, 5, 6, 7, 8, 12, 14, 24, 27, 29, 31, 32, 33, 34, 38, 39, 41, 42, 43, 44, 50, 52, 60, 61, 62, 65, 66, 67, 68, 69, 70, 71, 72, 73, 74, 76, 78, 84, 86, 87, 89, 90, 91, 92, 94, 100, 103, 104, 106, 109, 113, 114, 117, 118, 119, 120, 128, 129, 131, 132, 133, 134, 142, 149, 150, 152, 154, 155, 156, 157, 158, 159, 160, 161, 164, 165, 166, 167, 171, 172, 173, 174, 175, 176, 177, 179, 180, 181, 182, 183.

Royal Danish Library:
17, 20, 21, 23, 25, 26, 28, 45, 53, 88, 151, 153.

The National Danish Archives:
37.

The Danish National Museum:
178.

The Historical Archives of Faaborg City:
93, 95, 96, 97, 102, 105.

The Lemvig Museum:
110.

The Hall of History Museum, Schenectady, New York:
83.

The Harvard Yenching Library, Cambridge, Massachusetts:
122, 123.

Xinhua News Agency, Beijing:
1.

Great Northern Telegraph Company:
15, 63, 64, 138.

Cartoons by Sapajou:
111, 130.

From books and articles:

Charles J. Ferguson. *Andersen, Meyer & Company, Ltd. 1906-31.* (1931):
35, 40, 55, 101, 112, 116, 143, 144, 145, 146, 147, 148, 162.

Louis Meyer. *Bedstefars rejse til Amerika.* (1916):
56, 57, 58.

Waldemar Bache. *Dagbogsblade fra Kronprinsens Rejse.* (1931):
135, 136, 137, 139, 140, 141.

Udenrigsministeriet. Asiatisk Plads (1980):
9, 11.

Pan Ling. *In Search of Old Shanghai* (1983):
13, 49.

F.L. Hawks Pott. *A History of Shanghai.* (1928):
16

A. Svedstrup. *De Danskes Vej.* (1902):
18, 19, 30.

H.N. Andersen. *Tilbageblik.* (1914):
22.

Erik Nyström. *Det Nya Kina.* (1913):
36, 46.

Louis Graves. *Willard Straight in the Orient.* (1922):
54.

James Hsioung Lee. *A Half Century of Memories.* (1968):
59, 126.

Allister Macmillan. *Seaports of the Far East.* (1923):
99.

A. Kamp. *De Danskes Vej.* (1951):
127.

Hollington K. Tong. *Chiang Kai-shek. Soldier and Statesman.* (1938):
107.

Jonathan D. Spence. *The Search for Modern China.* (1990):
124.

Edmund Grut. *Kina i Støbeskeen.* (1947):
125.

China Trade Monthly. 1947:
169.

Zhong Wenxian. *Mao Zedong.* **(1986):**
98, 163.

Percy Jucheng Fang & Lucy Guinong J. Fang. *Zhou Enlai.* **(1986):**
108.

A Photo Album by Soong Qing Ling Foundation. *The Great Life of Soong Qing Ling.* **(1987):**
47, 48.

Fu Gongyue. *Old Photos of Beijing.* **(1989):**
51.

Official Guide for Travellers to the Orient. **(1918/1919):**
75.

Robert D. Turner. *The Pacific Empresses.* **(1981):**
85.

Shanghai Boiler Works, brochure. (1993):
77, 168, 170.

Bernard Gorowitz and George Wise. *The General Electric Story.* **1876-1986. (1989):**
79, 80, 81, 82.

Lou Rongmin. *The Bund, History and Vicissitudes.* **(1998):**
115.

C.E.G. Gad's Publishing Company, Copenhagen, Denmark:
maps – figures no.10 and 121.

Index

The following index includes names of persons, companies clubs, and associations mentioned in the book, from pages xi to xiii, pages 1 to 301 and in the genealogical table on p. 306. Vilhelm and Kirsten Meyer and their four daughters as well as Andersen, Meyer and Co. are only referred to in the index the first time they are mentioned in the book, and when they are show in the illustrations. An f after a page number means that the name is mentioned on this and the following page, whereas ff means this and the following pages. Page numbers in italics refer to an illustration.

For Product Safety Concerns and Information please contact our EU
representative GPSR@taylorandfrancis.com Taylor & Francis Verlag GmbH,
Kaufingerstraße 24, 80331 München, Germany

Printed and bound by CPI Group (UK) Ltd, Croydon, CR0 4YY
08/05/2025
01864400-0001